NS Basic Programming
for Palm OS

The easiest way to program your Palm!

Michael J. Verive

National Library of Canada Cataloguing in Publication

Verive, Michael J., 1960-
   NS Basic programming for Palm OS : the easiest
way to program your palm! / by Michael J. Verive.

Includes index.
ISBN 0-9695844-6-6

   1. BASIC (Computer program language) 2. Palm OS.
I. Title.

QA76.8.N48V47 2002   005.265
C2002-901903-6

Table of Contents

Acknowledgments

In 1676, Sir Isaac Newton was credited for writing "If I have seen further than others, it is by standing upon the shoulders of giants." I'm no Isaac Newton, and I haven't necessarily seen further than others, but this book would not have been possible without the help of several giants who deserve credit (no royalties – but credit nonetheless) for their contributions to the reviewing and content of this book, and for their support of NS Basic programmers in general. Here they are, in alphabetical order:

Eston Bond
Ron Glowka
Dan Hall
Douglas Handy
Christien Lee
Adrian Nicolaiev
David Orriss

And of course, George Henne and the crew at NSBasicCorporation.

I'm sure that there are many others whose names belong on this list, but you know what they say, "Memory is the first thing to go." (I can't remember the second thing!)

Chapter I – Introduction

I have to admit that I've been slow to embrace some technologies. Like mice, color printers, and CD burners. However, once I started using them, I wondered how I had gotten along without them.

So, it shouldn't come as a surprise that I wondered what everyone saw in the Palm Pilot (and its many incarnations, imitations, and spin-offs). Big deal. Save a few phone numbers, keep a calendar, jot down short messages. And all using a "Graffiti" language that everyone had a love/hate relationship with. To make matters worse, all this was on a wallet-sized computer with a (gasp!) monochrome screen that was hard to read in bright light or dark night.

Then I got one. A Handspring Visor Deluxe, followed by the Palm IIIc, m100, m105, Sony Clie...you get the picture. I was hooked. More than just hooked; I knew that I had to control them. Program them.

Not being a C programmer (and not really *wanting* to become one just to program my Palm OS device), I looked at the other options. I could go with an expensive forms-based system, or one of several freeware/shareware lay-out-the-screen-and-write-some-code (and hope for the best) systems. There was even Forth and a simple Basic interpreter, but I wanted more power and control over my code than their environments could provide, and didn't want to spend most of my programming time coding the locations of screen objects.

I stumbled on NS Basic for Palm OS during one of my web searches, and was more than a little curious. The list of functions, especially database, string, and arithmetic functions, was impressive. A demo wasn't available at that time, but the price was low enough to make it a "not-too-risky" venture. If the program lived up to its advertising, it could be the next best thing to sliced bread. At the worst, I was out the small purchase price. Besides, I still had a lot of old Basic code lying around that I wanted to "recycle", so a Basic system seemed to be the right choice.

The original IDE (integrated development environment) was a bit clunky, and not very forgiving, but the learning curve was very manageable (it was close enough to the Visual Basic IDE), and before I knew it I was cranking out some pretty simple – and some not so simple – programs.

NS Basic (I won't keep using the full name "*NS Basic for Palm OS*" since this book doesn't deal with the Newton or Windows CE versions of NS Basic) has since evolved into a robust, powerful language with a rich programming environment. Like virtually every "flavor" of Basic, NS Basic has a few quirks. Some you'll love, and some you'll hate. Such is life.

Why Basic?

The reasons many of us keep coming back to Basic include:

- Originally created as a **B**eginner's **A**ll-purpose **S**ymbolic **I**nstruction **C**ode, Basic is easy to write (at least a lot less cryptic than APL, Pascal, C, and FORTRAN, to name a few powerful yet not very verbose languages. But, if you like verbose, there's always COBOL!)

- Easy to debug (error messages are usually fairly informative – but very compiler/interpreter dependent!)

- Fairly portable – once you know common Basic syntax, you can apply that syntax to almost any Basic compiler/interpreter and be about 90% correct

- Good collection (also compiler/interpreter dependent) of functions for control of text/graphic layout, file handling, and sound/music generation, without having to rely too heavily on external libraries for most functions

Basic is like a pair of well-worn jeans – comfortable, maybe not always in fashion, but easy to feel at home with. Many of us also have a large investment in our Basic code, whether in the form of old school projects, personal "pet" programs, or professional applications – and nobody (except warped assembly language and C programmers) actually enjoys "reinventing the wheel". Face it – we love our clunky old code, and we'll try our best to find a way to revive it!

From its humble beginnings to its present standing as a professional language deserving of at least a little respect, Basic is here to stay. And when it comes to hammering out a quick app, it's hard to beat.

SideBar Basic was developed at Dartmouth College in 1964 under the direction of J. Kemeny and T. Kurtz. It was meant to be a very simple language to learn and also one that would be easy to translate.   In addition, the designers wished it to be a "stepping-stone" for students to learn one of the more powerful languages at the time. There are a large number of web sites dedicated to the history of Basic, and a great place to start is www.fys.ruu.nl/~bergmann/history.html.

This book assumes that you know a little about Basic programming, although you will be given so many programming samples (with really good documentation – I promise!) and templates that even new programmers should have little difficulty getting up and running. Whenever practical, screen shots will be provided as well. With a little history and humor to keep it all in perspective.

By the way, although many of you will be able to read this book and understand the concepts without your copy of NS Basic running, I strongly encourage you to try each of the techniques as you read them. Some of the programs build on previous ideas, and although you won't have to enter a single line of code for them (if you use the included projects), there's no substitute for digging into the code while you're reading.

It's a Zen thing.

Installing NS Basic

Minimum Requirements

In order to install and run the NS Basic IDE, your system will have to meet these basic requirements:

-   Operating System: Windows 95, 98, Me, 2000, NT, or XP.

-   Hard Drive space: Approximately 10 MB for NS Basic and its sample files. Approximately 75 MB will be required if all of the additional materials on the CD are installed.

-   Mouse or similar pointing device. Not strictly needed for installing, but essential for placing objects on the IDE screen. Important for maintaining sanity.

-   Palm or compatible device running Palm OS 3.0 or above (certain functions require the use of OS versions 3.3 or 3.5 or above. I'll let you know in the specific sections when the OS is an issue.) If you don't have a Palm device, you can use one of the versions of the Palm OS Emulator (POSE) included on the CD. We'll discuss the pro's and con's of testing with POSE later, in the appendix "Running POSE".

-   HotSync cradle/cable, and HotSync or similar file transfer utility to transfer programs and databases to your Palm device. The ability to HotSync isn't strictly needed to install and run NS Basic, and isn't necessary if you are only using POSE. However, without HotSync or another file transfer utility, you won't be able to use your NS Basic applications on your actual Palm device.

-   Coffee...lots of coffee.

To install NS Basic, refer to the instructions in the INSTALL.TXT file on the included CD. Word of advice – unless you have a *really* good reason to change it, use the default installation paths during the installation process. You might otherwise have difficulty loading and compiling applications written by other users.

> **Note** Some of the applications mentioned in this book or included on the CD ("Add Field Test", "BannerDemo", "Composer", "CreatorID List", "Directory", "General Template", "PDB Reader", and "Popup Text Changer"), and many applications written by other NS Basic programmers use additional code libraries that are only available to registered NS Basic users. Compiled versions of my applications are provided, along with their shared libraries, but you'll need to register and obtain the full NS Basic package in order to include these libraries in your projects. I'll let you know which applications in this book use these

libraries, and how you can tell by looking at an application's source code
which libraries are required.

When you get a little curious, look at some of my projects for an idea of the different
things you can do with NS Basic. These include a Tic-Tac-Toe game, a graphical
EtchSketch that is similar to the old "Etch-a-Sketch" toy (but without the messy
aluminum powder that spills out when you accidentally drop it down a flight of concrete
stairs), a Mouse Race game that uses bitmaps as sprites (movable images), a Memo Pad
style app that allows memos up to 32000+ characters, a simple doodling program, a
music composer, and others. I'll even include templates that you can use for developing
your NS Basic apps (these templates – in the "template" directory - include code for
using menus, the Palm clipboard, and other common functions). All of the other code
examples, including projects and code modules can be found in the "projects" directory,
with bitmaps in the "bitmap" directory. I was originally going to place code for each
chapter in a separate directory, but several projects are mentioned in multiple chapters,
and there's really no sense in duplicating projects.

So, if you're ready, let's get started.

SideBar I take a lot of pride in my work. I also take responsibility for
any errors that find their way into the manuscript. So, here's my
promise: No bad code, period. I take full ownership of every piece of
code for every project in this book, unless I specifically state that the
code came from someone else. I also promise to comment each project
as thoroughly as possible without getting petty – I'm not going to
comment every line of every project. Neither of us will survive that!

To make life easier for us all, updates, corrections, and sample code will
be available at the book's support web site:

http://www.nsbasicprogrammingforpalmos.com

If you DO find an error, let me know, and I'll correct it if I write a second
book, and give you credit (you were hoping for a refund, or at least a
free pizza, weren't you?). I can't guarantee any refund, since that's up
to my publisher and their lawyers. And we don't want to start talking
about lawyers.

Chapter II - What I meant to say was...

Throughout this book you will run into abbreviations, phrases or words that you may be unfamiliar with. To help you decipher what I'm talking about, the following should be helpful:

Abbreviations, terms, and mnemonics

API

An acronym for **A**pplication **P**rogramming **I**nterface (sometimes referred to as Application Programmer's Interface), the API is a set of routines built into the operating system to provide standard methods to accomplish common programming tasks. API's also make programming simpler, as they isolate the programmer from many of the mundane details. NS Basic provides various levels of API support, from the ability to call API functions directly, to many statements and functions that provide a simplified "wrapper" for many of the API routines.

Argument

No, we're not getting into a heated discussion here. In programming "lingo," an argument is a value passed to a subroutine, function, or program. For instance, if you want to determine the square root of a number, you would write something like this:

```
x=SQRT(y)
```

In this example, y is the argument for the square root function.

ASCII

An acronym for **A**merican **S**tandard **C**ode for **I**nformation **I**nterchange, ASCII codes are more-or-less standard codes that provide numeric representation of alphanumeric and punctuation characters. I say "more-or-less" because there are different implementations of the ASCII standards (making them less *standard*, but I didn't make the rules, so don't get angry at me!). The low 7 bits of the 8-bit ASCII code are the most consistent, with the high bit used for extended ASCII in some systems. The Palm OS Font tables in the appendix show the various characters associated with the ASCII codes for each font.

Bit

Short for **bi**nary dig**it**, a bit is the smallest unit of information represented by a computer – comparable to a switch being on (1) or off (0). It would be cumbersome and very time consuming to perform all computing operations one bit at a time, so longer combinations of bits (including nybbles, bytes, words, double words, etc.) are used as well. NS Basic variables have different bit lengths; byte variables use 8 bits, numeric variables consist of 16, 32, and 64 bit lengths, and string variables can contain up to 32766 characters of 8 bits each. User-defined types (UDT's) and arrays can exist as combinations of the other variable types, so their lengths are variable.

Byte

A byte is defined as 8 bits. Since each bit position can have one of two (2^1) values (on or off), a byte can have 256 (2^8) different values. Since the English and most international alphabets (including upper and lower case characters), the digits 0-9, and the common punctuation marks can be defined using fewer than 256 different values, characters are usually defined by a single byte each. To see how geeky programmers can be, see *nybble*, below.

Case-insensitive, Case-sensitive

THIS SENTENCE IS IN ALL UPPER CASE LETTERS. while this is in all lower case letters (e e cummings would have been proud). Case-insensitive means that the case (capitalization) doesn't matter. Case-sensitive means that lower and upper case characters are not viewed as being equal The Creator ID, for example, is case-sensitive, so the Character ID's of "aple", "Aple", "APLe", and "ApLe" are different 4-character strings. NS Basic keywords are case-insensitive; the commands "Beep" and "bEEp" would be identical to the NS Basic compiler (NS Basic's code editor maintains keywords in "proper" case – first letter capitalized – by default, but you can change this). However, the Palm Creator ID's, database names, and database types are case-sensitive.

CD

Compact Disk (you already knew that!). When I refer to "the CD" I mean the CD included with this book. This CD includes NS Basic, numerous programming examples, accessory programs to make your programming life easier, and some miscellaneous junk that was cluttering the hard drive in my laptop. Although the CD shipped from NSBasic Corporation contains some of the samples found here, any mention of "the CD" in this book refers to the CD that accompanies this book, and not any CD that may have come from NS Basic, Palm, Handspring, Microsoft, or other vendors.

IDE

Integrated Development Environment. Before languages like NS Basic, we had to use our favorite text editors, then take the edited text and run it through preprocessors, compilers, interpreters – and repeat the tiresome process for every syntax error. The NS Basic IDE allows you to graphically design forms, enter/edit code, and compile without forcing you to use a different tool for each step. Syntax errors usually bring you to the spot in code where the error occurred, streamlining the debugging process. The NS Basic IDE allows you to access many of your favorite tools, and can send the finished application directly to POSE for testing, or to your Palm device. There are times when you'll want to separate many of these tasks, but having the capability to do them together is one feature you'll come to appreciate.

GUI

Pronounced "gooey", GUI stands for **G**raphical **U**ser **I**nterface. Back in the early days, all screen and printer output was performed using only alphanumeric output (letters and numbers). We didn't have mice, and there were no "buttons" or other interactive screen elements. We used the Tab and cursor (arrow) keys, or their keyboard equivalents, to position our cursor on the screen for text input. Eventually, people got a little tired of looking at simple text, and produced crude graphics using text characters. Soon, more graphical systems (such as Apple's Macintosh) gradually became more acceptable, both for display and for user interaction. "Press any key..." was replaced by "Click the [OK] button", and operating systems started using graphical "windows" to improve the "look and feel" of their applications. Although text-based systems are still very functional, most of us prefer to break up the monotony with appropriate use of graphics. As we'll discuss later, graphics can improve the appearance of an application, or be a distraction, so they should be used appropriately. The Palm OS GUI is familiar to most users, so I'll show you how to use this familiarity to your advantage.

Nybble

No, I didn't make this up! Since a byte is 8 bits, and a nibble is a small bite, somebody thought it would be cute to call a 4-bit value a nybble (a "small byte"). This is one reason why the world thinks programmers are geeks. Maybe this is why some programmers spell nybble as "nibble" instead. It's *still* geeky. NS Basic doesn't provide built-in functions to deal with nybbles, and I don't think you'll miss them all that much.

OS

Operating **S**ystem. Although I've made every attempt to be as clear as possible when I'm referring to the Palm OS or the Windows OS, in general I'm referring to the Palm OS when I say "OS" in this book. I guess you could refer to an operating system guru as the "Wizard of OS" (sorry – I couldn't resist the pun!).

Windows

Windows can have at least three meanings when dealing with NS Basic programming. It may refer to one or more of the Microsoft Windows ™ family of operating systems, or to NS Basic graphics windows. Windows are also where readers of any *other* book on NS Basic programming should toss those books (just kidding – don't take everything so literally!!!). Actually, it's important to study different sources, and see what fits your programming needs the best.

Word

A word is a bit hard to define (no pun intended), but it is alternately used to define a 16 bit (2 byte) value, or the largest number of bits that the computer's processor or memory bus can transfer at one time, which is 32-64 bits or higher on most personal computers used today. Since the definition of a word is so open to interpretation, it's best to refer to values by the number of bits or bytes used.

| SideBar | There are a number of web sites that contain *much* more comprehensive glossaries than this, including www.glossary-tech.com. Not only is it a great place to look up unfamiliar terms or abbreviations, but it's also one of the best cures for insomnia you'll ever come across.

Conventions used in this book

Not only can some of the abbreviations and terms appear unfamiliar at first, but so can the layout of the information in this book. Although not everything presented in the book will appeal to everyone, I've included code examples, tips, warnings, notes, and other tidbits of information that I hope will be interesting or useful at least to *somebody*. You might think otherwise, though, so here's how you can separate the wheat from the chaff (I think that's my only biblical reference in this book):

Code will be set aside like this:

```
For LoopCounter=1 to 100
    'do something really useful
Next
```

Code that spans more than one line will use "_", the "continuation character" (for the book, or in code, although you don't need to include it when you're typing, and you won't see it too often in my code):

```
For ReallyLongString=1 to 10
    ReallyLongString=ReallyLongString+"abcdefghijklmnopqrstu
vwxyz_
    01234567890"
Next
```

Useful tips (you know, stuff that will probably make it into the manual someday, but I hope I beat NS Basic to it) look like this:

| Tip | Since Button text is always center-justified, consider using frame-less Buttons as headers for rows of fields, labels, or other objects.

If there's a particularly nasty bug or programming practice that you should be forewarned about, you'll see words of caution as:

| Caution | In order to avoid public humiliation (and improve sales), always beta test your applications before releasing them (certain PC operating system vendors may disagree)!

There will occasionally also be small tidbits of information that aren't really tips, but don't have potentially serious enough consequences to qualify as cautions, and you'll see these notes set off this way:

Note You don't have to use code modules for subroutines – they can be placed in your app's StartUp code, a Form's Before, After, or Event code – virtually anywhere.

Face it – programming can be boring, and reading about programming even more so (if that's possible). So, once in a while I'll throw in a little history or loosely-related information to try to keep things interesting. Since these references may not appeal to all audiences, you can spot them (and ignore them, if you want) set off from the rest of the text as sidebars like this:

SideBar If you think 2MB or 8MB of memory is limiting, consider the following. My first "personal computer" was a Timex Sinclair, a small book-sized computer with 2KB memory (you could get an additional 16KB memory module if you wanted to do some "serious" programming). I thought I was in heaven when I got my Commodore 64 (with 64KB memory)! I don't have either of these computers anymore, but I wish I did – they're both fetching pretty good prices on many online auction sites.

Chapter III - Important Concepts

(for me, at least)

You might think that it's somewhat presumptive of me to tell you what the important concepts are. Especially since I'm not a professional programmer (and you *might* be). But I'm willing to bet that a large proportion of those of you who buy and read this book aren't professional programmers, either. We're a pretty diverse group – physicians, electricians, hobbyists, taxi drivers, amateur kite flyers, etc. We didn't study lots of programming theory, algorithm development, the history of bits, bytes, words, double words, hex, octal, and other mundane topics. We program our computers because we have a specific task in mind, and don't always have the time to experiment as much as we'd like to (except for hobbyists, who program for the "fun" of it; and that's just sad). We're more interested in the *product* than the *production*. This book is written for us, the professional non-programmers. But you programmer types are welcome, too. Just take the next few paragraphs with a grain of salt. And, if that salt's on the rim of a margarita glass, that's even better.

As you'll soon see, programming the Palm OS devices will stretch your programming talents, and will force you to carefully plan every aspect of program design – whether you're a professional programmer or not. The current crop of Palm OS devices aren't terribly fast, have 8-16 MB or less of memory, usually have 160 pixel by 160 pixel screens that are slightly larger than a thumb's length high by a thumb's length wide (yes, I checked), and have no physical keyboard or numeric pad for direct data entry. Although at first these may seem like limitations, they actually help you focus on writing compact, efficient code, and keep the screen less cluttered.

OK, I lied. These limitations are REAL, and until you get used to them, they can be a real pain. The only true advantage to the small screen and lack of keyboard is that you learn to maximize program function with minimal user input/output. You deal with small sections of a program at any one time, which can help you debug and streamline your code.

Palm OS and NS Basic-specific Programming

Programs are databases

It may seem a little odd at first, but for reasons that I'll explain later, a Palm program is actually a specific type of Palm OS database. In fact, as far as the Palm OS is concerned, ANY file on the device is a database - not just "any old" database, but a database that must conform to the Palm OS specifications. The Palm OS launcher (the part of the operating system that, among other things, determines what application to run when you tap on an icon) expects to find certain identifying and application-specific information at specific locations within the database. If it can't find this information, it won't know what to do with the database. From the typical NS Basic programmer's standpoint, however, only a few of these tidbits of information are important to maintain control over: the Creator ID, the internal Palm OS name (not necessarily the same as the filename), and the data type.

Creator ID

The Creator ID is fairly simple to understand in principle – it's a case-sensitive (that is, UPPER and lower case characters are different, so "A" is not the same as "a"), 4 character (no more, no less) string of characters used by the Palm OS to identify an application. Although at first it seems that this would severely limit the number of possible ID's, a little math shows that these 4 ASCII characters (if we limit ourselves to numbers and upper/lower case letters, although the Palm OS allows ASCII characters from 33-127) can provide 62 different possible characters per position, or $62*62*62*62 = 14,776,336$ different Creator ID's. Although Palm has reserved the ID's that are in all lower case letters, there are still plenty to go around for the rest of us.

Caution When I first started programming using NS Basic, I ignored the "all Creator ID's must be unique" warning, and created different programs with the ID of "TEST" – and loaded them on the Palm Emulator. Actually, I didn't *ignore* the warning, but just thought that it was a *suggestion*, not a necessity. After all, I was the creator, so as long as I stuck to my own Creator ID, I'd be OK, right? Wrong! My apps crashed and burned. It turns out that the Creator ID identifies the *program*, not the *programmer*, as the creator! Since the Palm OS uses the ID to identify the program, more than one program with the same Creator ID will confuse the launcher, and you'll be in for some unpredictable behavior. Take my word for it, and make sure your Creator ID's are unique. NS Basic's IDE even provides a link to the Palm Creator ID registration Web page, so if you have an Internet connection, you can check for an unused Creator ID while you're programming, and register your own ID, to help prevent future conflicts.

By the way, not only do programs have Creator ID's, but so do other Palm OS files/databases. Luckily, non-program databases (e.g., PDB files) don't *need* to have unique Creator ID's, since a program may have several databases with the same Creator ID. In fact, keeping the Creator ID of your program and its associated files the same helps maintain consistency in your programming, and has another advantage; deleting a program from the Palm also removes the associated databases with the same Creator ID. This helps avoid having "lost" databases hanging around wasting valuable Palm memory.

Note Although deleting an application also removes its associated databases, beaming with Palm OS 3.5 and earlier doesn't work that way. You'll have to beam databases separately using BeamBox or another third-party beaming application. However, starting with Palm OS 4.0, there's a "bundle" bit that can be set on apps to have their databases beamed along with them based on Creator ID. Unfortunately, it's too early to tell if the usual beaming apps will consistently pay attention to this bit – and it's not something that NS Basic has exposed to the programmer (yet).

So, if you haven't already done so while programming in the NS Basic IDE using the Creator ID link, when you're about to distribute that "killer app" of yours, check with Palm's Creator ID Database (currently at http://www.Palm OS.com/dev/tech/Palm OS/creatorid/) to see if your ID is available. Better still, go ahead and register your ID while you're there. It doesn't cost anything, and you can rest assured that your ID is safe. As long as everybody else follows the rules, that is!

Database/Program Name

You might think that, like the Creator ID, the internal Palm OS name of your program needs to be unique – and you're correct (however, the program's name can be up to 31 characters long, so it's HIGHLY unlikely that you'll ever come close to running out of names). In addition, like the Creator ID, the internal Palm OS name for the programs and databases is case-sensitive. You can look upon this as a blessing or a curse – you'll see why when we get to database access. Palm also has recommended a standard practice of appending the Creator ID to the end of database names (even though it doesn't apply this standard to its *own* databases!).

> **Caution** Don't confuse the internal Palm name with the "external" filename used by Windows, with its filename+extension (*filename.ext*) format. The Palm OS expects to find the name of the database within the database header, which is where it gets placed when it's created by your NS Basic application. This internal name may or may not be the same as the Windows filename, and doesn't need to have an extension (e.g., .pdb, .prc, .exe) at all.

Develop a naming convention that works for you, stick with it, and you'll be safe. Or at least you won't be up at 2:00 am wondering why your program won't read the database "CustData" when you named it "custdata" in the first place. (There's a Windows utility called PDB Info on the CD that will show you the internal Palm OS name, Creator ID, and other information for any Palm OS program or database).

> **Caution** You can't use *all* 255 ASCII characters in your database/prc names. You need to stick with the characters from ASCII 32-126, or POSE and the Palm devices may refuse to load them!

Data Type

You don't need to be too worried or concerned about restrictions placed on the 4-character Data Type. There don't appear to be too many applications that really use this information, anyway, but for most purposes it's best left as "data" for databases, "libr" for libraries, and "appl" for applications. If you are using a third-party application to create PDB or PRC files, and have control over the data type, keep in mind that the Palm OS launcher displays programs only if they have the type "appl". Library files such as MathLib, which have the data type "libr" aren't displayed. Although NS Basic allows you to change the data type, it's of little importance to the beginning NS Basic programmer, but I included the info here for completeness. I'm just that kind of guy!

Tip When you start extending NS Basic using shared libraries, you'll see that you can use the data type to your advantage to hide applications by giving them a data type other than "appl", and you can group databases using any arbitrary data type. For now, keep it simple, and save the experimenting for later.

Object-Oriented vs. Top-Down Programming

I suppose there are a number of programmers today who have only programmed using object-oriented languages with feature-rich code editors. However, it wasn't too long ago that we wrote programs using punch cards (cards that went through a mechanical "punch" to create holes for an optomechanical reader to identify and decode later). We wrote one line per card, with line numbers:

```
100 PRINT "Initialization section"
110 (some other code)
120 (more code)
130 (you get the idea)
```

We would then place the completed decks of these cards into the optomechanical readers (way back in the dinosaur era) to read them one card at a time. The line numbers weren't as important for the card reader as they were for us programmers. Large stacks of cards tend to get hard to handle (especially if you're a klutz like me), so dropping and scattering a stack of 400 cards without line numbers would have sent countless programmers screaming. Not that rearranging 400 cards *with* line numbers was all that much fun, but those were the times we thanked our favorite Divine Being for line numbers, and vowed to forever be more careful.

Unless we were writing an extremely simple program, it was imperative that we first sat down and diagramed the program, using flowcharts (we'll discuss them later) or "pseudo-code," prior to actually creating a single line of code. There was a start, an end, and one or more (usually *many* more) steps between the two, with the program executing instructions from the "top-down" to the end.

Many of the initial steps in the program (conveniently known as the "initialization" subroutine or section) dealt with housekeeping routines such as setting up variables, file access, and initial printer or screen output for the user. Once the user gave some feedback, the program acted on that feedback, and eventually worked down the flowchart to the end of the program.

Programming with object-oriented languages such as NS Basic is somewhat different. There is still initialization code (usually put in the program's initial startup code, or run as part of each form's "before" or "after" code), but you'll write the bulk of your program's code to respond to actions performed on or by program objects. If this seems a bit confusing, it's actually much clearer in practice than in writing. (By the way, I will often refer to the terms "form" or "screen" in this book. When used to describe an NS Basic form, they refer to the same object, so the terms can be used interchangeably).

Using objects to control program flow results in code that's easier to maintain (in theory, at least). Each object's code typically performs a specific task, which logically is associated with that object. However, since you may not have control over the order in which objects are used, many error-checking and data-validation steps may be necessary to assure that crucial code is not skipped. You may also find yourself repeating similar code for different objects (and often on different forms), but much of this code may be placed in code modules, subroutines, or functions that are accessible from any form or object in your program.

As you study the different programs included with this book, think of how you would accomplish the same programming task with the older style of top-down programming (most of the highly graphical programs would be extremely difficult to code in this manner).

Structured Programming

Just because you aren't doing top-down programming doesn't mean you can forget about structure. After all, you can scatter just as many GOTO's in NS Basic as you can in other "flavors" of Basic. In fact, as you design the layout of your program, it's easy to get lazy and "code-as-you-go" without much concern over structure. However, a little thought into your program's goals and objectives can save hours of re-coding later. It's *much* easier to work out a program's structure prior to the initial coding than it is to try to restructure it later (especially when you start adding new options and error-checking).

Structured programming breaks a program's tasks into sub-tasks, usually in the form of subroutines. A basic rule (no pun intended) is that every subroutine should perform one main task, and should have only one entry point and one exit. You'll find, after programming for some time, that many of these subroutines are "reusable" enough to place in code modules that can be used by any of your programs. Maintaining these subroutines as separate code makes them easier to debug and modify as needed (we'll discuss subroutines and functions later – I just wanted you to get a feel for them). Each object's code is a subroutine by itself, and you'll soon understand how these subroutines become part of a larger program.

Flowcharting

Many of us programming "dinosaurs" learned to both bless and curse flowcharting. For those of you who don't know what a flowchart is, it's a graphical representation of a program's flow, or how to get from point A to point B (to point C, to point D, and so on...). Before most of us ever wrote a single line of code, we would sit down and diagram each section of the program.

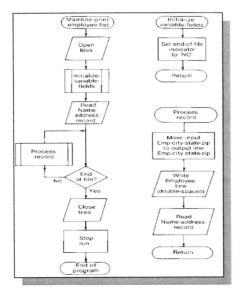

Breaking the programming task into individual logical blocks this way made it easier to manage the different routines. Remember, we were writing code one line at a time using punch cards (or slow video terminals or line printers). We didn't have mice to select blocks of text – we didn't even have word processors, just simple text editors that weren't very forgiving. Making changes to code was a long, laborious task, and not one to be taken lightly. Cut and paste didn't exist (unless you used scissors and actual paste!); everything was done one line at a time.

And we walked to and from school, 12 miles in the snow, uphill both ways...

Although today's word processors and code editors have come a long way (the editor in NS Basic helps you structure your code through color-coding keywords, comments, etc.) there's still no substitute for taking the time to prepare your program's flow before writing the actual code. You don't need to use flowcharts, but you should at least take the time to outline the important steps in your programs. That will make them more readable and maintainable later (and any programming technique that can help you maintain your sanity is worth the extra effort).

The Palm OS is "Event-driven"

This is one of the more difficult concepts for new Palm OS programmers to understand. However, it's important to understand what this means, as it will affect the execution of your programs' code.

As we previously discussed, older "top-down" programs executed one instruction after another, in the order that the instructions appeared, from the top line of code to the bottom (except for code that branched to another location, but the code was still executed sequentially). The Palm OS takes a different approach. Code is still executed in the order it is encountered, but the operating system uses an "event queue" to determine what code to execute next. Instead of a program flowing from line to line, the program instead tells the operating system "I have an event for you to take care of, when you're don't with what you're doing". By submitting events to be handled by the operating system, a Palm program allows the operating system to determine when the code for the event should be executed. When you tap on a button in an application, that application tells the Palm OS to handle the button tap when it's done with its current task.

How does the Palm OS keep track of its events? It maintains an "event queue", or internal list of events that need to be handled. Some of these will be events based on your user's actions, some may be events produced by the operating system itself, others can be generated by code in your applications, and so on. This allows the Palm to store events – you can think of the event queue as a sort of internal "To Do List".

Not only does the Palm OS handle this queue, but you can check to see if an event is waiting, what type of event it is, and even take over the handling of the event. This allows you to "trap" events, deciding which events the Palm OS should handle, and what you want to take over instead. Or, you can perform some processing based on an event, then allow the Palm OS to perform its own processing afterwards. As we'll see in the chapters on "Menus" and "Interacting with your user", being able to interact with the event queue gives you an awesome power over the Palm device. Don't worry - I'll warn you when you need to be careful of abusing this power.

Prototyping - know your audience!

Unless you are programming for your own pleasure (?), your final programs will most likely be used by people who may not understand why you designed them the way you did. As previously mentioned, the current crop of Palm OS devices (with a few exceptions) are limited by tiny 160 x 160 pixel screens – not the most conducive to the creation of highly graphical, "user-friendly" interfaces. Like Goldilocks visiting the home of Papa, Mama, and Baby Bear, your user may find your program objects too big, too small, or (hopefully!) "just right."

But, how will you know what "just right" is? Well, you have a few options:

- Write what you want – if your user doesn't like it, too bad!
- Write what you want – and be prepared to change what needs changing.
- Ask your user(s) throughout the design process for input.
- Create quick prototypes, or demos. (I'd call it creating "Pilot Programs" but the pun is too corny, even for me!)

Depending on your program and target audience, any of the above may serve your purposes well. Just realize that there's always more than one way to accomplish anything, so don't take criticism too personally. It's often someone else's perspective that allows us to see more clearly. Remember *who* you're programming for, and *why*.

Debugging/alpha/beta testing

Of course, once you finally write your program, it will be perfect, right? Maybe, but don't count on it. In fact, if possible, don't even allow yourself to be the person primarily responsible for evaluating, testing, and debugging your own software. Although you might be able to catch most syntactic errors (actually, the NS Basic compiler does a great job of that by itself), the logical or procedural problems are the ones that are the most difficult to find and solve.

Once you have the core syntax worked out, give the program to a small number of users (the *alpha* testing stage, when the program has the basic elements, but before you decide to "fine tune" the program) and ask them to find any errors. *Better still, bet them that they can't!* Given that kind of challenge (and a prize worth shooting for, like all the stuffed spinach pizza they can eat), testers will plug in the most unlikely, bizarre data, and do their best to utterly destroy the program. That's what you really need, after all, since *you* will probably try to use the data most likely to make your program work. The real world isn't so kind!

Once you've paid for all the pizza your budget will allow, you'll have the major weaknesses exposed. At this stage you're ready to fix the bugs, then "dress up" your program with the tiny details that only a programmer could love. Release the software to a larger group, preferably including some of your target audience, for *beta* testing to find the residual bugs. As with alpha testing, beta testing isn't meant to prove that the software is ready for distribution, but to find bugs. *In general, beta testing that doesn't reveal any bugs should be performed again with an entirely new group of testers.* You want bugs caught BEFORE the software hits its intended target audience.

When it's time to scrap it and start over

This is the most difficult step for any programmer to take. You've worked hard on your program, and despite all the modifications and revisions, it just "isn't right". This is where creating quick prototypes is very helpful, since you don't want to "kill your baby". In fact, if you create different prototypes, it's almost a guarantee that one or more will be thrown away. Better to throw away a quick-and-dirty prototype than a completed program, however, so don't be too attached to a particular user interface or design. Design your prototypes with the intention that some *will* be discarded. Edison didn't find the proper filament for the electric light in one try, so why should the design of a program be any different? If one design doesn't work, scrap it, and try a different approach. Don't think of it as failure, but as *eliminating that which does not work*. It's a step in the right direction!

Chapter IV - Your first project - "Hello, World!"

I don't know where, when, or why it became customary to start *every* programming book with an example that displays "Hello, World!", but I'm not about to rock the boat.

Before we go further, think of how you would accomplish this simple task. In the early days of Basic, this would be accomplished with the following code:

```
100 Print "Hello, World!"
110 End
```

This would send the string "Hello, World!" to the "default output device" – usually a screen or printer. The string would be displayed or printed at the current cursor position. You could clear the screen, print some blank lines, or position the cursor in various ways, but eventually your message would get through.

Palm programming with NS Basic is different in many respects, and this is no exception. Although NS Basic has methods to print this information directly on the screen, most screen "printing" that you will perform in NS Basic will be by modifying the Text property of an existing form object.

To see one way to get this accomplished, load the HELLO.PRJ file into the NS Basic IDE, press the [F5] key to create the HELLO.PRC file, and load it along with NSBruntime.prc (if you're not creating a "Fat App," where the runtime is bundled into your application's PRC file) and MathLib.prc (although it's not needed for this project, you should load it anyway, since we'll use it later) into POSE or your Palm OS device. You can also save, compile, and automatically load the program into the Install directory to be HotSync'ed on your actual Palm device, or have NS Basic directly load and run the program into POSE (based on your selections in Run, Compile Options in the IDE).

If you are running POSE and have told NS Basic to load and run the app, the "Hello, World!" program will start automatically. If not, you'll need to transfer the HELLO.PRC file to POSE or your Palm device (with runtime, as described above). The Palm OS launcher will place the program in the "Unfiled" program group (or *category*, in Palm OS lingo), so you may have to scroll through the icons or select "All" or "Unfiled" from the list of categories at the upper-right corner of the Palm Screen in order to see it. How you get there is unimportant (although tapping the little "Home" or "arrow" shaped Launcher "soft key" will skip the "Unfiled" section. Just thought you might want to know that).

Just get there, and tap on the Hello icon. The ever-popular "Hello, World!" message gets displayed.

Not too exciting, to be sure, but it's a nice start. We'll examine the code and describe just what happened. Once you can understand how NS Basic displays information, you're well on your way to creating a "real" program.

Return to the NS Basic IDE, and reload the HELLO.PRJ file, if necessary. You'll notice that on the main (only) form there is a single object with the name Fld1005:

This is a "Field" object, which is designed to hold text. Click on this field, and look at the list of properties (in the Property Explorer window, of all places!) to see what you can – and can't – change.

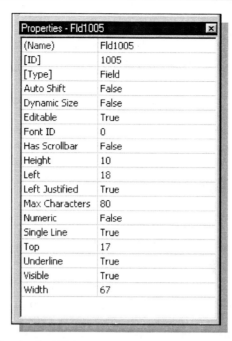

Properties - Fld1005	☒
(Name)	Fld1005
[ID]	1005
[Type]	Field
Auto Shift	False
Dynamic Size	False
Editable	True
Font ID	0
Has Scrollbar	False
Height	10
Left	18
Left Justified	True
Max Characters	80
Numeric	False
Single Line	True
Top	17
Underline	True
Visible	True
Width	67

Most of the information in the "Field Properties" box will be set at "design time" when you create or modify the project. In fact, all of these items (except Max Characters and Visible) can *only* be modified at design time, not during the running of your program.

Note I lied. You actually CAN modify some of the other properties at run time, but only by using API (Application Programming Interface) calls or "shared libraries" that act as a bridge to the API. The functions in the API aren't intrinsic to NS Basic, however, so the above statement is true if you stick with strictly NS Basic statements and commands. We'll explore the API later, and introduce you to the dark but wonderful world under the hood of the Palm OS API.

You have control, at design time, over whether the data is aligned to the left or right of the field (left or right justified), whether the field is underlined (and therefore visible even when it has no data), whether the field is limited to only one line (or can be a multi-line text field), or whether or not there is a "scroll bar" displayed to the right of the field (useful when there are more lines in the field than can be displayed at one time). You also have control over the number of characters that can be entered by the user (although you can place up to 32767 characters in a field programmatically. We'll explore all of the properties and methods later, in the chapter on NS Basic Objects.

Note If keeping track of all these properties sounds overwhelming, relax. The Field object has more properties than any other object, so it actually gets easier than this.

Experiment with any of these settings, and see what happens. Drag the field around, resize it, whatever you feel compelled to do. Go ahead – I'll wait. If things get a little messed up, just reload the HELLO.PRJ project from the CD.

Now, right-click on the field, and choose "View Code" to see the field object's associated code.

What? There's no code?

That's right; since the field object doesn't really DO anything in this app, there's no reason to give it any code. Instead, we have to place the code to display the "Hello, World!" message in the necessary location so that it gets run during the program's execution automatically. Although it might seem logical to put it in the program's startup code, it won't work there, since the field object won't be created until after its form is displayed, and that doesn't occur until after the startup code is completed. So, in order to show our "Hello, World!" message, we need to put code to change the text property of the Field object to "Hello, World!" in our main form's "After" code. This can be accessed in the Project Explorer (the list of objects at the right of the IDE screen) by right-clicking on "Form1004/Form1004(After)" and choosing "View After Code".

Note If this sounds complicated and confusing, relax. When we discuss the various code sections, this will all become clear to you. I promise!

Before we leave the project, take a look at the Project Explorer – there's a bitmap there, but the program doesn't display anything. Why have a bitmap that doesn't get displayed? The truth is, the bitmap *does* get displayed – as the Hello, World icon! NS Basic initially used a separate icon as a resource (part of the PRC file). NS Basic now incorporates ResIn (previously known as PalmRI) to allow the use of standard bitmaps (including BMP, GIF, and JPG files) for icons and bitmaps. Large icons (22x22 pixels) are displayed when the Palm launcher is in its standard, "icon" view. Small icons (15x9 pixels) are displayed when the launcher is in "list" view. It takes some creativity to create tiny, useful icons, but NS Basic supplies a good selection. I've even added a few, and I can't draw a stick figure of a stick!

While experimenting with the NS Basic IDE, you might have discovered that double-clicking an object brings up the code for that object. It's a shortcut you'll use time and time again. Explore the other parts of the NS Basic IDE. You won't cause any permanent damage – you've always got the CD to fall back on. Just come back to the book when you're done exploring.

Chapter V – Literals, Constants, Variables and Arrays

Without the ability to declare and change the values of different programming elements, programs would be unable to perform many useful tasks. In fact, they would be severely limited to whatever information the programmer had on hand at the time the program was written. Not very useful or "friendly," to say the least.

NS Basic has a modest collection of both constants and variables, including a very powerful user-defined variable type that at first might seem cumbersome, but is so flexible that time spent understanding and experimenting with this variable type will be well worth the effort.

Literals and Constants

Like other dialects of Basic, NS Basic allows the use of literals that are defined at design time. The following types of literals are supported:

NS Basic Literal Types

Constant	Example
Integer	16
Float	3.14159
String	"this is a string"
Hexadecimal (preceded by &h)	&h07

NS Basic also has a number of intrinsic, pre-defined constants. Most of these constants describe the status of a form object or event. Without wasting any more time writing about them, here they are (with more detail on each constant as we get to the appropriate object or event later):

NS Basic "built-in" Constants

NS Basic Constant	Function/description
nsbOn, nsbOff	Used to set/return pushbutton status
nsbYes, nsbNo	Used as Boolean values for yes/no
nsbChecked, nsbUnchecked	Used to set/return checkbox status
nsbNormal, nsbInverted, nsbGrey, nsbGray	Used as graphics pen type
nsbKeyOrButton	Used in determining GetEventType button or "soft-key" status
nsbPenDown, nsbPenUp	Used in determining pen status with GetPen
nsbWait, nsbNoWait	Used with Sound statement
True, False	Used as Boolean values (same as nsbYes and nsbNo)

NS Basic doesn't use the CONST statement to define constants for use in your programs. Instead, global variables (see below) can be defined and used much in the same way, except that they are defined during run time, not at design time. These global variables can lend considerable flexibility to your programming. We'll cover global variables in more detail in the next section.

> Caution Be careful about using too many global variables in your NS Basic programs. Some programmers declare all variables as Global, rather than dimensioning them as needed. During run time, NS Basic has to create space in a special database for each variable, so having a large number of Global variables (usually defined in the StartUp code) can create a long pause in the starting of your application. (Note – NS Basic may change their variable handling in the future, so at some point this may not be an important issue). For now, use globals when you need to have the same information available to multiple sections of your programs, but use them sparingly.

Variables

In their simplest terms, variables are merely placeholders for information that can change. Numerous variable types exist to allow programs flexibility in how information is stored, manipulated, and displayed. NS Basic supports most of the common variable types, but with some differences in the degree of precision compared to how those variables are used in Visual Basic and other languages.

NS Basic Variable Types (with Visual Basic comparisons)

Variable	NS Basic Description	Visual Basic 6 Notes
Integer	Used for whole numbers, whether positive or negative. Integers are stored in databases as 32-bit values.	Equivalent in size and precision to VB Long.
Short	Like Integer, but stored as a 16 bit value.	Equivalent in size and precision to VB Integer.
Float	Used for numbers that may contain fractional values. Floats are stored as 64-bit values.	Same as VB Double.
Double	Same as Float in computations and database storage requirements.	Same as VB Double.
Single	Same as Float except that Singles are stored as 16-bit values.	Same as VB Single.
Date	Used to store NS Basic Date values. NS Basic Date values are stored in databases as 64-bit floating point values.	No equivalent in VB.
Time	Used to store NS Basic Time values. Like Date values, NS Basic stores Time values as 64-bit floating point values.	No equivalent in VB.
Byte	Used to hold a single character (8 bits) of data. Unlike Strings, Byte values are NOT stored with a null (chr(0)) terminator.	Same as VB Byte.
String	Used to store alphanumeric data that can be greater than 1 Byte in length. Stored in memory and databases with null terminators after each String. String variables can be up to 32766 characters long.	Same as VB String, although VB strings can contain up to approximately 2 billion characters.
Database	Used to hold the "handle" of a database for subsequent file I/O. Physical databases must be dimensioned as Database type before file operations can take place.	Similar in function to the File Handle in VB.
Variant	Used to transfer information in SysTrapSub and SysTrapFunc statements. Undefined (and officially unsupported) for any other use.	The Variant in VB can refer to Date/time, floating-point number, integer, string, or object types.

Declaring variables

(Dim, Global)

Syntax:
   Dim var as vartype [* modifier]
   Global var as vartype [* modifier]

Description:
   Declares variables prior to their use

Although some languages allow you to create variables "on-the-fly," you must declare any variables before they are used in your NS Basic program, by using DIM or Global:

```
Dim MaxSeconds as Integer *6 ' 6 digits (used for display)
Dim Cost as float
Global PetName as String
Global FixedFloatResult as Float *12,3
' total of 12 digits, 3 past the decimal point (for display)
```

Optional "modifiers" can be used - for integer variables the modifier describes how many digits will be displayed, while for floating point variables the modifier describes how many digits will be displayed before and after the decimal point. The modifiers do not affect the actual value of the variable, just how it will be later displayed.

Where the DIM and Global statements are placed in your program determines how the declared variables will act. The DIM statement declares variables that will be used within a single subroutine. In fact, variables declared in a DIM statement in one subroutine will not maintain their values in other subroutines. They can't even be *accessed* outside of their own subroutines, unless they are used as arguments in subroutine or function calls (more on that later). Attempting to access a variable outside the subroutine that DIM'ed it will result in a compiler error. Although this may seem like a drawback, it helps keep local variables (variables used in a single subroutine) local. This also forces you to think about the variables before you use them (you're doing that already, aren't you?).

Variables declared with the Global statement are handled differently. Any variable declared as a Global variable will be accessible to any subroutine, form, or code module throughout the program (sorry – no "form-level" globals!). While it may be tempting to just declare all variables as Globals in this manner, it's a dangerous practice to use global variables in cases where local variables would work just as well. For instance, many functions return an integer result. It's tempting to use a global "result" integer variable for this purpose. However, you may need to call different subroutines or functions based on the value of this "result" variable, and these called routines may themselves require the use of a "result" variable. Using a global variable for all of these calls could alter the behavior of these routines (and keep you up late at night debugging them). Global variables have other potential drawbacks, as I mentioned previously in the section on Constants.

When naming your variables, keep in mind that NS Basic variable names must start with an alphabetic character, but can contain the letters a-z, the numbers 0-9, and the underscore character. NS Basic variable names are *case-insensitive* (e.g., LastName is the same as lastname), so you have quite a bit of flexibility in your choice of variable names. Use this to your advantage – calling a looping variable LoopCounter will make debugging much easier later on than if you simply use a single letter.

```
Dim ThisVar as String
Dim thisvar as String
' this will cause an error, since variable names aren't
'case-sensitive, and NS Basic won't let you Dim the same
'variable twice in the same routine
Dim UserDataEntry as string
Dim LoopCounter as Integer ' this makes it easy to read
Dim J as Integer ' in two weeks I won't remember what J was!!!
```

User-Defined Types (UDT)

Type

Syntax:
> **Type name**
> **Var1 as vartype [* modifiers]**
> **Var2 as vartype [* modifiers]**
> **'...**
> **End Type**

Description:
> **Defines a custom variable type to be used in a subsequent Dim or Global statement**

NS Basic supports User-Defined variable Types (referred to as UDT's) by using the Type...End Type declaration:

```
Type PersonnelRecord
   LastName as String
   FirstName as String
   Salary as Float
   VacationDays as Integer
End Type
```

Then, after the Type...End Type declaration, the new variable PersonnelRecord can be used later in code:

```
dim EmployeeInfo as PersonnelRecord
```

The individual components of each EmployeeInfo variable can then be accessed individually:

```
msgbox "Last Name: " + EmployeeInfo.LastName
msgbox "Salary: " + EmployeeInfo.Salary
msgbox "Remaining Vacation: " + EmployeeInfo.VacationDays
```

You can use UDT's in arrays, although the syntax might look a little odd at first:

```
Type Inventory
Itemname as string
     StockNum as integer
     OnHand as integer
     RawCost as float
End Type

Dim Paper(1000) as Inventory
InvValue=0
For I=1 to NumItems
   InvValue = InvValue + (Paper.RawCost(I)) * (Paper.OnHand(I))
Next
```

As you can see, UDT's are powerful variable types, partly because they can contain different types of information, but mostly because they make programming more structured and easier to debug. You can read and write UDT's like any other variable, so database applications can be very powerful, and easy to maintain by simply altering the structure of the UDT, rather than changing each and every database statement:

```
Type PersonnelRecord
   LastName as String
   FirstName as String
   Salary as Float
   VacationDays as Integer
End Type
dim EmployeeInfo as PersonnelRecord
'…code to prepare records
result=dbPut(EmployeeInfo)
'write last name, first name, salary, and vacation together
'if we didn't use the UDT, we'd have to explicitly
'read or write each piece of data like this:
'result=dbPut(LastName,FirstName,Salary,VacationDays)
'This line, and any other line referencing the data would have to
'be changed if the database structure changed later
```

Arrays

Syntax:
   Dim Arrayname(subscript1[,subscript2][,subscript3]) as vartype [*modifiers]
   Global Arrayname(subscript1[,subscript2][,subscript3]) as vartype [*modifiers]

Description:
   Declares arrays prior to their first use

NS Basic supports single and multidimensional arrays (with up to 3 levels of subscripts). These arrays can also be created using any of the NS Basic variable types, and can use modifiers as described for the Dim and Global statements:

```
dim Salary(100) as float*6,2
' use 6 digits, with 2 past the decimal point
dim TextBuffer(200) as byte
dim CompanyEmployeeRecords(1000) as PersonnelRecord
' PersonnelRecord previously defined as UDT
dim 3DMatrix(100,100,100) as float
dim 4DSpace(10,20,30,40) as integer
'this will cause an error, since NS Basic only supports arrays
'with up to 3 levels of supscripts
dim TableInfo(100,10) as string
```

NS Basic arrays must be dimensioned using literal values, not variables, since NS Basic does not support dynamic arrays (arrays that can have variable numbers of elements):

```
dim Price(1000) as float ' this is OK
dim NumItems as 1000
dim Price(NumItems) as float ' this is invalid
```

Also, unlike many dialects of Basic, NS Basic doesn't support LBound or UBound, functions which are commonly used to determine the Lower and Upper boundaries (occupied elements) of arrays. NS Basic DOES support the function NoOcccurs that returns an integer result equal to the maximum subscript for the indicated array and subscript:

```
dim result as integer
dim StringInfo(100,2) as String
result=NoOccurs(StringInfo,1)
' this will return 100 as number of elements for subscript 1
```

However, since NS Basic doesn't support dynamic arrays, there's little use for LBound or UBound, or even for NoOccurs, except in code that's being converted from other dialects of Basic. For now you'll need to maintain your own internal pointers for array element subscripts (it's good programming practice to do this anyway).

NS Basic arrays have a minimum subscript of 1, unlike many dialects of Basic which start with a base (lowest subscript) of 0. Also unlike some Basic versions, NS Basic doesn't allow you to change the base to 0. Maybe one day...

Arrays can be written to, and read from, databases as easily as other variables. You can use this to quickly initialize programs with arrays of information. The following code, which clears a 10,000 element string array, takes 19 seconds on my system:

```
Global HelpStrings(100,100) as string
Dim CurrentRow as integer
Dim CurrentCol as integer
For CurrentRow = 1 to 100
   For CurrentCol=1 to 100
      HelpStrings(CurrentRow,CurrentCol)=""
   Next
Next
```

Watching an application "do nothing" for 19 seconds seems like forever. Let's see if it's faster using database access. So, I'll save the array first (don't worry too much about the database code – we'll cover databases in detail later):

```
Dim dbfh as Database
Dim res as Integer
res=dbCreate(dbfh,"ClearedArray",0,"test")
res=dbOpen(dbfh,"ClearedArray",0)
res=dbPosition(dbfh,1,0)
res=dbPut(dbfh,HelpStrings)
res=dbClose(dbfh)
```

This code writes the 10,000 element array in less than half the time on my device. So far so good, but the real test is how quickly the data can be read. So, now that the database is present, I'll read it into the array:

```
Dim dbfh as Database
Dim res as Integer
res=dbOpen(dbfh,"ClearedArray",0)
res=dbPosition(dbfh,1,0)
res=dbGet(dbfh,HelpStrings)
res=dbClose(dbfh)
```

Similar to the database writing routine, reading the array also takes less than half the time as looping. This may not seem too important by itself, but which technique would you rather use to initialize or load an array? Better still, if you were the *user*, would you want to wait any longer than necessary? The defense rests.

Now that I've shown you how to read and write arrays to a database, I'm going to ask you to do something unusual. Forget what I just told you. Really! Can you think of why Palm might frown on transferring data this way? I'll give you a hint – memory. Why move a chunk of data around if you could just refer to it (and edit it) in place instead? Since the Palm uses system memory (which is very limited) and not disks to store data, there's little performance penalty in accessing the data directly (and doing so avoids having data occupy two places in memory at the same time).

So, don't *really* forget the database array input/output routines – just make good use of them, and only use them when necessary to increase performance when memory constraints aren't an issue. It's all about balance.

Size Matters!

Palm memory is quite limited, so attention needs to be paid to the storage requirements of variables, and the maximum size for each variable type. Single numeric variables are represented internally as 8-byte floating point values, while string variables can occupy up to 32767 characters each. Arrays require a small amount of overhead for storage, and each array must fit within a 64k block of memory. The maximum size of any array is limited by the total amount of memory (64k), and the number of elements (due to the overhead required). Since numeric variables are stored as 8-byte values, numeric arrays can contain up to 64k/8 records (actually 8185 by my testing). As previously mentioned, strings require a null-terminator for each string, so the maximum number of strings in a 64k space would be 64k/2, or 32000 elements. However, string arrays require additional space due to overhead as well, given by the formula:

Space required=elements*2+(length+1 for each assigned string)+4

So, a 10,000 item string array would require 20,000 bytes, plus the (actual length of the strings+1) for each string, + 4 bytes, which would leave 65535-20,004, or 45531 bytes for strings plus null terminators, equal to an average of 4.5 bytes per string. Obviously, then, arrays of larger strings would only accommodate fewer elements. Luckily, array elements that have not yet been assigned do not occupy system memory, and for most purposes your arrays will not approach these limits. If you expect that they might, consider using databases instead of arrays (will discuss databases later, but with a little planning Palm databases can be used as dynamic arrays).

Chapter VI - Programming Elements

Every element of an NS Basic program exists within a subroutine. Don't believe me? You can't write code for an NS Basic program that doesn't somewhere, somehow get executed between Sub and End Sub statements (actually, that's not true, but code that falls outside these statements will either cause the compiler to complain, or won't get executed at all).

Speaking of the compiler, NS Basic uses what's known as a "one-pass" compiler, which means that all code is seen and compiled from top to bottom, going through the program only once. Code is compiled by NS Basic in the following sequence:

- Project StartUp Code
- Code Modules
- Each form/screen in sequence as shown in the Project Explorer
    - Form "Before" Code (code before objects are drawn on the form)
    - Form "After" Code (code after objects are drawn on the form)
    - Form Event Code
    - Menu code in the order that the menus were defined
    - Code for each form object in sequence as shown in Project Explorer
- Project Termination Code

Caution Since NS Basic is a one-pass compiler, it's possible to attempt to call functions or subroutines before their actual code gets compiled – and this can cause you to spend hours debugging otherwise perfect code. We'll come across this when we discuss functions and subroutines (and we'll discuss ways to make this work to your advantage), but for now just keep this in the back of your mind.

Writing NS Basic programs is much like writing a number of routines nested in other routines. If you're used to writing programs in Visual Basic or other "object oriented" languages (purists will tell you that Visual Basic isn't *truly* object oriented, but that's an entirely different topic), you are already familiar with using the properties and methods of objects to determine the flow of program code. Contrast this with the old top-down, punch card method of programming, and it's easy to see how this programming model offers considerably more flexibility and power. This comes with added responsibility, though, but you'll get used to it.

Statements

With few exceptions, programming statements in NS Basic perform a single function per line. These statements may perform arithmetic operations, manipulate variables or objects, access databases, etc:

```
fldTechnicalInfo.text="The 555 Timer is a very versatile IC."
Salary=30000 + EmployeeBonus - CreditUnionFee
NumRecs=dbGetNoRecs(EmployeeDB)
```

Additionally, program statements may pass execution to other subroutines or functions:

```
Call TextToMemo("Write this to Memo Pad")
x=sqrt(y)
```

Statements can be part of a group of statements, as we'll see with the looping (Do...Loop, and For...Next) and decision making (If...Then...Else...EndIf, and Select Case...Case...Case Else...End Select) statements, in which case the groups must be complete (each Select must have an End Select, for instance). We'll cover these special statements later when we discuss program "flow."

There is currently a maximum length of 256 characters for program statements (although this may change in the future). Since long statements can be difficult to read and follow, NS Basic supports the use of the underscore ("_") character at the end of a line to instruct the compile to treat the next line as a continuation of the current line:

```
'example of long line broken into two
CalcResult=exp(x^6)+5*(x^4)+4*(x^3)-12*(x^2)_
+13x+3
```

Note that if you use the underscore character to continue a long string, you need to "close the quotes" on the previous string before continuing to the next line:

```
'this currently gives unexpected results:
InstructionText="Place tab A into slot B, then tab C into_
slot D, then place tab E into slot F"
```

Depending on how the options have been set on the compiler, the word "and" may be capitalized, since the text editor treats the continued line as though it was a statement containing the keyword "And". This may change in future versions, but for now keep this in mind, and continue strings like this:

```
'this currently gives unexpected results:
InstructionText="Place tab A into slot B, then"+_
"place tab E into slot F, and tape edge 12 to side 4"
```

We'll discuss working with strings in the chapter on "String Handling" later, but I wanted to introduce you to this concept now, while you're learning the details of working with the IDE.

Comments

Although not technically statements, you can also place *comments* in your code, either at the end of a line of code, or as stand-alone comments.

Comments in code are preceded by a single quote mark (just as in Visual Basic – eases the transition a bit, don't you think?):

```
' This is a comment line
FooBarArray(112)=45.6  ' this is also a comment
```

However, when the single quote is enclosed within double quotes, it becomes part of a string:

```
Message.text="Here's a sample of a single quote in a string"
```

Your comments don't become part of the compiled program; they are ignored by the compiler, and don't add to the size of the compiled application. So, use comments generously in your programming. What you program today might seem completely obvious to you now, but when you (or worse yet, your boss!) may have to debug your code weeks or months from now, *nobody* will be able to figure out what you meant by:

```
If k > z Then
   Fld1005.text=str(x+pow(i,j))+errmsg$(f)
Else
   Msgbox "err:" str(b)
End If
```

Make it a habit to comment your code as though you were writing the comments for someone else, and your comments will be more useful to you as well. Also, try to stay away from "abstract" variable names as in this previous section of code. Even if you comment your code thoroughly, your programs will be considerably more readable (and maintainable) if your variable names describe what you are using them for. For instance, you may have code that clears every item in an array used to represent a 100 row by 100 column table:

```
Dim CurrentRow as integer
Dim CurrentCol as integer
Dim TableArray(100,100) as string   ' used for 100x100 table
For CurrentRow = 1 to 100
   For CurrentCol = 1 to 100
      TableArray(CurrentRow, CurrentCol)="" ' clear table
   Next
Next
```

That code is nearly self-documenting, as opposed to:

```
Dim k as integer
Dim l as integer
```

```
Dim T(100,100) as string    ' used for 100x100 table
For k = 1 to 100
   For l = 1 to 100
      T(k,l)=""    ' clear table
   Next
Next
```

Each code section performs the same function, but you can easily see what is happening in the first code section even without referring to its comments.

Subroutines and Code Modules

Sub, Exit Sub, End Sub

Syntax:

> **Sub SubroutineName([arg1 as vartype][, arg2 as vartype][,...])**
> **[Statement1]**
> **[Statement2]**
> **'...**
> **[Exit Sub]**
> **[Statement3]**
> **[Statement4]**
> **'...**
> **End Sub**

Description:

> **Declares a section of code to be run as a separate routine**

We've already laid the foundation for the use of subroutines – every form, object, and event has code run as part of a subroutine. Your program starts with "Sub" and ends with "End Sub." Everything else falls somewhere between the two.

You may never need to write your own subroutines, especially if you are writing small applications. However, chances are that you'll eventually find yourself using some code fragments over and over. Rather than cutting and pasting every time that you want to reuse code, create small code modules for your most often used, favorite routines. For instance, I have routines that I use in almost every program. One writes data to the Memo Pad, and the other sends text to a printer using PalmPrint. Although I could probably recreate the routines each time I need them, why put myself through the agony? Instead, NS Basic provides an easy, concise way to include modules of routines in your programs. From the IDE, you can add existing modules, or create new modules, without ever leaving your current project. These modules can contain subroutines that are accessible from anywhere in your program.

To create your own subroutine, first open or create a code module in the IDE. If you are creating a new module, you'll see an empty window open up, so enter something like the following:

```
Sub <substitute your Sub name here>()
End Sub
```

Replace the <substitute your Sub name here> with the name of your subroutine, and place your code between the two lines. Remember that any variables you use must have either already been defined by the Global keyword in the program's StartUp code, or DIM them yourself in the subroutine before you use them.

```
Sub CalculateTip()
Dim TaxRate as float
'...code here
End Sub
```

Any variable that you DIM in your subroutine will be a local variable, and will be invisible to other parts of your program. You can even use DIM to create a local variable that shares the same name as a Global variable, but it will act as a local variable and not affect the value of the Global variable of the same name.

Subroutines can have values (arguments) passed to them, and can return values to the program as well. Consider a subroutine that would determine food for a pet:

```
Sub FindFoodType(Pet as Integer, Food as String)
Select Case Pet
    Case 1 ' dog
        Food="meat"
    Case 2 ' cat
        Food="fish"
    Case 3 ' alligator - hey, it's not MY pet!
        Food="whatever it wants"
    Case Else
        Food="unabel to determine"
End Select
End Sub
```

You can call this routine with either a literal value or a variable:

```
Dim CatMenuItem as String
Call FindFoodType(2,CatMenuItem)
```

Or

```
Dim PetType as Integer
Dim DogFood as string
PetType = 1 ' dog
Call FindFoodType(PetType, DogFood)
```

Note that subroutine arguments must match their type, not their names. Subroutines keep track of what variable type to use *by position*. There can be any number of subroutines in each module (up to the limit of the size of the code editor). These subroutines can even call other subroutines, as long as the *called* subroutine is listed before the *calling* routine.

> **Note** You don't have to use code modules for subroutines – they can be placed in your application's StartUp code, a Form's Before, After, or Event code – virtually anywhere. Subroutines in the StartUp

code can be called from any form or object, while subroutines in a Form's code can only be called in that form. I personally place my subroutines in code modules or the StartUp code most of the time, so that they will be available anywhere in the app, and they will get compiled before any of the form or object code.

Although subroutines are supposed to have only one entry and one exit point, there will be times when you need to exit a subroutine early. To do so, use Exit Sub (code from the EasyCalc+ project):

```
Sub ProcessKey(key as String )
'...
If firstDigit = 1 Then
    '...
Else
    If key="." Then
        If instr(1,fldAmount.text,".",0)<>0 Then
            MsgBox "Already have a decimal point in the amount."
            Exit Sub
        End If
    End If
    '...
End If
'...
End Sub
```

In reality, you can avoid the use of Exit Sub by rearranging If…Then…Else…End If statements, but the code may not be as readable.

With the ability to have many subroutines, you might be wondering how the OS keeps track of its steps. As it turns out, every call to a subroutine or function tells the OS to save a copy of its "return address" and other specific information that it will need for the trip back. If you use too many subroutine calls, the system will run out of space and come to a grinding halt. Try not to nest your subroutines too deeply, and don't use subroutines that call themselves (a technique known as *recursion*, which is not supported in NS Basic).

If a subroutine is in a code module, or compiled before being used elsewhere in code, calling a subroutine with a parameter can be done without using the Call keyword:

```
Call ReadData(dbkey)
```

is equal to

```
ReadData dbKey
```

Subroutines with multiple parameters can also be called in these two different ways:

```
Call Create3DGraph(x,y,z)
```

Or

```
Create3DGraph x, y, z
```

Functions

Function, Exit Function, End Function

Syntax:

> **Function FunctionName([arg1 as vartype][,arg2 as vartype][,...]) as vartype**
> **[Statement1]**
> **[Statement2]**
> **'[...]**
> **FunctionName=expression**
> **[Statement3]**
> **[Statement4]**
> **[Exit Function]**
> **'[...]**
> **End Function**

Description:

> **Declares a section of code to be run as a separate routine, returning a value in the name of the function**

NS Basic comes with numerous built-in functions, and supports additional arithmetic functions in the shared library "Mathlib." At the time of this writing, NS Basic supports over 100 different functions, including powerful mathematic and trigonometric functions, string/date/time manipulation, database management, and serial input/output functions. Add to these the special functions for responding to user actions and a handful of miscellaneous functions, and you'll never need to write another function.

Never say never! One of the most useful features of NS Basic (among other languages) is the ability to create new functions. To define a new function, create or open a code module, and start with the keyword "Function." For example, here's a simple function to calculate a restaurant tip:

```
Function TipCalc (MealCost as float) as float
TipCalc=MealCost*0.15
End Function
```

To call this function:

```
Dim AmountToTip as float
Dim DinnerCost as float
DinnerCost=val(fldDinner.text)
' get the cost of dinner from a field on the form
AmountToTip=TipClac(DinnerCost)
```

Note that unlike subroutines, the Function *name* is used to pass the return value to the program (which also means that functions can only return one value, while subroutines can return any number of values). Although this might take some getting used to at first, notice how this "user-defined" function acts just like any of the built-in functions? Functions can have other functions embedded within them, so it's easy to build on existing functions as needed. Just remember that functions within functions have the same memory hogging problem as subroutines (and, like subroutines, functions cannot call themselves – recursion isn't allowed in NS Basic).

Like subroutines, functions can be exited before you hit the End Function statement, using the Exit Function statement:

```
Function TipCalc (MealCost as float) as float
If MealCost > 100 then
   TipCalc=MealCost*0.2
   Exit Function
Else
   TipCalc =MealCost*0.15
End if
End Function
```

I don't think you'll need to use Exit Function often, but at least you'll know it's there.

Define

Syntax:

> **Define FunctionName as vartype**

Description:

> **Defines the type of information that will be returned in a subsequent function declaration**

Another feature of functions that I need to tell you about is that a function must be defined before it is used. Since the functions in code modules are compiled before most of the other program code, this won't be a problem – unless you need to refer to functions before they're actually seen by the compiler. This can occur if you have user-defined functions in the program StartUp code, or if you have code modules that refer to functions that occur later in the same or different module. Since functions always return a result, the compiler can't know what variable type to return if the function is used before it is compiled. To get around this, you can DEFINE a function before it's ever used. A good place to do this is in the program's StartUp code. Using our tip calculator function as an example:

```
Define TipCalc as Float
```

Since the compiler only needs to know that TipCalc returns a floating point result, it can use this information prior to actually compiling the TipCalc function.

Controlling the flow

Programs would be pretty boring – and not too useful – if there was no way to move through code except one statement at a time, in a straight path, from beginning to end. Life doesn't work that way, so why should programs?

Conditional statements

As in life, programs often have to make decisions based on a condition, and transfer control or perform some action as a result of that decision. NS Basic offers two similar methods for this type of "conditional" program flow: If...Then...Else...End If and Select Case...Case...Case Else...End Select. For all intents and purposes the two methods could be used interchangeably, but each is better suited to specific programming situations.

If...Then...Else...Elseif...End If (and everything in between)

Syntax:

If condition Then
    Statement1
    [Statement2]
    [...]
End If
or
If condition Then
    Statement1
    [Statement2]
    [...]
Else
    Statement3
    [Statement4]
    [...]
End If
or
If condition Then Statement1
or
If condition Then Statement1 Else Statement2
or
If condition1 Then
    Statement1
    [Statement2]
    [...]
ElseIf condition2 Then
    Statement3
    [Statement4]
    [...]
End If
or
If condition1 Then
    Statement1
    [Statement2]
    [...]
Else If condition2 Then
    Statement3
    [Statement4]
    [...]
    End If

End If

Description:

Allows execution of different code segments based on the result of a variable or expression

Different forms of the "If...Then...ElseIf...End If" construct exist in most programming languages. NS Basic supports many of these forms, starting with the simplest, one line "if this, then that" form:

```
If a=5 Then b=6
```

However, if you have more than one path to take in your code, you might need something a little more useful:

```
If a = 5 Then b=6 Else b=7
```

Or

```
If a = 5 Then
    b=6
Else
    b=7
End If
```

Either form of the command will work well. However, it should be easy enough to imagine that complex forms may be possible, including "nested" forms:

```
If i<1 Then
    i=0
    res=dbReset(pdb)
Else
    if k < 1 Then
        k=0
    End If
    res=dbPosition(pdb, i, k)
End If
```

By now you've probably noticed something about the indenting in these code segments. I indent each "level" to separate it from the surrounding code. This makes it easier for me to spot missing "Else" or "End If" keywords. Contrast the code above this paragraph with the following:

```
If i<1 Then
i=0
res=dbReset(pdb)
Else
if k < 1 Then
k=0
res=dbPosition(pdb, i, k)
End If
```

It's hard to see which statements "belong" to which If...Then...Else...End If blocks. Use indenting as you use comments – both can save you hours of debugging time! (Did you notice the missing End If?)

The If statements can also have multiple comparisons, although you'll see later that these comparisons are sometimes better handled by the "Select Case" statements:

```
If Weekday = "Monday" Then
    TaxPercent=0.05
Elseif Weekday = "Tuesday" Then
    TaxPercent=0.075
Elseif Weekday = "Wednesday" Then
    TaxPercent=0.10
Elseif Weekday = "Thursday" Then
    TaxPercent=0.15
Elseif Weekday = "Friday" Then
    TaxPercent=0.25
Else
    TaxPercent=0.30
End If
```

The conditions tested by the If statements can be any of the following:

AND

OR

NOT

>

>=

=

<=

<

<> (or "Not =")

or just an item in parentheses or alone, which would be evaluated as a Boolean "true":

```
dim ValidTime as integer
ValidTime=true
If (ValidTime) Then
    msgbox "Current Time:" + CurTime
End If
```

Multiple conditions can be evaluated simultaneously:

```
If (StockValue < 45) and (NumberOfStocks > 100) Then
    Msgbox "Sell!  Sell!  Sell!"
End If
```

For simple expressions, you can use the one-line version of IF...Then:

```
If fldHelpStatus.text="Help" then Call DisplayHelp()
```

Even slightly more complex statements can be handled on one line:

```
If fldMenuItem.text="Butter" then Fat="High" else Fat="Low"
```

You can't continue this forever, though:

```
If fldMenuItem.text="Butter" then Fat="High" elseif_
fldMenuItem.text="Yogurt" then Fat="Medium" else Fat="Low"
```

NS Basic considers this "stacking" of If statements on the same line, and won't allow it. But, even if you *could* stack them on the same line, the statement would be far too difficult to read. Like most programming, the more elegant syntax wins out.

Speaking of elegant syntax, there's a subtle difference between NS Basic's syntax for ElseIf and what you may be used to. Actually, it's not a problem with ElseIf, but with Else If. Confused?

Consider the following:

```
If RecNo > 1000 then
   Msgbox "Too many records"
Else If RecNo > 500 then
   Msgbox "More than 500 records"
Else
   Msgbox "Less than 500 records"
End if
```

Looks OK, doesn't it? Try it, and the compiler will complain (quite abruptly, too!), that there's an If without a matching EndIf. NS Basic looks at the code as though it was written like this:

```
If RecNo > 1000 then
   Msgbox "Too many records"
Else
   If RecNo > 500 then
      Msgbox "More than 500 records"
   Else
      Msgbox "Less than 500 records"
   End if
```

Written like this, it's easy to see that NS Basic expects an additional End If, since it treats the Else If (the two word form) as parts of separate If...Then...Else...End If blocks. So, to make the code work as originally written, you'll need to modify it:

```
If RecNo > 1000 then
   Msgbox "Too many records"
Else If RecNo > 500 then
      Msgbox "More than 500 records"
   Else
```

```
      Msgbox "Less than 500 records"
    End If
End if
```

Now, the syntax is correct, although it looks a little awkward. Stick with the one-word ElseIf form instead, and avoid this hassle altogether. Trust me on this. If NS Basic ever decides to get rid of the non-standard two word Else If construct, your apps will need revision if you include it. Why not avoid this in the first place? Besides, your code should be as standard and "portable" as possible.

You'll use the If...Then...Else...Elseif...End If variations often. Get familiar with them, indent at each new level, and try to make your statements as simple as possible.

Select Case...Case...Case Else...End Select

Syntax:

> **Select Case variable**
> **Case val1**
>   **Statement1**
> **[Case val2**
>   **Statement2]**
> **'...**
> **[Case Else**
>   **StatementElse]**
> **End Select**

Description:

> **Allows execution of different sections of code base on the value of a variable**

There will be many times when the If statement is too long and wordy, especially when there are many possible values for a single variable, and different actions to take according to each value. It is often simpler (and easier to read and debug) to simply select the variable in question, then compare it with the various values. This is exactly what the Select Case statements do, and do well. Take the previous multiple If...Then...Else...Elseif...End If code:

```
If Weekday - "Monday" Then
    TaxPercent=0.05
Elseif Weekday = "Tuesday" Then
    TaxPercent=0.075
Elseif Weekday = "Wednesday" Then
    TaxPercent=0.10
Elseif Weekday = "Thursday" Then
    TaxPercent=0.15
Elseif Weekday = "Friday" Then
    TaxPercent=0.25
Else
    TaxPercent=0.30
End If
```

Although this code is fairly simple to follow, if you need to modify it later, it's easy to get a little lost. Using the Select Case...End Select statements may be somewhat easier to follow:

```
Select Case Weekday
   Case "Monday"
      TaxPercent=0.05
   Case "Tuesday"
      TaxPercent=0.075
   Case "Wednesday"
      TaxPercent=0.10
   Case "Thursday"
      TaxPercent=0.15
   Case "Friday"
      TaxPercent=0.25
   Case Else
      TaxPercent=0.30
End Select
```

Note that the "Case Else" is optional, but it's a good idea to include it, even if only to add some code to display a message when an unintended value finds its way into the Select Case statement.

NS Basic's Select...Case construct doesn't allow for less-than or greater-than, as permitted in some versions of Basic:

```
Select Case Salary
   Case < 20000 ' this will cause the compiler to stop with_
                  a syntax error
   '...
End Select
```

Also, you can't use expressions in the Case line:

```
Select Case Salary
   Case (5*BaseSalary) ' this will also cause a syntax error
   '...
End Select
```

Still, even with these limitations, you'll find the Select Case...End Select construct easy to use and fairly "self-documenting" (especially if you indent each level, as above).

Looping

Computers excel at doing repetitive tasks. They don't get bored, don't need to stop for coffee breaks, don't complain to the boss about working in a dimly lit room that smells because someone dropped a burrito last week and didn't clean it up...oops, got a little side-tracked there for a moment.

All programmers, at some point, realize that the computer can be used to perform multiple or repetitive tasks that would be too time-consuming and/or boring for a human to perform, especially if these tasks had to be performed day by day, week by week, etc. It's also common for programmers to have code that needs to be executed multiple times, either for a fixed or variable number of iterations, or until a condition is met (or for as long as a condition remains). This may involve filling an array with known values, reading a database until the last record is read, or controlling an external device (keeping a basement sump pump running as long as there is water up to a certain level on the floor). NS Basic includes support for several methods of performing code in this repetitive manner, with different application for each method.

For...Next...Exit For

Syntax:

For loopvariable = val1 to val2 [step interval]
    Statement1
    [Statement2]
    '...
    [Exit For]
Next

Description:

Executes a section of code for a specified number of iterations

The "For...Next" loop, as it is often called, is a looping strategy present in virtually all dialects of Basic, in one form or another. The loop starts with a variable of a certain value, and steps through the code, incrementing the variable, until the variable exceeds a target value:

```
Dim errorcode as integer
Dim RecordCount as Integer
For RecordCount = 1 to 5
   errorcode=dbReadNext(EmployeeDB,dbKey,dbRecord)
   'database has already been opened
Next
```

This code would read 5 records from the EmployeeDB database (assuming that these records exist).

The loop counter (RecordCount, in this case) must be numeric, but it can be any numeric variable type. Although in this example my loop counter was incremented by the value 1, the For...Next loop can take an additional parameter "Step" to determine how to increment the value of the counter (in this case a variable of type "Float"):

```
Dim x as float
Dim y as float
For x=5 to 6 step 0.1
   y=sin(x)
   call Graph(Y)
Next
```

The Step parameter can also be used to decrement, or decrease the number of the loop counter:

```
Dim x as float
Dim y as float
```

```
For x=6 to 5 step -0.1
   y=sin(x)
   call Graph(Y)
Next
```

Actually, if you want to decrement a loop counter, you *must* use the Step parameter. The following code will skip past the loop, although it appears that it should run 10 times:

```
Dim x as integer
Dim sum as integer
sum=0
For x=10 to 1 ' missing "step -1"
   sum=sum+x
Next
msgbox "sum: "+str(sum)
```

The For...Next loop can use variables for the upper or lower boundaries of the counter, and for the step command. From the GraphDemo project:

```
For IndexX=MinX to MaxX ' loop through x values
    PlotX=160*((IndexX-MinX)/Xdiff)
    ' scale x to the screen from 0-159
    '... other code here...
Next
```

But what if you need to exit out of the loop before the loop counter hits its target? Luckily, the For...Next loop has a statement "Exit For" that allows you to leave a loop early:

```
For PokerBet = LowAnte to HighAnte
   BetAmount=PokerBet*CurrencyValue
   If BetAmount > 500 Then
      Exit For ' too rich a bet for me!
   End If
Next
```

For...Next loops can also be nested. From the TableDemo project:

```
Sub ClearTable()
StatusField.text="[ ...initializing...] "
For CurrentRow=1 to MaxRow
    For CurrentCol=1 to MaxCol
        TableDataArray(CurrentRow,CurrentCol)=""
    Next
Next
CurrentRow=1
CurrentCol=1
StatusField.text="[ Ready] "
DisplayTableInfo
End Sub
```

Notice the indenting; just as in the use of If...Then...Else...End If, indenting makes it easy to see *at a glance* which code belongs to which loop counter.

Important points to remember about the For...Next loop

Iterations (times through the loop)

If the start and end values for the counter are equal, the loop will get executed once (remember, the loop continues until the counter *exceeds* the target value). If you need to avoid execution of the code in the loop, either check the values and avoid the loop altogether, or use "Do...Loop...Exit Do" instead (described in the next section).

Syntax

Some forms of Basic require the use of the variable name after the Next keyword:

```
For X=6 to 5 step -0.1
    Y=sin(X)
    call Graph(Y)
Next X ' this will cause an error in the NS Basic compiler
```

This is neither required nor supported in NS Basic. You can get around this and still use the variable name as a comment:

```
For X=6 to 5 step -0.1
    Y=sin(X)
    call Graph(Y)
Next ' X
```

Although this may help you debug your code later, proper indenting *alone* will easily set blocks of code apart from each other, so you can tell which loop belongs with which counter.

Don't use a loop counter after the loop ends

The value for a loop counter cannot be relied upon to keep its value outside of the loop, or after the loop ends. To demonstrate this, create a new project, place a single field on the form, and name the field fldCounter. In the main form's "After" code, place the following:

```
Dim counter as Integer
For counter=1 to 10
    fldcounter.text=str(counter)
Next
fldcounter.text=str(counter)
```

Compile the project, transfer it to POSE or your Palm OS device, and run it. Surprised? The loop continues until the counter exceeds the target value, so in this case the counter equals 11 after the loop. However, it's bad practice to expect the counter to be a certain value after the loop, so if you need to keep track of the number of loop iterations, or cycles, use a separate variable.

NEVER explicitly change the value of the loop counter

Leave that for the loop to perform automatically. If you call another routine or function in the loop, be certain not to inadvertently change the value of the loop counter:

```
global ArrayIndex as integer
global NameArray(100) as string
For ArrayIndex=1 to 100
    call CheckName
Next

Sub CheckName()
If NameArray(ArrayIndex)="The Boss" then
    ArrayIndex=ArrayIndex+1 ' skip over the boss's name
end sub
```

Not only is the value of ArrayIndex not defined outside of the loop, when you return to the loop after incrementing the value, it gets incremented again, and may contain an invalid array subscript. You can avoid this by potential pitfall completely by using local (non-Global) variables for loop counters, and avoiding the use of the loop variables outside of the loop.

Do...Loop...Exit Do

Syntax:

> **Do**
> **or**
> **Do [UNTIL condition]**
> **or**
> **Do WHILE condition**
>   **Statement1**
>   **[Statement2]**
>   **'...**
>   **[Exit Do]**
> **Loop**

Description:

> **Executes a section of code while, or until, a specified condition is met**

The Do...Loop construct is considered by many programmers superior to the For...Next loop, since it does exactly what it says, with no assumptions. In many cases, it's also faster than the For...Next loop, since manipulation of the looping variable may be more efficient.

```
counter=1
NumRecs=dbGetNoRecs(EmployeeDB)
Do Until counter=NumRecs
    res=dbReadNext(EmployeeDB,dbKey,SalaryData)
    counter=counter+1
Loop
```

The Do...Loop can also test for various conditions, not just loop until a variable meets a certain condition, but while a variable is within a specified range:

```
EmployeeSalary=0 ' initialize the test variable
Do While EmployeeSalary < 50000
   res=dbReadNext(EmployeeDB,dbKey, EmployeeSalary)
   ' read up to the boss's salary
   MyBonus=MyBonus + EmployeeSalary/100
   ' skim a little off the top
Loop
```

or written to run continuously until a condition causes an "Exit Do" statement to be executed:

```
Do
   res=dbReadNext(EmployeeDB,dbKey, EmployeeSalary)
   if res<>0 then
      ' we've hit the end of the database, or some other error
      res=dbClose(EmployeeDB) ' close the database
      Exit Do ' and exit the routine
   else
      if EmployeeSalary > 50000 then
         StockPrice=StockPrice+1
         ' add for each high salary employee
      end if
   end if
Loop
```

This flexibility allows the Do...Loop to be used in virtually any situation that would normally use the For...Next loop, and in many situations where the For...Next loop would be too cumbersome. Additionally, the precautions taken when using the For...Next loops as described above do not exist with the Do...Loop constructs. There are probably few, if any, situations when a Do...Loop cannot be used in place of a For...Next loop.

Jumping

Testing for conditions and executing code based on conditions is one way to alter program flow, but often you'll need to jump to an entirely different segment of code. Sometimes you'll want to call a routine and then return to the original code, and at other times you'll want to bail out and just transfer control to a different section of code entirely. We'll discuss two ways to do this, along with a way to jump to a completely different form as well.

GOTO, GOSUB

Syntax:

    GoTo Label
    GoSub Label

Description:

Transfers program execution to a different section of code (and, with GoSub, returns to the next code statement after encountering a Return statement)

GOTO allows you to perform a complete, "no holds barred" jump to an entirely different section of code. All you need to do is supply the label (a unique name followed by a colon ":") for the section of code that you want to jump to, and "Voila!" – you're there.

```
'... some program code...
GOTO CalculateBonus
'...
CalculateBonus:
```

The GOTO and the code being jumped to must exist in the same subroutine. Also, any code immediately following the GOTO won't be executed, unless there's another GOTO that jumps to that section of code. Sounds painful, and it is. Code with numerous GOTO's that jump back and forth is often referred to as "spaghetti code," since it's about as easy to follow as a strand of spaghetti in a bowl full of pasta. For instance, let's say we just wrote a program to write restaurant reviews. A portion of the code might look like this:

```
Sub RestaurantReview()
dim TipPercent as float
dim TipAmount as float
dim BillAmount as float
dim SalesTax as float
dim Service as string
'...preceding code to obtain rating
If Service = "Poor" Then
    GOTO NoTip
Elseif Service = "Fair" Then
    TipPercent=0.10
    GOTO CalculateTip
Elseif Service="Good" Then
    TipPercent=0.15
    GOTO CalculateTip
Elseif Service="Great" Then
    TipPercent=0.25
    GOTO CalculateTip
Else
    TipPercent=0.20
    GOTO CalculateTip
End If
ContinueProgram:
'other code goes here
GOTO LeaveRestaurant
NoTip:
    Tip=0
GOTO ContinueProgram
GOTO LeaveRestaurant
CalculateTip:
    Tip=round((BillAmount-SalesTax)*TipPercent,2)
GOTO ContinueProgram
```

```
LeaveRestaurant:
'...
End Sub
```

Although you might be able to figure out what you meant looking at this code in a week or a month, trying to modify this code later (especially if someone ELSE has to do the modifications) may require a few cups of coffee (or wine, or whiskey…). A better way to code the routine would be to use GoSub, which runs code elsewhere in the routine, but continues with the next line of code when it encounters a "Return":

```
Sub RestaurantReview()
dim TipPercent as float
dim TipAmount as float
dim BillAmount as float
dim SalesTax as float
dim Service as string
If Service = "Poor" Then
    Gosub NoTip
Elseif Service = "Fair" Then
    TipPercent=0.10
    Gosub CalculateTip
Elseif Service="Good" Then
    TipPercent=0.15
    Gosub CalculateTip
Elseif Service="Great" Then
    TipPercent=0.25
    Gosub CalculateTip
Else
    TipPercent=0.20
    Gosub CalculateTip
End If
 'other code goes here
'LeaveRestaurant code can now follow without using GOTO
'...
Exit Sub ' use this to prevent "falling through" to the_
subroutines
'----
'subroutines follow
'----
CalculateTip:
    Tip=round((BillAmount-SalesTax)*TipPercent,2)
Return
'----
NoTip:
    Tip=0
Return
End Sub
```

The code for the main routine is more streamlined and easier to maintain, as is the code for the other calculations. There's even another way to do this with functions, which we'll cover later. But for now, recognize that GOTO is best avoided. Careful planning of program flow prior to writing the actual code will help keep you from the unnecessary use of GOTO.

SideBar What's that? You don't want to take my word on this? If I haven't convinced you to avoid GOTO's as much as humanly possible, perhaps this will (courtesy of Karen Watterson at APress):

The Infamous "GoTo" - Well-known Dutch computer scientist Edsger W. Dijkstra (author of several college texts) opined against GoTo's in his famous and often-cited classic article "Go To Statement Considered Harmful" in 1968. You can read the original on the ACM Web site at http://www.acm.org/classics/oct95/. Dijkstra was the 1972 ACM Turing award winner (do an internet search, or refer to http://www.turing.org.uk if you're not familiar with Alan Turing and the Turing Test). Dijkstra's ACM citation explains how, in the late 1950's, he was one of the principal contributors to the development of the ALGOL and that he "is one of the principal exponents of the science and art of programming languages in general, and has greatly contributed to our understanding of their structure, representation, and implementation. His fifteen years of publications extend from theoretical articles on graph theory to basic manuals, expository texts, and philosophical contemplations in the field of programming languages."

Another giant figure in computer science is Donald Knuth, and his rebuttal ("Structured Programming with GOTO Statements", Computing Surveys, Volume 6, 1974, 261--301) to Dijkstra's comments on GoTo's is almost as famous as the original document. By the way, Professor Knuth, the inventor of the TEX typesetting language and author of the classic "Art of Programming" series of books on algorithms, has a home page at http://www-cs-faculty.stanford.edu/~knuth/ and there's a funny cartoon about him and his alleged book, Donald Knuth's Big Dummies Guide to Visual Basic, at http://www.ibiblio.org/Dave/Dr-Fun/df200002/df20000210.jpg.

(Thanks, Karen!)

NextForm - a special form of GOTO?

Syntax:

NextForm "formname"

Description:

Exits the current form, loads the specified form, and continues execution with that form

Unless your program is a small, highly focused application, it's likely that you will need more than one form for input or display of program information. Although you could create a large number of different objects on a single form, and use the Hide and Show methods to only display the objects you need (simulating different forms), at some point you will want to create a program with more than one form. To transfer control from one form to another, use NextForm with the name of the new form:

```
Nextform "formname"
```

The program control then gets passed to the form referred to in the "formname" parameter. Once the new form is loaded, any code following the NextForm statement in the calling form will NOT get executed.

Caution NextForm doesn't *immediately* jump to the named form, but sends the necessary events to the event queue to close the current form, load the next form, then open the form. So, if there is code following a subroutine call that executes the NextForm statement, that code will be executed – and usually with unexpected results. Consider the following code snippet:

```
Sub Form1003_After()
Global x as integer
X=5
If x=5 Then
    Call ShowNextForm()
    X=6
End If
End Sub

Sub ShowNextForm()
NextForm "frmNext"
End Sub
```

If you check the value of X in frmNext, it will be 6, not 5. Now, I had to do a little jumping around to make this happen, but if NextForm acted exactly like GOTO, this wouldn't happen. That's why I consider it a *special* form of GOTO.

Therefore, NextForm will usually be used at the end of a section of code, called as the result of a button or menu selection, or executed as the result of a list selection, with no subsequent code.

Unfortunately, NextForm doesn't accept variables in the "formname" parameter. So, if you need to branch to different forms based on the value of a variable, you'll need to use either If...Then...Elseif...End If or Select Case...Case...Case Else...End Select (of course, you *will* use meaningful form names, won't you?):

```
Select Case WeekdayForm
   Case "scrMonday"
      Nextform "scrMonday"
   Case "scrTuesday"
      Nextform "scrTuesday"
   Case "scrWednesday"
      Nextform "scrWednesday"
   Case "scrThursday"
      Nextform "scrThursday"
   Case "scrFriday"
      Nextform "scrFriday"
   Case Else
      Nextform "scrWeekend"
```

```
End Select
```

Notice also that NextForm doesn't provide for passing any values to the called form. You'll need to use global variables or databases to save data for use in multiple forms.

> **Note** You may see the command *NextScreen* in older NS Basic programs. It's the same as NextForm, but was created when NS Basic referred to different forms as "screens". The two are interchangeable, at least at the time of this writing.

Running external programs

At some point you may want your programs to be able to call other programs, whether you're just writing a "shell" type of program that can launch other programs, or to run another program that you've previously written, or just to take advantage of the functionality of an existing program without having to "re-invent the wheel." NS Basic allows you to do this in one of two ways – "Chain" and "AppLaunch."

Chain

Syntax:

Chain CardNo, AppName

Description:

Loads and executes the specified application

"Chain" is the more straightforward of the two, and is used to call either NS Basic or non-NS Basic apps. To execute the Chain command, all you need to know is the "card number" and program name you wish to chain to. The "card number" parameter is a Palm OS way to specify which card a program or database "resides" on. The Palm OS has the ability to access "native" or onboard memory, which by default is card 0. Knowing that no amount of memory is ever enough for everyone, Palm designed a way to specify which physical memory card a database or program (programs are databases, remember) would exist on. For now, you should stick with card number 0, unless you know that the application you are Chaining to exists on a different card:

```
Chain 0, "NewProgram"
```

Actually, Palm warns against "hard coding" the card number, and suggests that a variable be used instead:

```
Dim CardNo as integer
CardNo=0
Chain CardNo, "NewProgram"
```

The program name in the Chain statement is the internal Palm name, not necessarily the name of the program as displayed on the Launcher. If you're writing your own programs, you have access to this name (it's the actual name of your program, visible in the IDE under your program's Preferences). If not, you can use the PDB Info program supplied with this book/CD to determine the internal name for any program (PRC) or database (PDB).

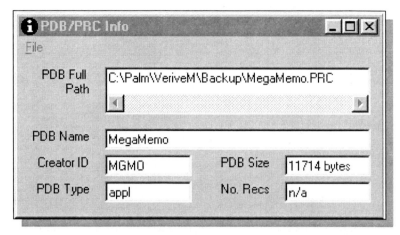

As control is passed to the chained program, the NS Basic program that issued the Chain command ends, any variables are destroyed, and all databases closed. Save any information you wish to have accessed by the chained program in a database, then read that database with the chained program. You could also use the system clipboard to transfer data, and the NSBSystemLib shared library makes this a piece of cake. This and other shared libraries are discussed in the chapter "Extending NS Basic."

> **Tip** Although MegaMemo as shown above is an application with the type "appl", it could have had the type "libr" and still be valid in a Chain statement. This can be useful if you decide to create a "menu" style application that calls other smaller applications. You might not want the individual applications visible on the Palm screen. However, applications with the type "appl" are shown with their icons (or default icons if none are present in the PRC resource), so you'd need to change their type from "appl" to a different type. PDB Info not only displays the PDB Type, but also allows you to change it as needed. Use "libr" instead, and you can Chain to the application even though it won't be visible on the Palm screen (using the Palm launcher).

AppLaunch

Syntax:

ReturnCode=AppLaunch(CardNo, AppName, LaunchCode, StringData)

Description:

Temporarily transfers execution to the specified application, passing a "launch code" and data string, then resumes execution after the launched application terminates

AppLaunch, the other method for transferring control to another program from NS Basic, works in a completely different manner. Instead of stopping the calling program and transferring control to the chained "target" application, AppLaunch instead passes a command (launch code) and string data to the called program, but returns control back to the calling NS Basic application. The target application cannot be a NS Basic application, and it must be able to accept the information passed to it.

One of the more popular uses of AppLaunch is to send string data to PalmPrint, from Steven's Creek Software (www.stevenscreek.com). PalmPrint provides applications a method of printing to several different IR-enabled printers (an infrared adapter is also available for standard, non IR-enabled printers). NS Basic doesn't have printer support built in, but instead can use AppLaunch to send any string data "transparently" to PalmPrint:

```
dim result as integer
dim CardNo as integer
CardNo=0
result=AppLaunch(CardNo,"PalmPrint",32768,"Print this string")
```

PalmPrint's documentation gives 32768 as the command to print string data, so this will cause PalmPrint to immediately send "Print this string" to an IR printer (additional codes and formatting options can be found in the chapter "Special Topics"). Since it would be cumbersome to write this out each time string data needed to be printed, a small subroutine can be designed and placed in a code module to call from any object or form:

```
Sub PalmPrint(PrintString as String)
Dim CardNo as Integer
Dim LaunchCode as Integer
Dim result as Integer
CardNo=0 'usually 0, but Palm suggests not hard-coding it
LaunchCode=32768 ' command passed to PalmPrint to print a string
result=AppLaunch(CardNo,"PalmPrint",LaunchCode,PrintString)
' make the call and return the result
If result<>0 Then
    result=alert("Print Error", "Error printing to
PalmPrint",3,"OK")
EndIf
End Sub
```

Then, to send a string to PalmPrint, just use the following:

```
Call PalmPrint(DataString) ' assuming DataString is valid string
```

By the way, as long as the subroutine is in a code module, or compiled before being placed elsewhere in code, calling a subroutine with a parameter can be done without using the Call keyword:

```
PalmPrint DataString ' assuming DataString is valid string
```

Ending your NS Basic application

Stop

Syntax:

Stop

Description:

Terminates execution of an NS Basic application

Ever notice that you don't "Quit" or "Exit" most Palm OS applications? You just tap or click your way from one application to the next, and they (usually) faithfully obey. The Palm OS is quite forgiving this way. You don't even have to explicitly close files! Not that I encourage that kind of "devil-may-care" attitude, but it's nice to know that the system is smart enough to keep track of many of the little details. Actually, it's not just a matter of being smart. Open files, subroutine pointers, and the other "little details" consume large amounts of precious memory and resources. Keeping the system clean by managing these background tasks is one of the Palm OS's treasures.

However, if you are intent on ending your applications completely, you can do so with the "Stop" command:

```
Stop
```

It's that simple. Your application will execute its Termination code, shut down, and return you to the Palm Launcher screen. Any subroutine "returns" will be removed from memory, and all open files will be closed (but it's still a good idea to make sure you have already closed them yourself in code – you're less likely to run into trouble that way).

> **Note** The Termination Code section is where you should save the data and other components of your application's current "state" if you want your users to return to the same spot where they left off. We'll cover this topic of "saving state" in the chapter on "Special Programming Topics."

Chapter VII - Projects and Forms

Once you have NS Basic's IDE (integrated development environment) installed on your Windows system, you'll find that the highly visual IDE makes designing with forms and objects straightforward, allowing you to place objects on a screen layout that provides a pretty accurate representation of the Palm device's screen.

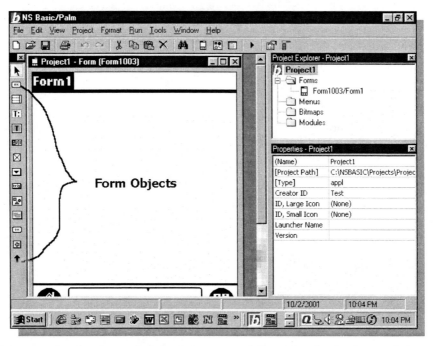

Objects can be placed anywhere on the screen, and dragged and resized as needed. As briefly mentioned earlier, these objects have *properties* and *methods* used to configure and manipulate them, and code associated with them as well.

All objects, whether we're referring to programming objects or real, physical objects, can be described by their characteristics and their actions. Object characteristics are known as *properties*, and they describe the object; these properties include name, ID number, position, size, visibility, editability, text, number of characters allowed, numeric or not, etc. Not all properties can be used to describe all objects, which parallels real life objects.

Once you place objects on a form, you can adjust the properties that will determine their behavior when they are initially displayed. Code placed in different sections of the form can also modify many properties of these objects, as can the objects' own code. Since each object's code is a subroutine, it can be called like any other subroutine (although without parameters passed), reducing the need for redundant coding.

Not only do objects have properties to describe them, they have actions, or *methods* that the object can carry out or have performed, including hide, show, clear, redraw, setfocus, etc. Some methods and properties share the same name (text, selected), which may at first be confusing, but will become clear as we explore them in context. For your convenience, Appendix B lists the current NS Basic objects, with their properties and methods.

Before we delve into NS Basic object programming, we need to discuss the project and its forms. Although not objects in the strictest sense, the project and its forms have properties and code associated with them, so in this respect they act as objects.

The NS Basic Project

An NS Basic project, like the human body, has an anatomy (as a doctor I get to make this analogy!). Without getting too specific (or disgusting), just as the skin contains the rest of the body, the NS Basic project contains the code for all of the application. Also, just as the body has systems of related organs, your project will consist of related objects and code. The project's properties help describe the application, so we'll cover that area first.

Your NS Basic project has two "properties" that you *must* have control over: the project name and Creator ID. As previously mentioned, these properties must be unique, as the Palm OS uses these to identify and load applications with its launcher. The name you give your project here becomes the internal Palm name for the final application (PRC) file. The Palm OS requires that this name be alphanumeric and no greater than 31 characters long (32 with the null terminator). A separate "Launcher Name" can be given to your project to be displayed on the Palm screen. You may also specify large and small icons for the launcher (the large icon is displayed by the launcher when apps are shown in "icon" view, and the small icon used when the launcher is in "list" view), and a "version string" that can be used to track program changes. This additional information is stored in your program's PRC file, but does not affect how it runs.

Startup and Termination Code

As we'll see with forms and objects, projects contain code sections. Code for projects (other than the code within the forms and objects of the project) is contained in two code sections: startup and termination. Startup code is run before any forms or objects are created, so this is a great place for you to put GLOBAL statements, initialize arrays, check for the presence of databases, etc. However, any references to forms or screen objects before they are created will be flagged by the compiler as errors (or, if not caught by the compiler, will result in program crashes).

> **Tip** Although you might be tempted to place all of your initialization code in the startup section, this can result in a considerable delay in the "perceived" starting of your program, since all that your user will see is a blank screen. Since screen objects and forms can't be

used to display progress (they haven't been created in the program yet), you are somewhat limited in the ability to let you user know that the program isn't frozen. You can use message boxes and alerts, as well as the "object-less" commands DrawBitmap (see the project "splash.prj"), DrawChars, DrawLine, DrawRectangle, FillRectangle, and graphics window commands (CreateWindow, DestroyWindow, EraseWindow, and SetCurrentWindow). These commands may be very useful in the startup section to give some form of "status" message to your user, especially if a significant delay is expected (anything more than several seconds can seem like a very, very long time to an unsuspecting user!). The CD includes a project ("Progress Bar Test.PRJ") that demonstrates the production of vertical and horizontal progress bars, which are extremely useful for letting your users know, graphically, how your application in proceeding. Keep in mind that any information presented to the user in this way during startup will be overwritten when the first form loads.

The other code section "owned" by the project alone is the termination code. Code in this section is run when the program is terminated for any reason (any reason except for program crashes, that is!), or if the user switches to another program by pressing one of the application buttons (the four buttons for the Datebook, Phone Book, To Do List, and MemoPad/Note Pad apps). You'll most likely use the termination code section to save information that will be needed the next time the program is run, especially if you want your user to be able to leave your program, run some other program, then return to the previous spot in your initial program. See the "Save State" project for a demonstration of this programming technique.

Like the startup section, the termination code cannot refer to any form or object (by the time you get to the termination code, your forms and objects may have been "destroyed"), so visual feedback to the user must be through the same methods used in the startup section. Unfortunately, the termination code can't be used to return to the program using NextForm in case the user decides not to exit. However, the Chain command can be used to call an external program from the termination code, including the calling program itself. Combine the techniques in the Save State project with code to Chain to the calling program, and you can have the user return to the previous spot in your program instead of exiting. This requires considerable control over variables and database status, but it can be done.

Caution You can easily create a situation where your user can't leave your program at all! I wouldn't suggest using the Chain command in the termination code to call the same program until you have some experience in NS Basic programming. Unless, of course, you like resetting your Palm!

Forms

Continuing with the anatomy analogy, if the project represents the skin, then forms can best be though of as the different organ systems of the body. Forms should contain related objects that work together to accomplish a specific task. You can create your projects with virtually any number of forms, although they must contain at least one.

Although not technically NS Basic objects, forms also have properties and code associated with them. Since every other object gets placed *on* these forms, understanding forms is fundamental to NS Basic programming.

> **Note** You might at some time wonder if it's possible to have a "formless" NS Basic program. After all, it's conceivable that you might want to write a program such as one that takes a predefined database, performs some function (such as sorting, printing, etc.), and then ends without requiring any user intervention. As you've already seen, you can display a large variety of information to your user before any forms are loaded or displayed. At the time of this writing, you must have at least one form in your project. This form doesn't have to have any code (look at the Splash project), but it must exist.

Forms have a small number of properties, and even a smaller number of properties that currently have any utility for most applications. Load the Hello project, and look at the "Properties" for the first (in this case, only) form.

Of the properties listed, only the Form Name, Form Title, Default Form, and Show Titlebar properties are likely to be useful (at least when you start programming). NS Basic support forms of different sizes, but for now resist the urge to change the Left, Top, Width, and Height properties. Better still, go ahead and experiment with these values. The default form is small enough already – it's unlikely that a smaller form is going to have any advantages (except for Modal forms, which aren't fully supported as of this writing).

When your form is first created in the IDE, it's assigned a 4-digit ID (in this case 1004). All Palm OS objects have unique ID numbers. For the most part, NS Basic isolates you from the ID (you can't select or change it in the IDE), but there are a few instances where it will be important to know an object's ID, and I'll let you know when that information will be important.

The form's Name and Title initially are set to "Form" followed by the ID number. You'll probably want to change one or both of these, especially if you will be displaying the form's Title (by setting "Show Titlebar" to TRUE in the form's Properties). NS Basic doesn't have a command to change a form's title during runtime, so you'll have to set it during your program design (the Palm OS API has commands for setting and displaying a form's title, but we'll cover that in the section on API calls). Since the default title area consumes nearly 10% of the screen, you may wish to leave the title blank, leaving the top of the screen clear for later use.

If you plan on using more than one form in your application, you'll want to give your forms more descriptive names than their defaults. Not only will this make your forms easier to identify during programming, but NS Basic refers to a form's name when switching from one form to another:

```
If Salary < 50000 then
   NextForm "frm1040EZ"
else
   NextForm "frm1040A"
end if
```

Many programmers use the first few characters of an objects name to refer to the type of object, like "frm" to refer to the form object, "pop" for popups, "lst" for lists, etc.

In this example, the different names not only tell NS Basic which form to load, but also let you as a programmer know at a glance what type of object is being manipulated (although in this case the NextForm command gives it away!).

> **Tip** It's tempting to sit down and design your forms from scratch and "on-the-fly" as you are programming, but with a screen that's only 160 pixels high by 160 pixels wide, you don't have room for a large number of objects. Additionally, if you start out designing forms with numerous objects, and later decide to change these objects, you could have a lot of code to modify. Also, since you can only fit a small number of objects on a form without it becoming too cluttered, it may be useful to group related objects on separate forms. For instance, if you were designing a program for managing a checking account, you might want to use one form for entering and modifying information, another form for displaying monthly/yearly totals, etc. Keeping the number of objects to a minimum, and grouping objects according to function helps keep forms uncluttered, and helps in maintaining structured, uncluttered code as well.

Form Code

Forms have code associated with them, and this code exists in one of three sections that are executed at various times in a form's "life" – before the form is displayed, after the form is displayed, and during any event that occurs on the form. How quickly a form displays depends to a great extent on how much code is in the various sections of the form, so careful attention to code placement may make the difference between a sluggish application and one that appears quick and responsive.

"Before" Code

A form's "before" code section contains code that is executed when the form is loaded but before it is displayed (and before the form's objects are displayed). Since the form's objects aren't displayed yet, you can't access their visual properties or methods, but can initialize list and popup items, create form-level global variables, etc. Your form's "before" code will be run any time the form is displayed, whether the form is the project's default form (and therefore run at startup, after the project startup code), if the form is called using NextForm, or if the Redraw command is issued for the form.

> **Caution** The Redraw command does not simply redraw the form objects and their contents, but runs the form's associated "before" and "after" code. This is extremely important to remember, but is barely mentioned in the manual. Don't say I didn't warn you!

As with your project's Startup code, a form's "before" code is executed before any form objects become visible. Because of this, you should avoid lengthy database or array initializations, or other code that will needlessly delay visual reinforcement to your user. Make use of the "object-less" graphics methods mentioned in the section on project startup code if needed to give some feedback to your user during time-consuming operations. Make it informative and entertaining, and your users might not even mind the wait!

SideBar Years ago I learned what was called the "seven second rule." On the average, users will wait approximately seven seconds with no feedback before they start to worry that the program is "stuck," at which time they start clicking the mouse, hitting the return key, tapping the Palm screen, etc., to get some feedback. Cinematography has a variation of this rule, where viewers lose interest in a scene if the camera angle doesn't change after seven seconds. Webmasters have learned that this applies to web pages as well (viewers lose interest if a page doesn't load within seven seconds). If you don't think seven seconds is that long, look at a clock and imagine, when the second hand gets to the "12" that your app has just started. Now imagine staring at an empty screen as the seconds tick by: 0...1...2...3...4...5...6...7 - getting a little anxious? Benchmark your programs on actual Palm devices, not just the POSE emulator, to see if there are any sections that need some additional user feedback to prevent this frustrating situation.

"After" code

Your form's "after" code is where you will most likely place most of your form and object initialization code, as you only have control over both visual and non-visual properties and methods of the form and its controls once the form has been created. As in the form's "before" code, your variables declared as Global in the "after" code are available to all objects and subroutines in the form. The same caveats apply here regarding lengthy initialization – your user is probably ready to start interacting with your program by now, so finish as much of the "housekeeping" as possible. If additional initialization routines are necessary, you may be able to incorporate them into the code for some of the screen objects on an "as needed" basis. For your first few projects these delays are not likely to be much of a problem, but as you develop larger, more complex programs you may wonder why your apps seem sluggish. Careful planning and attention to visual details will keep both you and your users satisfied.

"Event" Code

The "Event" code section requires some explanation, as it's treated differently than any other code section. Unlike code that you can call as a subroutine or function, or code that's directly attached to an object, the Event code section is called whenever a system event occurs, including tapping the screen, selecting one of the silk-screened "soft keys" or pressing a "hard" button, or certain system events. In this section you can "capture" a key or event, perform some action, then either allow the normal action to occur, or tell the OS that the event has been "handled" by your own routine. For instance, you may notice when you first create your NS Basic apps that tapping the silk-screened "menu" key doesn't automatically pull up a form's menu, although one may have been created. Or, you might want to use a different calculator than the one assigned to the calculator soft key – especially if you want this calculation to be part of your program. You can intercept the tap that would otherwise run the Palm Calculator app, perform the calculation, and return to your program (actually, you never left, but you get the idea). You might also want to create your own program Launcher or Find command to be run within your program. By intercepting the screen taps or button presses, you can create your own custom routines to enhance or replace the existing routines. Since the code in this section is specific for the form that it is placed on, once your program has finished running (or a new form is called), the previous settings are left intact.

You may wonder just how this section is used in your program, and how the program "knows" that there is an event that needs to be handled. The Palm OS provides an "event queue" that contains information regarding the event that "called" the Event code routine. The GetEventType function can be used to determine the nature of this event:

```
dim res as integer
Ans=GetEventType()
```

The value returned by GetEventType will be 1 (or NsbKeyOrButton) if a key or button was pressed, 2 (or NsbPenDown) for a PenDown event (stylus pressed on the screen surface), 3 (or NsbPenUp) for a PenUp event (stylus lifted from the screen surface), 4 (or NsbJogDial) if the "jog dial" is pressed on the Sony Clie device, or greater than 24832 if the Event code was called from an event in a shared library.

One of the most commonly used functions you'll want to perform in the Event code is displaying a form's menu. Since the 160x160 screen limits the space available for screen objects, it's useful to have the "menu" soft key instead of having to place a "Display Menu" button control just for the purposes of displaying your form menu(s). Additionally, users of other Palm OS programs are familiar with using the menu key, so using a common interface will make your applications immediately more intuitive and less frustrating for your user (and anything that's intuitive is also more likely to be used!). We'll discuss this later in the section on NS Basic Menus, but a brief overview now will give you an idea how the Event section is used.

To call a menu (let's assume you have a menu named "mnuMain"), you need to have code in the Event section of the desired form that determines that a key or button was pressed, then you only have to determine if the menu key was selected, and perform the appropriate action (in this case, the DrawMenu command):

```
dim key as string
If GetEventType()=nsbKeyOrButton then
    ' if key/button was "pressed"
    key=getKey() ' if so, get the key value
    select case asc(key) ' and compare it with known values
        case 5 'menu key on silkscreen area
            MenuDraw "mnuMain" ' draw the menu
            SetEventHandled
            ' don't let the Palm OS do anything else with it
        case else
    end select
End If
```

The GetKey function will return a nonzero value if a key or button is pressed, which is the value associated with the key or button. In this case we were only interested in a key/button press to issue the MenuDraw command (although we were only looking for the value 5 in this example, you can see a complete list of hardware and silkscreen buttons in the description for GetKey). Looking at these values shows that you have considerable control over the code run for the different keys or buttons that can be pressed, including the on/off and cradle HotSync buttons. It may be tempting to write code for each of these keys and buttons, but unless you have a really good reason to interrupt or replace the normal functions, try to avoid getting too fancy – at least until you have a good grasp of the power and complexity of event handling.

> **Caution** There's a bug in the Palm OS event handling. Actually, it's not a bug, but it acts like one. Let's say that you trap all possible button taps and ignore them, so your program will only allow screen taps. If your program displays a Message or Alert box, pressing one of the previously trapped keys will perform the keys usual function. Why does this happen? The Message and Alert boxes are actually small modal forms (modal forms are forms that force user input to themselves, and don't allow the user to continue until the modal form is removed). Since they are forms, the Message and Alert boxes have their own event handlers that won't have the button trapping that your initial form had (since you don't have control over their event handling routines). Therefore, when the Message or Alert boxes are displayed, you lose control of the event handler. Once the user presses a button on the Message or Alert box, and your previous form regains control, your event handler will be active. However, if the user presses one of the Palm hard buttons or soft keys, your program may lose its "focus." This is an insidious problem, especially if you are writing a game that uses the Palm's buttons as game controls. Avoid the use of Message and Alert boxes in these programs. Chances are that you will want to use more graphical methods of presenting information to your game players anyway, but you need to know about this to maintain control in your programs that try to trap these buttons.

Note in the preceding example that I've also included the SetEventHandled command. Since my code handles everything that needs to be done to display and activate the menu, I neither need nor want the Palm OS to try to determine what to do with the menu soft key tap. In other instances you may want to write a routine that performs part of the processing for a screen tap or button press, then pass the event to the Palm OS for the usual processing. In that case you would omit the SetEventHandled command.

Not only can your program intercept keystrokes and button presses, but you can obtain the position and status of a screen tap by using the GetPen command. By using the following code in your form's Event code, you can determine the X and Y coordinates of the last stylus action, along with whether it was a tap or a lift (PenDown or PenUp event) that triggered the event:

```
dim XPos as integer
dim YPos as integer
dim PenStatus as integer
GetPen XPos , YPos , PenStatus
'returns pen status as the NS Basic variable
'nsbPenUp or nsbPenDown
```

This code can be used to trap stylus taps anywhere on the screen, enabling you to perform functions not directly supported by NS Basic objects. For instance, the code for a Field object is only run when the user leaves the field. But what if you need to run some code when your user enters a field? By using GetPen and comparing the X and Y coordinates with the left, top, width, and height of a field, you can determine when a user has entered a field, and execute code at that time.

```
dim XPos as integer
dim YPos as integer
dim PenStatus as integer
GetPen XPos , YPos , PenStatus
if (XPos>=40) and (XPos<=120) and (YPos>=20) and (YPos<=30) then
   'user has tapped the area from X 40 to 120, Y 20 to 30
end if
```

If you have a field 40 pixels from the left and 20 pixels from the top, with a width of 80 pixels and height of 10 pixels, this code will allow you to perform your own code upon entry to the field. Your field's code remains unchanged, and is still run when the user exits the field.

> **Tip** Don't use SetEventHandled in this case. If you do, your user won't be able to enter your field at all (the Palm OS wouldn't pass the tap to the field object, so it wouldn't know that it was entered)!

Since this processing consumes valuable clock cycles, putting too much code in the Events section of a form can make your program sluggish and unresponsive. Use the Events section only when necessary, and minimize the amount of time spent in this section's code. We'll discuss the GetKey, GetEventType, GetPen, and SetEventHandled statements in more detail later.

"Unload" Code

Sorry – this is a cruel joke (I'm so ashamed!). There is no "Unload" code section (although there may be in future versions). For now, be sure to perform any "maintenance" functions (saving data, closing databases that were opened for this form, etc.) prior to using NextForm to jump to a different form.

Chapter VIII - Screen Graphics

Although NS Basic makes working with forms and objects easy and powerful, there are many of what I refer to as "form-less" or "non-object" graphics commands. With these commands, you can create and manipulate graphics windows, rectangles, and lines, display bitmap images, and place text at any location on the screen. Not only are these screen graphics commands extremely useful for routine graphics display, being "form-less" and "object-less" they can be used even before any form or object is displayed in your application (during your project's Startup code, for instance). However, unlike screen objects, these graphics do not respond to screen taps directly. You'll need to include code in the Events section of your form to handle these screen taps (or allow the taps to get passed through to any form objects underneath the graphics).

Graphics Windows

Graphics windows in NS Basic are used to create subsets of the screen in which graphics are displayed. Although the same effect can be obtained with clearing an area of the screen by hiding the objects in the area, and placing graphics in the cleared area, the real advantage windows is that all graphics commands are *relative* to the window's coordinates rather absolute (or relative to the entire screen). Why is this important? Imagine creating a routine to display a number of items at the upper left corner of the screen, using each object's left, top, width, and height to generate the necessary X and Y coordinates. Now, if you decide that this information would be better placed on the bottom right corner, you'd have to rewrite the coordinates for each object, which would take additional time and run the risk of introducing errors. However, if you graphics windows, all you have to do is change the window's coordinates – the objects drawn in the window will remain in their relative positions. You can even have multiple windows, and vary the display to each window as needed (even allowing the user to select which window to draw in). In addition, erasing a window's graphics is easily performed by erasing the window itself, rather than erasing the individual objects. Removing the windows completely ("destroying" it) causes the underlying screen to return to its previous state cleanly and with very little processing overhead.

Creating and Selecting Windows

CreateWindow, SetCurrentWindow

Syntax:

CreateWindow "WindowName",Left,Top,Width,Height
SetCurrentWindow "WindowName"

Description:

Create a "virtual" window for graphics display. Set the window to be used for subsequent graphics display.

Thankfully, most of the windowing commands are self-explanatory. To create a new graphics window, simply issue the command CreateWindow with the name and coordinates of the desired window:

```
CreateWindow "winGraphics",X,Y,Width,Height
```

This creates a new window "winGraphics" that can be used for graphics commands. No changes are made to the current screen display at this time, however, including clearing the window area. You have to do this yourself (see "Erasing Windows" in the following section). Similarly, the graphic window doesn't have a visible border, title bar, or other visual elements that you are used to if you program in Visual Basic or most other programming languages.

The main purpose for graphics windows is that any graphics drawn in a graphics window will be drawn with their left and top values relative to the x and y values used in the CreateWindow line. For example:

```
CreateWindow "winGraphics",10,20,60,80
SetCurrentWindow "winGraphics"
DrawChars "New Window", 5,10 ' draws string in window area
```

will create a 60 pixel wide by 80 pixel high window "winGraphics" with its top left corner 10 pixels from the left and 20 pixels from the top of the current form, and place the text "New Window" 5 pixels from the left and 10 pixels from the top of the window, or at actual positions of 15 pixels from the left and 30 pixels from the top of the form.

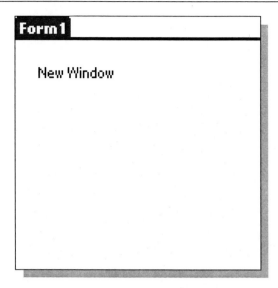

Tip Note the use of the SetCurrentWindow command. Although you might expect that you could use CreateWindow to "create a new separate graphics window to be used for subsequent graphic commands" (straight from the manual!), you can't *guarantee* that these graphics will actually go to the "current" window unless you explicitly control for it. You may have more than one window, for example, and might lose track of which is the current window.

Ready for some ***good*** news? The name of the graphics window doesn't have to be a literal value – it can be a string variable as well. The use of a variable rather than a literal is supported by all of the graphics windows commands. Also, if you're going to use a string literal, it isn't case-sensitive, so all of the following are equivalent:

```
CreateWindow "winGraphics",10,20,60,80
CreateWindow "WINGRAPHICS",10,20,60,80
CreateWindow "wingraphics",10,20,60,80
```

Erasing Windows

EraseWindow

Syntax:

> **EraseWindow**

Description:

> **Erase the contents of the current graphics window**

Once you have a graphics window created, you'll want to use it. However, if you create a window on a form that already has objects displayed in the area you want for your window, you'll probably need to clear this area (unless you want to superimpose your window's contents over the existing form) As mentioned above, creating the window doesn't clear its contents. The EraseWindow command will clear the current graphics window. As before, use SetCurrentWindow to assure that you are erasing the correct window:

```
CreateWindow "winGraphics",10,20,60,80
SetCurrentWindow "winGraphics"
EraseWindow
DrawChars "New Window", 5,10
' text will be drawn in a cleared window
```

Destroying Windows

DestroyWindow

Syntax:

DestroyWindow "WindowName"

Description:

Erases and removes from memory the specified graphics window

No, we're not trying to drive Bill Gates out of business. We've created our graphics windows, drawn some text or other graphics in them, and erased them. When we're through with them, rather than just erase them, we need to destroy our windows to release the Palm resources.

```
DestroyWindow "winGraphics"
```

DestroyWindow also destroys any text, bitmaps, lines, or rectangles placed in the named window. Additionally, the command causes the screen contents to be refreshed, so any object(s) under the destroyed window are redrawn (actually, the entire form is redrawn).

One last point concerning graphics windows: the compiler may let you create more than one window with the same name, or erase, set, or destroy nonexistent windows. The use of a global flag to determine whether or not a window is present will help prevent nasty crashes:

```
Global WindowExists as integer
WindowExists=false ' set this to indicate whether or not_
our window exists
'...some code...
If WindowExists=false Then
    CreateWindow "winGraphics",10,20,60,80
    WindowExists=true
End if
```

```
'...some code...
If WindowExists=true then
    SetCurrentWindow "winGraphics"
    EraseWindow
    DrawChars "New Window", 5,10 ' draws text in a cleared window
End If
'...some code...
If WindowExists=true then
    DestroyWindow "winGraphics"
End If
```

Drawing Graphics

NS Basic supports a small number of graphics commands for directly drawing onto a form or window. With these commands you can draw lines and rectangles (filled, or empty with border), or place text and bitmaps at any desired position on the form/window. With a little clever programming, you can also easily draw single pixels or circles as well.

Drawing Lines

DrawLine

Syntax:

DrawLine xStart, yStart, xEnd, yEnd[,penType]

Description:

Draws a line on the current form or graphics window

Line drawing in NS Basic is quick, simple, and a powerful way to set screen sections apart for visual emphasis. The syntax is straightforward:

```
DrawLine xStart, yStart, xEnd, yEnd, penType
```

where xStart and yStart are the distance in pixels from the left and top of the form (or window, if the line is being drawn in a graphics window) for the start of the line, and xEnd and yEnd the pixel positions for the end of the line. NS Basic doesn't require that the end positions be greater than the start, so the following are equivalent:

```
DrawLine 10,20,100,120
DrawLine 100,120,10,20
```

By default, DrawLine will draw lines as solid black. You can supply an additional parameter, the "penType" value, to draw lines in black, gray, or the same as the background ("white"):

```
DrawLine 10,20,120,20,nsbNormal ' draw a black line
DrawLine 10,50,120,50,nsbGray ' draw a gray line
DrawLine 10,50,120,50,nsbGrey ' for the non-USA programmers!
```

```
DrawLine 10,80,120,80,nsbInverted' draw line in background color
```

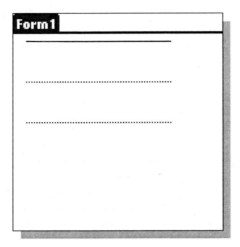

Drawing Pixels

NS Basic doesn't have a command to draw single pixels, but it's simple enough to simulate:

```
DrawLine 10,20,10,20,nsbNormal ' draw a black pixel at 10,20
```

You can even create your own DrawPixel command:

```
sub DrawPixel (x as integer, y as integer)
    DrawLine x,y,x,y
end sub
```

You can place this subroutine in your program's startup code, or in a code module. For casual use this may be helpful, but the use of subroutines involves additional processing overhead. Also, since you can't pass NS Basic special variables such as nsbNormal to subroutines, you will need to add additional code if you wish to draw pixels with the pen types nsbGray or nsbInverted.

> **Tip** You can still use the penType parameter to draw using nsbNormal, nsbGray, or nsbInverted, but be careful – using nsbGray draws in gray by alternating black and white pixels:
>
> ```
> DrawLine 10,20,10,20,nsbGray ' black pixel at 10,20
> DrawLine 10,21,10,21,nsbGray ' white pixel at 10,21
> DrawLine 11,20,11,20,nsbGray ' white pixel at 11,20
> DrawLine 11,21,11,21,nsbGray ' black pixel at 11,21
> ```
>
> In other words, the only pixels visible when using nsbGray are those in which both x and y positions are either even or odd. If one position is even and the other is odd, a pixel is drawn using the background "white" color, and will be indistinguishable from the background.

Drawing Rectangles

DrawRectangle, FillRectangle

Syntax:

>**DrawRectangle xStart, yStart, Width, Height[,CornerRadius][,penType]**
>**FillRectangle xStart, yStart, Width, Height [,CornerRadius][,penType]**

Description:

Draws a rectangle with the specified parameters on the current form or window

If you've ever had to draw even simple geometric figures line-by-line, you'll appreciate the NS Basic commands for drawing filled or empty ("border only") rectangles. The syntax is similar to the DrawLine command, but uses the width and height of the rectangle, and an additional parameter to describe how to draw the corners of the rectangles:

```
dim x as integer
dim y as integer
dim width as integer
dim height as integer
dim CornerRadius as integer
'DrawRectangle X,Y,Width,Height,CornerRadius,penType
'pen types nsbNormal, nsbGray, nsbInverted are optional
DrawRectangle 20,40,20,40,4,nsbNormal
DrawRectangle 50,40,50,50,0,nsbGray
```

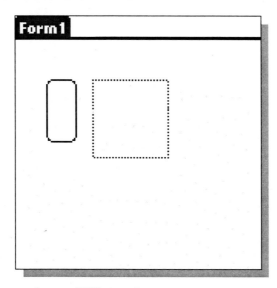

To create filled rectangles, use FillRectangle:

```
'FillRectangle X,Y,Width,Height, CornerRadius,penType
FillRectangle 20,40,20,40,4,nsbNormal
FillRectangle 50,40,50,50,0,nsbGray
```

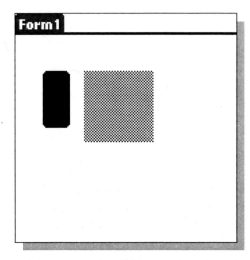

You can erase an area of the screen using FillRectangle, using nsbInverted as the pen type:

```
FillRectangle 20,40,20,40,4,nsbInverted
```

To erase the entire screen:

```
FillRectangle 0,0,160,160,0,nsbInverted
```

Encapsulate this in a subroutine, and you can easily create a CLS command:

```
Sub CLS()
   FillRectangle 0,0,160,160,0,nsbInverted
End Sub
```

You say you want to leave the title alone, yet erase the lower part of the screen? Since the form title and underline take up the first 15 screen lines (0-14), try this:

```
Sub ClearLowerScreen()
   FillRectangle 0,15,160,145,0,nsbInverted
End Sub
```

Like the DrawLine command, rectangles can be drawn with penType of nsbNormal, nsbGray, or nsbInverted. The additional CornerRadius parameter treats the corner as being one-fourth of a circle (technically an "arc" of 90 degrees), with CornerRadius the radius of the circle that would be drawn if all 4 arcs came together.

Drawing Circles
NS Basic doesn't provide DrawCircle or FillCircle commands, but they're not too difficult to create from the DrawRectangle and FillRectangle commands. Since the

CornerRadius parameter used in these commands creates an arc of a given radius, all that's necessary to do is determine the center of the circle, and use the radius of the circle to determine the boundaries of the rectangle that would contain the circle. Using the radius as the CornerRadius parameter causes the corners to gently curve together to create the final circle.

It sounds a little confusing as a description, so maybe a little code will help:

```
DrawRectangle X-R, Y-R, 2*R, 2*R, r-0.5, nsbNormal
```

This would draw a circle of radius R at center X,Y. Using actual values to give you an example, how about a circle drawn at the middle of the screen (80, 80) with a radius of 40? We'll even create DrawCircle and FillCircle subroutines, and use them as though they were built-in NS Basic functions (place routines in code modules):

```
Sub DrawCircle(x as integer, y as integer, r as integer)
DrawRectangle X-R, Y-R, 2*R, 2*R, r-0.5, nsbNormal
End sub

DrawCircle 80,80,40
```

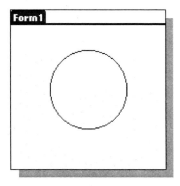

```
Sub FillCircle(x as integer, y as integer, r as integer)
FillRectangle X-R, Y-R, 2*R, 2*R, r-0.5, nsbNormal
End sub

FillCircle 80,80,40
```

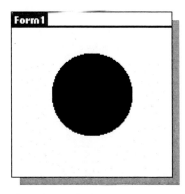

Notice that the CornerRadius parameter is not exactly R; the actual distance from the center pixel needs to be adjusted by a half-pixel in all directions to account for the size of the center pixel (even though it's not drawn). You can use the nsbGray and nsbInverted penType to draw in gray or the background color. As with DrawPixel, you can place these small routines in your project's startup code or a code module, but if your programs need to be as quick and responsive as possible you'll want to avoid subroutines (whenever possible). Once you get the rest of your code bug-free, change any reference to subroutines with "in-line" code for speed.

Drawing Text

DrawChars, Cursor, Display

Syntax:

> **DrawChars CharString,Left,Top**
> **Cursor Left, Top**
> **Display var1[,var2][,var3][,...]**

Description:

Used to position and display text on the current form or window

There are two ways to place text directly on a Palm screen without using any of the built-in objects: DrawChars and Display.

As we mentioned briefly before (when discussing the windowing and screen graphics commands), DrawChars is used to place text at a given form/window location using the default font:

```
DrawChars "New Window", 5,10
```

You have no control over the text once it's displayed. It cannot be edited, right justified, underlined, have its font changed, word-wrapped etc. In other words, this command is best used for placing short text messages on a form or window. Since the DrawChars command does not use a form object, it can be used before any forms are loaded, as in your project's startup code. Like the DrawLine and DrawRectangle commands, DrawChars also supports the use of the penType parameter to draw the text in black (nsbNormal), gray (nsbGray), or in the background color (nsbInverted). However, unlike the DrawLine and DrawRectangle commands, using nsbInverted as penType with DrawChars displays the characters in the background color but with a black "background" (white characters on a black background). You can take advantage of this characteristic of DrawChars to create a very visual "flashing" string: use DrawChars with the same text at the same position, but with alternating nsbNormal and nsbInverted:

```
Dim LoopCounter as Integer
For LoopCounter = 1 to 10
    DrawChars "Watch me flash!",5,30,nsbNormal
    Delay 0.2
    DrawChars "Watch me flash!",5,30,nsbInverted
    Delay 0.2
Next
```

The Delay statements are necessary to keep the text from flashing so rapidly as to be unnoticed. Experiment with the number of loop iterations (cycles) and delay to produce the desired effect. Alternatively, you could create a loop that continues to flash the message until the user taps on the screen or presses a button:

```
Do While SysEventAvailable()=0
   DrawChars "Watch me flash!",5,30,nsbNormal
   Delay 0.2
   DrawChars "Watch me flash!",5,30,nsbInverted
   Delay 0.2
Loop
```

The other method of displaying information without relying on form objects is through the use of Display:

```
Display var1 [ ,var2,var3...]
```

Unlike DrawChars, Display displays any variable or literal value at the current form/window cursor position. Because it does not require the conversion to string format to display numeric values (required for DrawChars), Display is a faster method for the display of numeric data. However, you need to explicitly control the cursor position through the use of the Cursor command:

```
Cursor 10, 30
' sets the cursor to x,y - in this case
' 10 pixels from the left, 30 pixels down
Display ItemTotal
```

Because it is so limited, you probably won't use Display much. You can't change the font, penType, or any of the other characteristics of the displayed values. It was initially included to help with debugging, but except for its speed it's not very useful. Like the Print command in most versions of Basic, Display places its information sequentially on the form/window. However, unlike the Print command, although you can use commas to separate multiple variables on the same line, they won't be spaced out by tab stops (the usual behavior for most versions of Basic). If fact, they won't be spaced out *at all*:

```
Dim a as integer
Dim b as integer
Dim c as integer
a=5
b=16
c=25
Cursor 5,40
Display a,b,c
```

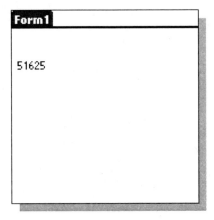

will NOT display 5 16 25, but instead 51625 – not quite what was intended. If you are going to display multiple values on the same line, separate them by spaces or some other delimiter:

```
Display a," ",b," ",c
```

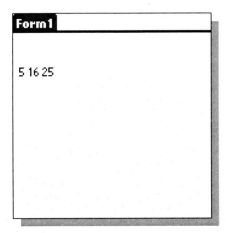

Display also doesn't automatically advance the cursor to the next line (probably since there aren't predefined "lines" on forms or windows). You'll need to use the Cursor statement to position the Display statement each time:

```
Dim a as integer
Dim b as integer
Dim c as integer
a=5
b=16
c=25
Cursor 5,20 ' 5 pixels from the left and 20 from the top
Display a
Cursor 5,30 ' down another 10 pixels to spread the "lines" apart
Display b
Cursor 5,40 ' I think you get the idea by now...
Display c
```

Since there's not much power in the Display statement, you'll probably not use it much. It's just nice to know it's there.

Drawing Bitmaps

DrawBitmap

Syntax:

DrawBitmap BitmapID,Left,Top

Description:

Draws a bitmap image on the current form or window at the specified location

NS Basic provides two ways to display bitmap images. One method is to create a bitmap object on the form, load a bitmap into the project, and modify the bitmap object's "Resource ID#" property to reflect the resource ID of the actual bitmap. This method is discussed in more detail in the section on using the Bitmap object.

> **SideBar** NS Basic uses ResIn to allow support for BMP, GIF, ICO, EMF, JPG, and WMF formats. Using other image editing programs, you should be able to convert virtually any image to a format compatible with NS Basic for use in your NS Basic applications. The Mona Lisa probably won't look too good on a 160x160 monochrome device, but you might like it. After all, beauty *is* in the eye of the beholder!

The other method for displaying bitmaps is through the use of the DrawBitmap command, which takes the resource ID of a bitmap that has been already loaded in the IDE, and the X and Y coordinates of the top left corner where the bitmap will be displayed as parameters:

```
DrawBitmap 1004, 10, 50 ' a bullseye, as bitmap ID 1004
```

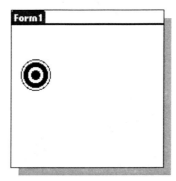

You can also use a variable to hold the bitmap's resource ID:

```
Dim BitmapID as integer
BitmapID = 1023
DrawBitmap BitmapID,10, 50
```

This will draw the bitmap with ID 1023 on the current form or window 10 pixels from the left, and 50 pixels from the top. The bitmap will be drawn at its original size in pixels, so bitmaps larger than 160x160 pixels cannot be completely displayed on the majority of Palm devices.

You can take advantage of this to "scroll" through a bitmap that's larger than the actual screen. If you make either or both of the x and y values negative, the left/top edges of the image will be shifted off-screen, with the image appearing scrolled left/up. The same effect can be accomplished using graphic windows, as the bitmap will be displayed relative to the window coordinates, with the off-window edges invisible to the user. The following screen, from the "Scroll Sample" project, illustrates scrolling a map that's considerably larger than the viewing window:

Most of your bitmaps will probably NOT be the size of the entire form, although form size bitmaps can be used to place background graphics on the form. You'll need to use the Show method for any objects that you wish to display on top of the bitmap, since the act of drawing the bitmap "covers" any underlying form objects:

```
DrawBitmap 1006, 0, 0 ' draw 160x160 bitmap at 0,0 to fill form
btnContinue.Show ' button hidden by bitmap, need to show it
btnQuit.Show ' ditto
```

The bitmap does not become part of the application until it is compiled, so changes can be made to it at any time, using your favorite paint program or bitmap editor. The next time you compile your application, the revised bitmap will be used.

> **Tip** The enclosed CD contains utilities (including Code Tools, Paint Shop Pro, ResIn. IrfanView) for converting and editing bitmaps, both prior to and after the compilation phase (as part of your application's PRC file). I suggest making any modifications to bitmaps before compiling them. Any changes made to your bitmap resources in the PRC file won't be saved automatically to your original bitmap that was used during compilation, so re-compiling the project means re-editing the bitmap. Why go through the work twice?

Animating bitmaps

Since you can draw a bitmap at any form or window location, it's fairly simple to provide some animation to your program:

```
Dim X as integer
For X = 0 to 100
   DrawBitmap 1006, X, 40
Next
```

If the bitmap with ID 1006 were a small car, this would create the illusion of the car driving across a portion of the current form or window:

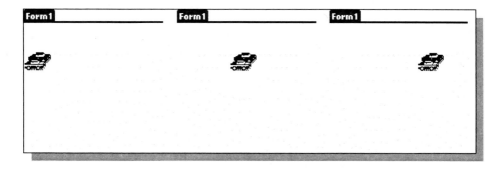

> **Tip** If you use this form of animation to move an object, be sure that the object has a clear border equal of a width equal to the number of pixels moved, or the image will leave a "trail" as it moves.

You could compare the coordinates and size of the bitmap with the positions of other screen objects to determine if a "collision" occurred. It's easy to create even multi-level, highly graphical games using this technique. Be sure to leave a clear border of at least enough pixels to erase (overwrite) the previous pixels when drawing a bitmap near its pervious position, or you will leave a "shadow" or "tail" of the image (try the code above with a bitmap that doesn't have a clear border, then with one that does as a comparison).

In addition to drawing the same bitmap in different positions, you can draw different bitmaps in the same position for a different effect. Using the same image but with different brightness (again, this is something for an external image editor, not NS Basic, since there is no "brightness" parameter), you can make an image fade in or out:

```
Dim image as Integer ' we'll use this for our bitmap resource id
Dim loopcount as Integer ' loop through the code a few times
For LoopCount=1 to 5
For Image = 1009 to 1012 ' our bitmaps have consecutive id's
     DrawBitmap Image,0,0 ' draw at the top left
     Delay 0.2 ' delay to prevent flicker
Next
For image = 1012 to 1009 step -1 ' display them in reverse order
     DrawBitmap image,0,0
     Delay 0.2
Next
Next
```

The above code, from the "Fader" project, uses four bitmaps of different brightness and displays them consecutively to alternately fade the image in and out.

The Delay statement is used to create a more pleasing display, since there may be noticeable "flicker" with some of the faster devices, or if the application is running in POSE on a very fast computer.

You can even create a "mini movie" player by taking consecutive bitmaps and displaying them rapidly one after the other. You can place the resource ID's in an array, then loop through the array, using the stored resource ID's. However, a faster method would be to load each bitmap into your project, one after the other, without creating any other object in the NS Basic IDE during the bitmap loading process. This causes the bitmap resource ID's to be assigned sequentially, making it easier to loop through the ID numbers directly, rather than using an array. This technique is used in the "MiniMovie" project.

Bitmaps are stored in the final PRC, so there is a practical limit on how many bitmaps can be stored. Eventually some form of image compression/decompression will be available for NS Basic programmers. For now, keep an eye on the size of your program's PRC, and weigh the pros and cons of using bitmaps in your projects from the user's point of view. Used judiciously bitmaps can add variety and interest to your applications without undue memory and/or performance demands.

Chapter IX - NS Basic Objects

NS Basic supports most of the standard Palm OS objects, including bitmaps, buttons, checkboxes, fields, gadgets, labels, lists, popups, repeaters, scrollbars, selectors, and the lowly shift indicator. Table support isn't yet included in NS Basic, but I'll give you a workaround.

Bitmap

Graphics can make or break a program. Used appropriately they can add interest and clarity to your programs. Used poorly, they can slow your program to a crawl, obscure an otherwise clear app, and send your users elsewhere.

NS Basic provides two means by which to display a previously designed image, or bitmap, on a Palm device (there's actually a third method as well, but this additional method is pretty sneaky, and is covered later in this chapter in the Signature Capture section of the Gadget object). In the Screen Graphics chapter we discussed the use of the DrawBitmap command, which could be used to place a bitmap anywhere on a form or window. By moving the bitmap, or quickly changing bitmaps, we could create pretty effective animation. However, these bitmaps suffered from the fact that they were one-sided – the user couldn't interact with the bitmap. In addition, you as the programmer couldn't perform one very simple task – you couldn't hide the bitmap. Once it was drawn it couldn't be easily removed without erasing or removing the form or window that it was on, or overwriting it with a "blank" bitmap, or some other time-consuming method.

The Bitmap object allows a different level of graphics functionality. It also adds a little confusion, but if you're willing to play with them a bit, you'll come to understand some of their power.

First of all, try to forget that the Bitmap object is called a "bitmap" at all. It's NOT a bitmap, but actually more of a "placeholder" for a bitmap to be added separately. To use a Bitmap object, you first place it on a form, then move and resize it to the desired Top, Left, Width and Height (it will resemble a small checkerboard at this point).

At this point, the Bitmap object doesn't have any actual image assigned to it. To add the image, right click on the Bitmap folder in Project Explorer, and select "Add Bitmap". You will be allowed to select bitmaps in a variety of formats, from any location on your system.

Tip Just because you *can* add an image from any directory and drive doesn't mean you *should*. Trying to keep track of all of the different images and projects can be difficult. I suggest either keeping all projects and bitmaps in their own directories, or keep them in the default NS Basic locations. Especially when you first start, don't get too fancy.

When you add these images, you'll notice that each one gets assigned an ID number. This ID is known as the Resource ID (the bitmap is stored as a "resource" in the PRC file, and given an internal ID). In order to "link" or assign these bitmap images to the Bitmap objects, place the ID of the actual bitmap image you wish to see in the "Resource ID" property of the Bitmap object. This Resource ID for the Bitmap object is assigned at design time, and cannot be changed during runtime. The bitmap does not become part of the project until it is compiled, but remains separate. This allows you to make any necessary changes to the bitmap without having to reload it each time. If you need to remove the image from your project, simply right click on the bitmap in Project Explorer, and select "Remove Bitmap".

Note If you do a lot of work with Bitmap objects, you'll probably forget to assign the Resource ID of a bitmap image to the Bitmap Object once in a while. Your application won't compile, and you'll get a fairly verbose message "A form bitmap object has not been assigned a corresponding resource id # of a valid bitmap file" message confirming your mistake (along with the warning that your "program will abort if loaded to the Palm device"). However, the final PRC won't be created, so the "abort" warning might be a bit harsh!

You can't change the position or size of the Bitmap object at runtime, either. So, since you have to do all of this at design time, and can't move it or resize it at runtime, what's the advantage of using the Bitmap object?

Unlike bitmaps drawn using DrawBitmap, the Bitmap object can have code attached to it – it responds to stylus taps (specifically, the penUp event). In addition, you can use the Hide and Show methods with the Bitmap object, unlike DrawBitmap. This makes it easy to create graphical "buttons" your user can interact with. The MegaMemo project takes advantage of this during cut, copy, and paste operations to provide the user with a familiar user interface. Sure, we could use Button objects with the captions "Cut", "Copy", and "Paste" – but what fun is that?

Like most other NS Basic objects, the Bitmap object's code is run when the user taps on the Bitmap. The Bitmap object doesn't give any visual feedback, though, so you might want to provide either audible feedback, or "flash" the Bitmap during the beginning of the Bitmap's code:

```
bmpChoice.Hide
delay 0.1
bmpChoice.Show
```

This code snippet from the Bitmap Explorer project makes the Bitmap invisible for one-tenth of a second, then makes it visible again (for more emphasis, you can create a loop that flashes the bitmap multiple times). As an added benefit, the Bitmap, like other NS Basic objects, is protected from additional taps when it's invisible.

> **Tip** You don't have to set the size of the Bitmap object if all you are using it for is an image "placeholder". Images that are bigger than the Bitmap object will be displayed, and will respond as though the Bitmap object were the same size as the image (the actual images are neither scaled nor cropped to fit the Bitmap object). Images that are smaller will only take up a portion of the Bitmap object – but the remaining "empty" object area will respond to stylus taps as well. However, if the Bitmap is *smaller* than the image, only the taps that fall *within* the Bitmap's borders will trigger the Bitmap's code – taps outside of the borders, even if your user taps on the image, will be ignored by the Bitmap, and will "fall through" to any underlying objects.

As we'll see in "Extending NS Basic", Bitmaps and other objects have a new "ID" property, which can be retrieved using .ID:

```
ObjectID=bmpTarget.ID
```

This ID number is used with SysTrapSub, SysTrapFunc, and shared libraries (also described in "Extending NS Basic") to identify the object in many of the Palm OS API functions. Use of the API is best left to C programmers, but we'll describe the general concepts and give examples (and some stern warnings) in "Extending NS Basic". So, to be complete, I've listed the ID property for the various objects, but we won't go into it in great detail – that's beyond the scope of this book.

Button

Just as Fields are the most useful and versatile objects for displaying text to users (as you'll see later), Buttons are the easiest, most intuitive way for users to interact with Palm applications.

Buttons are rectangular objects with rounded corners, they may or may not have a visible frame (and not, then, even *look like* a button), and may or may not have text. The text of a button typically lets the user know what action will be taken if the button is pressed, like "Write New", "Update", and "Clear", in these buttons from a phonebook app:

Buttons have code associated with them that is executed after the button is tapped (specifically, when the button is released). The button gives visual feedback by changing its background from white to black (or blue, on color systems), letting the user know that it has been pressed.

Like most other NS Basic objects, buttons are placed on your form by selecting the Button object from the toolbar, then clicking on the form where you want the upper-left corner of the Button. You can resize Buttons as needed by either visually moving the button and dragging one of the button's resizing handles, or by modifying the Left, Top, Width, and Height properties in the IDE. Button text, or label, is modified at design time in the IDE, or can be changed during run time through the button's Text property:

```
btnLoadData.text="Load Data"
```

You can also decide at design time what FontID you want to use for the Button text. This font cannot be changed at run time using standard NS Basic commands (although the API contains support for changing for font. See the section on "Extending NS Basic" for more details on using the Palm OS API). If you are using the LED or Symbol fonts, you may not be able to place the text you want at design time, but can place it on the button at run time:

```
btnUp.text=chr(1)  ' if using font #5, will display solid up arrow
btnUp.text=chr(3)  ' displays a grayed up arrow in font #5
btnSetAlarm.text=chr(20) ' displays small alarm clock in font #3
btnInfo.text=chr(4)  ' displays the info icon in font #4
```

Button text is always center justified (you can view this as a blessing or a curse). If the button is not wide enough to hold the entire text string, the text will be "cropped" on both sides to avoid spilling over the boundaries of the button, as in this button that's too small for the text string "Too Much Text Here":

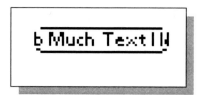

 The NS Basic manual and Palm OS make reference to the "AnchorLeft" property, which is used by some controls to determine which direction the control should expand to accommodate longer strings. This property currently has no effect on the Button object, or any other object whose text is center justified. NS Basic includes this support to comply with the Palm OS. Store that in your bag of tips!

Because a button's text is always centered, you may wish to use a button instead of a field as the heading for lists or vertical collections of fields. However, if you create a button with a frame, your users will want to tap it, even if it doesn't do anything. You can design your buttons with or without frames, and whether these frames are bold or not, in the NS Basic IDE by selecting the "Frame" and "Non-bold frame" properties:

Note that the "Non-bold frame" property only applies if you have "Frame" selected as well. Plan the frames and their bold/non-bold properties carefully, since they can't be modified at run time.

> **Tip** You may have to do some minor "tweaking" with the position and size of buttons, since how they appear in the IDE may not match exactly how they will appear on the actual Palm device or in POSE. However, use the X and Y display in the IDE to position your buttons (and other objects) – this will help you maintain both alignment and spacing.

Buttons have a few methods available at run time, and you might have guessed them already: Hide, Show, Redraw, and Text. We've already covered Text, and the others are pretty self-explanatory.

```
btnOption1.Hide  ' make button invisible
btnCalcTax.Show  ' show the previously hidden button
btnStart.Redraw  ' redraw button if overwritten or erased
```

Like other objects that support it, the Redraw command will only cause the Button to become visible if it was not hidden previously. The Button is also inactive (does not respond to stylus taps) when hidden.

Unfortunately, Buttons can only contain text, and not bitmaps or other graphics. However, you can always create your Buttons without text, and display characters or graphics over them. However, when the Button is tapped, it briefly changes to white text on a black background:

(or blue on color systems when the Button contains text, black when blank), then to its previous state, so any graphics drawn over Buttons will need to be redrawn if you wish to emulate a graphical Button.

At first, keep your Buttons simple, and experiment until you feel comfortable enough to start doing anything out of the ordinary. Remember - users expect Buttons to act like Buttons, so don't get too carried away!

Like the Bitmap and other objects, Button's have an ID property which can be retrieved using .ID for use with calls to API functions:

```
ObjectID=butCalculateRent.ID
```

Use of this ID number is described in the chapter "Extending NS Basic", and is best left to programmers knowledgeable in the use of the Palm OS API functions.

CheckBox

A common situation you will be faced with is the need to offer your user with a choice of two or more options. Often, these choices will be mutually exclusive; only one option can be selected at any given time. For example, the following screen is from a Palm-based computer dating service (OK, we're not curing cancer or developing a high-efficiency cold-fusion energy source...but who says we can't have a little fun?):

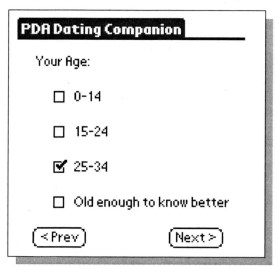

Obviously, the user must belong to only one of the age groups listed. Similar choices could be made regarding gender, favorite color, etc. Note also that by using the Checkbox you can also allow your user to use a single click to enter either discreet data or a range of data (such as age, above). By checking the status of the Checkbox, you can avoid more time-consuming range checking. Compare this code, using the Checkbox concept:

```
If chkAge0to14.status=nsbChecked then
    'code if 0-14
ElseIf chkAge15to24.status=nsbChecked then
    'code if 15-24
ElseIf chkAge25to34.status=nsbChecked then
    'code if 25-34
Else
    'code if 35 or older
End If
```

with this code using the actual user age:

```
UserAge=val(fldAge.text)  ' get age from user entry in field
If UserAge < 15 then
    'code if 0-14
ElseIf UserAge < 25 then
    'code if 15-24
ElseIf UserAge < 35 then
    'code if 25-34
Else
    'code if 35 or older
EndIf
```

The CheckBox avoids having to use the conversion from text to numeric age, and is slightly faster in the comparisons (in general, equality comparisons are more efficient than comparisons using "less than" or "greater than" – but this is dependent on the compiler/interpreter used). However, the speed advantage comes at the expense of screen space – the multiple CheckBoxes take up far more space than a single field for user entry of age. You'll need to decide which technique suits your individual applications best.

Well, I got a little ahead of myself, but you've gotten a glimpse of the usefulness of the CheckBox. You've seen that you can determine the status (checked or unchecked, or as NS Basic puts it: nsbChecked or nsbUnchecked) of a CheckBox, but there's much, much more.

For starters, you place the CheckBox on a form by selecting it in the IDE, and clicking the form at the location you wish to place the CheckBox. The default CheckBox is unchecked, and has the text "Checkbox" as its label. Not too useful, but using the properties you can set the initial text, AnchorLeft property (you'll probably want to leave this set to "True"), selected status (True or False, the equivalent of nsbChecked or nsbUnchecked), size, and location.

You can also set the Group ID, which is where you determine which of a number of CheckBoxes are grouped together in a mutually exclusive arrangement (that is, if only one value can exist at a time, only allow one choice – this eliminates the need for you *or your user* to assure that only one selection has been made). You'll notice that the default Group ID for CheckBoxes in the IDE is "0". This might give the false impression that all CheckBoxes with Group ID of "0" are mutually exclusive, but in reality a Group ID of "0" allows the CheckBoxes to act independently of other CheckBoxes on the same form. In other words, NS Basic and Palm don't assume that you want the CheckBoxes assigned in any specific manner, so you're given a way to allow them to act independently by default, but can easily group CheckBoxes together later if desired. Smart!

Tip PushButtons act in the same manner, and can be interchanged with CheckBoxes for a different "look and feel" based on how you want to present feedback to your user. In fact, both PushButtons and CheckBoxes can share common Group ID's, making for some visually interesting forms! Keep it simple, though, since a confused user isn't likely to be a happy (or productive) user.

You can have multiple groups of CheckBoxes, each acting separately as mutually exclusive groups:

```
 PDA Dating Companion

 Your Age:         │  Gender

    ☐  0-14        │     ☐  Male

    ☐  15-24       │     ☑  Female

    ☑  25-34       │     ☐  Undecided

    ☐  Old enough to know better

  ( < Prev )                ( Next > )
```

Just make sure that each set of CheckBoxes has its own non-zero Group ID. Also, make sure that each set of CheckBoxes has at most one CheckBox marked as Selected (doing otherwise will only confuse you and your users!). You can do this at design time, or through code at run time:

```
chkAge0to14.status=nsbChecked
chkAge15to24.status=nsbUnchecked
chkAge25to34.status=nsbUnchecked
chkAgeOver34.status=nsbUnchecked
chkGenderMale.status=nsbUnchecked
chkGenderFemale.status=nsbChecked
chkGenderUnknown.status=nsbUnchecked
```

In addition to the Selected property, you can also set or retrieve a CheckBox's Label property:

```
chkGenderMale.label="Dude"
chkGenderFemale.label="Chick"
chkGenderUnknown.label="???"
'now they have slightly less "stuffy" labels
```

You'll probably never need to use the Label or AnchorLeft properties, but it's nice to know about them ahead of time.

In case you're wondering, yes – you can change the font used to display the CheckBox's label. Just select the FontID in the IDE that corresponds to the font you wish to use. This is a design time decision, however – you can't change the font at run time (without using the API calls, that is – but that's in the chapter on "Extending NS Basic"). Make sure you leave enough room for the largest text that you're going to place in the CheckBox (especially if you plan on changing it at run time).

You might be surprised to find out that the CheckBox has code associated with it. Since you will probably be checking the status of CheckBoxes in *other* code, it seems almost redundant to have code associated with the CheckBoxes themselves. However, judicious use of a CheckBox's code can avoid the need for the If...Then...ElseIf...EndIf statements as shown above. Let's take the example above, with the Age and Gender choices. Since there was specific code to run based on the status of these CheckBoxes, why not just run the code when the CheckBoxes are selected or deselected, rather than wait until later? This is particularly useful if a global variable is set based on the value of mutually exclusive CheckBoxes.

Like most other NS Basic objects, CheckBoxes can be created in the IDE as visible or invisible (i.e., their Visible property is set as True or False). Similarly, the Redraw, Hide and Show methods can be used to, well, redraw, hide and show them:

```
chkGenderMale.Hide ' in case you only want non-males selected
chkGenderMale.Show ' ok, you changed your mind
chkGenderMale.Redraw ' in case we need to redraw the item
```

Keep in mind that the CheckBox is inaccessible by the user when hidden, although you can still access its properties and methods in code (like other NS Basic objects). Additionally, if the CheckBox is hidden, the Redraw method has no effect.

Like the Bitmap and other objects, the CheckBox's ID property can be retrieved using .ID for use with calls to API functions:

```
ObjectID=chkAgeRange.ID
```

Use of this ID number is described in the chapter "Extending NS Basic", and is best left to programmers knowledgeable in the use of the Palm OS API functions.

Field

The Field is probably the most important form object to understand. It is incredibly versatile, easily accessible, and the object you'll use the most to retrieve information from, and display information to your user.

In its simplest form, a Field is simply an object placed on the form where a user can enter data. In fact, it's the ONLY object that allows the user to directly enter alphanumeric information (that is, if you allow editing of the Field's contents). As the programmer, you have control at design time over a Field's numerous properties, including Name, Left, Top, Width, Height, FontID, maximum number of characters entered, justification, underline status, single or multiple line status, dynamic size, scrollbar, AutoShift, visibility, and numeric status. Here's a screen shot from the Field Explorer project, demonstrating various fields, in all their glory:

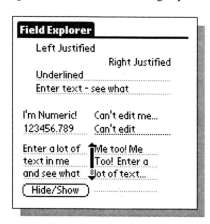

At runtime you have fewer options, but virtually anything that can be done with text, you can do with the Field object. So, instead of rambling on and on about it, let's explore the Field object.

With the NS Basic IDE running, start a new project (name it whatever you want – it doesn't matter) and place a single Field on the form near the upper left hand corner. To resize the field, click on it, grab a resizing handle, and move it to resize. Note that you can resize the Field in any direction, but for now, just make it wider.

Even at its widest, though, the Field object would be pretty limited if you could only display one line's worth of information. Look at the properties of the Field object, and you'll see several properties that govern just how much information can be placed or viewed in the field: Maximum Chars, Single Line, Has Scrollbar, and Dynamic Size.

Maximum Chars refers to the number of characters that the user can enter, NOT the number of characters that are visible. If Single Line is checked, then the number of characters visible is limited by the size of the field. If Single Line is left unchecked, then the number of characters visible is determined by the number of lines visible (based on the height of the Field and the size of the font being used) and whether or not Dynamic Size is checked.

Sounds confusing? Actually, it's not difficult to understand. If you want a single line of text limited by the width of the Field, make sure Single Line is checked (but be sure that your user's text will fit in the allotted space). If you want a single line that will scroll text horizontally if the user enters more text than will fit in one line, keep the Field one line high, but check Dynamic Size. If Dynamic Size is checked AND the Field object is more than one line high, text longer than one line will wrap to the next line, and will scroll horizontally if longer than the total Field length as displayed.

If "Has Scrollbar" is checked, then a vertical scrollbar will be added to the right of the Field and used to scroll the text up or down as needed. Just make sure that you leave enough room (7 pixels) to the right of the Field for the scrollbar.

> **Tip** If there is a "scrollable" object on a form (such as a Field, List, or PopUp with a visible scrollbar), NS Basic will automatically assign the hard "up" and "down" buttons on the Palm device to that object. If there is more than one scrollable object, each object will scroll simultaneously with the use of the hard buttons.

So, by varying the position, width, height, and a few other properties, it's pretty easy to get complete control over how much information can be entered or viewed in Field objects. Additionally, you have control over the *kind* of information (alphanumeric or strictly numeric) by checking or unchecking Numeric. Oddly enough, Fields with Numeric checked will only accept positive numbers (it's a Palm OS restriction, not NS Basic). In order to enter negative numbers, leave Numeric unchecked, and perform data validation after the Field information is entered. See the TestNum function for details. For an alternate method of data entry that allows both positive and negative numbers to be entered in a Field, check out the AltNumEntry project supplied on the CD.

To access a Field's contents, use the text method (even if the Field is declared "Numeric"). If you need to convert the value to a numeric form, use the Val function:

```
Dim TestData as string
Dim TaxRate as float
TestData=fldUserData.text ' retrieve the text from the field
```

```
TaxRate=val(fldTaxRate.text) ' convert text to a numeric value
```

Assigning string data to the Field is performed in a similar manner. You can restrict the text that your user enters to a specific number of characters using MaxChars (text added programmatically doesn't have this limitation, and can be up to 32k in length). Numeric data needs to be converted to a string prior to placing it in a Field (even if the Field is declared "Numeric"):

```
Dim TestData as string
fldUserData.MaxChars=80
'limit user-entered text to 80 characters
fldUserData.text=TestData
fldTaxRate.text=str(TaxRate)
fldSalary.text=format(EmployeeSalary, "$nn,nn0.00")
' use format to convert value to string
```

So, how can you tell if a user entered numeric data, expecially when you want to allow negative numbers, and for that reason can't set the Field's Numeric property to True? Here's where TestNum is the most useful.

TestNum

Sytnax:
   TestNum (StringData, SignOption, NoDigitsBeforeDecPt, NoDigitsAfterDecPt)

Description:
   Tests a string to verify that it meets various criteria

Since NSBasic doesn't have a "mask" option for Fields to restrict or format user input, TestNum allows you to easily test a string *after* it is entered to see if it meets criteria for:

Sign: If the SignOption argument is " " (blank), then the string must not have a leading positive or negative (+ or –) sign. If SignOption is "+" or "-" then your user can enter a leading + or – sign.

Number of digits before the decimal point: This argument determines the maximum number of digits allowed to the left of the decimal point. Use this option sparingly!

Number of digits after the decimal point: Also self-explanatory, this argument restricts the number of digits your user can enter to the right of the decimal point.

TestNum returns a code of 0 if all conditions are met, or a non-zero return value if any of the tests fails (or if the string is non-numeric).

```
Dim result as integer
Dim SkinTemp as string
SkinTemp=fldSkinTemperature.text
'allow a numeric value with 3 digits to the left, and 1_
to the right of the decimal point, and don't allow a sign_
(can't have negative temperature!)
If TestNum(SkinTemp, " " , 3, 1)<>0 then
```

```
    Msgbox "Error in skin temperature - please check value"
    fldSkinTemperature.SetFocus
End if
```

TestNum should be used when you want your users to have the most flexibility in entering numeric data (remember, a Field set to Numeric won't accept a negative sign), while allowing you to validate the Field's contents prior to continuing.

As stated above, placing text in a Field through code rather than by on-screen data entry allows you to ignore the Maximum Chars property – fields can contain up to 32767 characters. The same rules regarding how the Field displays the characters apply as though the user placed the characters there.

The other difference between assigning text to a Field with code and having your user enter the information occurs when the user exits the Field. The field object's code is triggered when the user *exits* the Field (unlike other programming languages that run code when the Field has the focus). Whether a Field obtains its focus when a user taps on the Field, or through code:

```
    fldUserData.SetFocus ' focus set to this field
```

the Field's code will be run as soon as the Field is exited. This will occur when another form object receives the focus, either by user action or through code. In this way a Field's contents can be checked for validity before moving on to another section of your program. However, the Field's code is NOT run if the program is exited by tapping one of the Palm device's buttons or "soft keys" to run another application.

If needed, you can "trap" the screen taps and button presses, make any necessary changes, then continue processing. You can also determine when a Field has been entered by comparing the X and Y coordinates of any stylus tap (penDown event) on your form with the left, top, width, and height of your fields, and run any desired code when the user taps within the boundaries of your Field (see the section on Form Event Code for more details).

You can align ('justify") text at the left side or right side of the Field. Field objects are created initially as left justified, since most of your Field information is likely to be text rather than numeric. However, you may wish to use right-justification for numeric Fields, or for special circumstances when you want text right justified. You'll need to decide this at design time, since justification cannot be changed while your application is running. The Field property "Left Justified" is selected by default; change this if you want to create right justified text.

Tip You may wonder why there's no "Center Justify" option. Since the Palm OS fonts are not fixed-width fonts, attempting to center justify text in a field would involve multiple API calls to determine the width of the text in the current font, the coordinates of the current field, and some "pixel pushing" to center text. It would only work for text that was shorter than the field, and would also involve considerable extra processing. Luckily, a Button object's text is always center justified, so you can use a button (without a frame) to simulate a center justified field. Since button text is not likely to change frequently, there's little performance penalty in using buttons for occasional centered text.

Since Fields are commonly used to enter sentences, and not only words and phrases, the AutoShift property is one you'll find handy. When your user enters text into a Field that has AutoShift checked, the Palm OS determines if a new sentence is starting (such as after a period, question mark, or exclamation point), and capitalizes the first letter of the next sentence. If you have a Shift Indicator (discussed in more detail later) on the form, it will automatically reveal the shift status of the field. You can set the AutoShift property of a Field at design time, but currently you cannot modify this property when the application is running.

The Field object is also a great way to display information to the user that you don't need (or want) to be modified. Leave the Editable property unchecked, and your user can see any alphanumeric information entered into the Field, but will be unable to modify it. However, as the programmer, you can make any changes to the Field information in code, regardless of the status of the Editable property. You can even make the Field visible or invisible, by using the Hide and Show methods:

```
fldUserData.Hide
fldUserData.Show
```

If a Field has been partly or completely erased or covered by a screen object (e.g., bitmap, graphics window) it can be made visible with the Redraw method:

```
fldUserData.Redraw
```

Note that if a Field is hidden (either set as not Visible at design time, or through the use of the Hide method), the Redraw method has no effect.

Like the Bitmap and other objects, a Field's ID can be retrieved using .ID for use with calls to API functions:

```
ObjectID=fldDataEntry.ID
```

Use of this ID number is described in the chapter "Extending NS Basic", and is best left to programmers knowledgeable in the use of the Palm OS API functions.

As you can tell, Fields are versatile, powerful Palm OS objects. To see how each of the Field properties and methods appears in a running application, load and run the "Field Explorer" project on the included CD.

Gadget

The Gadget is a very simple object – it is merely a rectangular area that responds to a stylus tap. By itself the Gadget has nothing to display. No text. No graphics. No checkbox. No...you get the idea. In version 1.12, NS Basic added Signature Capture methods, bringing the Gadget back into respectability.

Note OK, maybe I'm being a little harsh on the poor Gadget. I never got too excited about an invisible control that had less functionality than an empty bitmap, or frame-less, text-less button. But, that's just me. You can form your own opinion.

To use a Gadget, select it from the IDE, and set its size and position in the usual way. Other than the position and size, you have only one property that can be set at design time

– the name. As usual, give your Gadget a name that will make it easy to use and debug. The gadget will be represented by a rectangle in the IDE, but will be invisible on the actual device. If you want to place text or an image on the Gadget you'll need to make note of the position and size of the Gadget, and write your code accordingly. Since the only reason to use a Gadget under text or graphics is to allow user interaction, take care not to go outside the boundaries of your Gadget, or your users will encounter areas that should respond to stylus taps, but don't.

You can determine where your user tapped in the Gadget by using the GetPen command in your Gadget's code:

```
Dim X as integer
Dim Y as Integer
Dim PenStatus as integer
GetPen X, Y, PenStatus
'now x and y contain the horizontal and vertical coordinates
'where the user tapped the stylus
'if you check PenStatus, you'll find that this code is called
'when the stylus leaves the screen (PenUp = 3), not when it
enters.
'It's a minor point, but you might want to know anyway!
```

You can use this location feature to create "clickable maps" where instead of buttons, your user can select any area in an overlying graphic (for example, a street map), and compare the X and Y values to determine the region tapped in. The Gadget doesn't provide any feedback to the user, so make sure your Gadget code is responsive enough to avoid additional user taps. You can take advantage of the Hide and Show methods:

```
gdtMap.Hide
gdtMap.Show
```

You can also use the Redraw method, but the Gadget itself is invisible, so there's nothing to redraw. :

```
gdtMap.Redraw
```

Redraw and Show currently have the same effect – the Gadget will respond to user taps.

Tip The Gadget will still allow signature capture (described below) regardless of the Hide, Show, or Redraw methods.

Like the other objects, a Gadget's ID property can be retrieved using .ID for use with calls to API functions:

```
ObjectID=gadSignatureCapture.ID
```

Use of this ID number is described in the chapter "Extending NS Basic", and is best left to programmers knowledgeable in the use of the Palm OS API functions.

Signature Capture

The most awaited feature in NS Basic for quite some time had been the ability to capture signatures or other user-created graphics. Starting with version 1.12, NS Basic added four methods to the Gadget object to allow simple capture, storage, and display of signatures and graphics (although these methods can be used for signatures or other graphics, NS Basic refers to these methods for signature capture, so I'll stick with their nomenclature).

> Caution The only caveat – and it's extremely important – is that the Gadgets used for capturing and displaying a captured signature MUST be the same size. No bigger, no smaller, but exactly the same size. Neglect to follow this advice, and I can't be held responsible!

Signatures are captured as strings containing a modified Palm OS bitmap, so you'll need to use Dim or Global to declare the string. This string is like any other string, and can be written to or read from databases, saved and stored in arrays, etc.

```
Global CapturedSignature as String ' I use global so all objects
can access the string
```

To prepare for signature capture, create a Gadget in the IDE, positioning and sizing as usual. In your code, use the EraseSignature method to clear the Gadget prior to capturing the signature:

```
gdtSignatureArea.EraseSignature
```

To capture the signature, you need to Start a capture session, then End it to save the signature string:

```
gdtSignatureArea.StartSignatureCapture
'...some other code...
CapturedSignature=gdtSignatureArea.EndSignatureCapture
```

Once captured, the signature string can be copied, saved in an array, written to a database – anything you would normally do with a string. However, since the string contains a compressed bitmap image, you should avoid any manipulation of the string's contents.

To display the signature, simply use the DisplaySignature method, taking care that the signature string exists:

```
If len(CapturedSignature) > 1 then
   gdtSignatureArea.DisplaySignature CapturedSignature
End If
```

You can also set a flag when the signature is captured, and only allow the display of the signature if the flag is set:

```
Dim GotSignature as Integer
Dim CapturedSignature as String
gdtSignatureArea.EraseSignature
```

```
GotSignature=false ' clear the flag to avoid errors
gdtSignatureArea.StartSignatureCapture
'...some other code...
CapturedSignature=gdtSignatureArea.EndSignatureCapture
GotSignature=true ' now it's OK to display
If (GotSignature = true) and len(CapturedSignature) > 1 then
    gdtSignatureArea.DisplaySignature CapturedSignature
End If
```

This avoids the error of attempting to display a signature that hasn't been captured. However, you can still have a fatal error if you use the EndSignatureCapture method before you prepare the Gadget with the StartSignatureCapture method. One more flag, and we're ready:

```
Dim GotSignature as Integer
Dim CaptureStarted as integer
Dim CapturedSignature as String
gdtSignatureArea.EraseSignature
GotSignature=false ' clear the flags to avoid errors
CaptureStarted=false ' ditto...
gdtSignatureArea.StartSignatureCapture
CaptureStarted=true ' set flag to allow EndSignatureCapture
'...some other code...
If CaptureStarted=true then
    CapturedSignature=gdtSignatureArea.EndSignatureCapture
    GotSignature=true ' now it's OK to display
End If
'...some other code...
If (GotSignature = true) and len(CapturedSignature) > 1 then
    gdtSignatureArea.DisplaySignature CapturedSignature
End If
```

You can append a signature on top of an existing signature by using the StartSignatureCapture method even after a signature has been captured. Using the EndSignatureCapture method will then capture the revised signature.

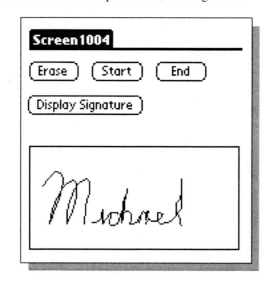

Since the signature capture feature can be used for any graphics, you can easily create a simple doodling program with a Gadget and very little code. Bitmaps, text and other screen graphics can be drawn directly on the Gadget (very easy to do if you first create a graphics window the same size as the gadget, since any graphics drawn in the window will be drawn relative to the window, and will not "spill" over the edge of the window) and saved as part of the "signature string," making for a versatile graphics capture. Also, since you can save the graphics at any time, then continue capturing additional graphics, you can use a string array or database to hold the compressed bitmap string, allow the user to save partial work, and by incrementing or decrementing the array or database record pointer and using the DisplaySignature method, provide multiple levels of Undo/Redo. Add database functions to save and retrieve the array (if you're not already using a database for the captured strings), and you have a full-featured application.

Printing captured graphics strings remains difficult, as there are currently no tools for printing these graphics directly from the Palm screen (although, by the time you read this, there may be). So, printing these graphics involves converting them to standard Windows bitmaps, then printing them from the Windows desktop. The Sig2Bmp program, included in the "Accessory Programs" directory on the CD, is a shareware application that allows you to easily convert saved signature strings into standard bitmaps, which you can manipulate and print from Windows.

Note I take back all the ugly things I said before about the Gadget!

Label

The Label object provides the easiest way to place text on your forms at design time. Not as versatile as Fields, Labels have only a few properties and methods that are necessary to understand, and most of the time you'll only use a subset of them anyway.

Although they are limited, you'll find that Labels have some advantages over Fields. The most important advantage during design time is that the text of the Label is immediately available to set and see (at least when using Fonts 0, 1, 2, 7, and part of Font 6), unlike the Field whose text must be set during run time. Labels are also always left justified, making it easy to use them as row or column headers, titles, etc. (as in the "Memos available" title for the memo list in MegaMemo, one of the projects on the CD):

Labels are placed on your form by selecting them in the IDE, and positioning them as necessary. The initial text is placed using the Label's properties, at which time you can select the Label's FontID, and modify its position as well directly by choosing the Top and Left parameters. You don't have direct control over the size of a Label, however.

Labels are sized according to the length of the text placed in them, and the font used, so you only have *indirect* control over their size.

Note You can look at this a simplifying your programming, or as restricting it. That's almost a theological discussion, and won't make a difference in the final project. I wouldn't lose any sleep over it.

When assigning the initial text to a Label, consider whether or not you will be changing the Label's text while your application is running (for instance if you are using the Label to use as a header for a row of Fields, and you might want to update the Label with the header name):

```
lblRowHeader.text="Patient Height" ' assign text
```

> **Tip** Although the Label's text can be changed at run time, the Label will only accept as many characters as were used in the text placed at design time. Use additional spaces to "pad" your Label's text as needed to accommodate the longest text string that the Label will be expected to contain.

Like most NS Basic objects, Labels have code that is executed when the Label is tapped with the stylus. Since users typically won't be used to tapping on Labels (they're not objects that usually "do" anything), chances are that you won't use the code of a Label often. However, this would be a great place to put code to sort a row of Fields if the Label is the row header, or a "hidden" section of code for games, security, etc.

Except for its text and visibility, none of a Label's properties can be modified at run time. To make a Label visible or invisible, or to redraw it, you will use the Show, Hide or Redraw methods, respectively:

```
lblRowHeader.Show
lblRowHeader.Hide
lblRowHeader.Redraw
```

Note that if a Label is not visible (either by use of the Hide method, or if it was designed as invisible and the Show method was never used), Redraw will have no effect. Similarly, it will not respond to user taps.

> **Tip** This inability to be redrawn or respond to user actions while hidden is a common thread among objects. The code for the object is still accessible, however, and may be called like any other subroutine, regardless of whether the object is visible or not.

Like the Bitmap and other objects, a Label's ID property can be retrieved using .ID for use with calls to API functions:

```
ObjectID=lblTableHeading.ID
```

Use of this ID number is described in the chapter "Extending NS Basic", and is best left to programmers knowledgeable in the use of the Palm OS API functions.

List

The List object (and its cousin, the Popup) display one or more items to the user, usually for the purposes of making a selection. Lists are intuitive – what you see is what you get.

If there are more items in the list than can be displayed at one time (as seen above), the List displays small (*very* small) arrows near the top and bottom that, when tapped, "scroll" the contents of the List to reveal more items (you can also scroll the List using the up and down hard buttons on the Palm device, as long as there is no other object on the form that traps these buttons, like a Field with attached scrollbar). You can highlight any of the visible List items by code, or the user can highlight the item by tapping on it.

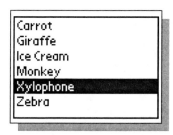

Like most objects, the List has code that is executed after the user taps on the List with the stylus. Although you can highlight a List item in code or by tapping on it, the List code isn't executed when you perform the selection in code – only when the user taps on it. However, since the List code is a subroutine, it can be called like any other subroutine, using the actual subroutine name (the name that shows up when you edit the List code).

You place and resize a List on the form like other objects: by selecting it in the IDE, and moving and sizing the List directly or by modifying its properties. Once placed on the form, the Font to be used for each List item can be selected, as can the List's initial Visible property.

> **Tip** Prior to Palm OS 3.5, Lists could not be consistently hidden, either by setting the initial property to make it invisible, or by using the Hide method (the Hide method was available, but didn't hide the List). As there are currently a large number of Palm devices using Palm OS 3.3 and earlier, keep this in mind when using Lists. If you need to be able to hide a List on systems using Palm OS 3.3, consider using a Popup instead. Oddly enough, although the Popup object can be thought of as a List with a Label and Button, the Hide and Show methods work properly with it in OS 3.3, and not the actual List object. Go figure.

Although Lists are initially created at design time, their contents are initialized and manipulated at run time. Lists must be initialized before you start to add items to them by the use of the Clear method (failing to Clear a List prior to using it is one of the most common errors new NS Basic programmers make with Lists):

```
lstMenuItems.Clear
```

This "empties" the List and prepares it for the addition of List entries, or items. Lists can contain string items only – they're inflexible in this respect. If you need to create a list of dates, times, or numeric values, you need to convert them to their string equivalents prior to placing them in a List. Similarly, you'll need to convert the strings back to numeric, time, or date values if you want to use them in that manner. To add an item to a List, use the Add method, which appends the item to the bottom of the List:

```
lstMenuItem.Add "Beef" ' add a string literal
Dim Dessert as String
Dessert="Ice Cream"
lstMenuItem.Add Dessert ' we can also add a string variable
Dim MenuArray(10) as string
Dim ArrayPointer as Integer
For ArrayPointer = 1 to 10
    lstMenuItem.Add MenuArray(ArrayPointer)
    ' elements in string arrays can be used as well
Next
```

Once you have worked with Lists, you may notice – especially with long Lists – that the List display seems to take a long time. This is no illusion. You can reduce this time delay by the use of the NoDisplay option, which prevents the List from being redrawn each time an item is added:

```
lstMenuItem.Add "Spinach",,NoDisplay
```

Caution Be careful with NoDisplay. You can populate a List entirely with the NoDisplay option, and the List will appear empty. However, the items are still there, and will respond to user taps or the use of the Selected method.

After you've added all the items, use the Redraw method to make the List's contents available (only necessary if you used the NoDisplay option):

```
lstMenuItem.Redraw
```

You will also make the List items visible if *at any time* you use the Add method without the NoDisplay option:

```
ListBox.Clear
ListBox.Add "Monkey",, NoDisplay
ListBox.Add "Giraffe",, NoDisplay
ListBox.Add "Zebra",, NoDisplay
ListBox.Add "Carrot",, NoDisplay
ListBox.Add "Ice Cream",, NoDisplay
ListBox.Add "Xylophone" ' now everything gets displayed
```

You might be wondering why there are two commas following the item being added, and the NoDisplay option. There is a briefly documented method, IndexNo, which can be used with the Add method. The full syntax would then be:

```
ListObject.Add itemstring,[ IndexNo] ,[ NoDisplay]
```

IndexNo is the position in the List that you want the item added. If IndexNo is omitted, each List item is added to the bottom of the List. You can reverse this order using an IndexNo of 1:

```
ListBox.Clear
ListBox.Add "Monkey",1, NoDisplay
ListBox.Add "Giraffe",1, NoDisplay
ListBox.Add "Zebra",1, NoDisplay
ListBox.Add "Carrot",1, NoDisplay
ListBox.Add "Ice Cream",1, NoDisplay
ListBox.Add "Xylophone",1 ' now everything gets displayed
```

As you see, you can have considerable control over the position of items in a List using IndexNo. Just be careful not to use an IndexNo that is greater than the number of items in the List + 1, and you'll be fine.

```
ListBox.Clear ' no items in the list now
ListBox.Add "Monkey",2, NoDisplay  ' this will cause a fatal error
requiring reset
```

If all this sounds confusing (and a pain), especially if you plan on having many items in your Lists, you're right. After all, why can't you just load the Lists (and Popup) at design time, avoiding the wait time altogether? Well, starting with 2.0.3, NS Basic added a List property to List and PopUp objects. From within the IDE, you can populate these objects with their initial items. You can still access these items as though they were placed there at run time, so there's really no penalty for performing the loading at design time.

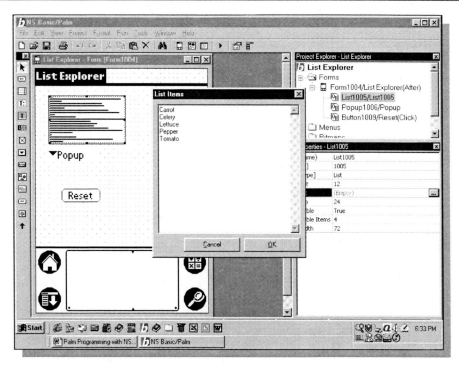

Lists are dynamic – they can shrink and grow as needed. "How can I determine the number of items in the List?" I'm glad you asked (OK, *I* asked, but somebody had to!). It's not always easy or desirable to maintain a variable to keep track of how many items the List contains. It's also not necessary, since you can determine the size of a List with the NoItems method:

```
Dim ListSize as integer
ListSize=1stMenuItem.NoItems
```

Once added, List items are retrieved by their integer position in the List, starting at "1". You can select an item in code, or retrieve a selected item's position using the Selected method:

```
Dim UserSelection as Integer
UserSelection=1stMenuItem.Selected ' retrieve the current_
selection
1stMenuItem.Selected=4
' set the 4th item as the selected one, and highlight it
1stMenuItem.Selected=0
' using 0 deselects the item, so nothing is highlighted
```

You can also remove a List item using its position with the Remove method:

```
1stMenuItem.Remove 3 ' removes the third item
```

Assigning an integer variable to the Selected property of a List is usually performed in the code section of the List item, to determine the user's choice. If the integer position is not important, but the text of the chosen item is, you can retrieve it using the Text method:

```
Dim ChosenItem as String
Dim UserSelection as Integer
UserSelection=lstMenuItem.Selected ' get the position
ChosenItem=lstMenuItem.Text(UserSelection)
' retrieve the text for the selection
```

You can also combine the Selected and Text methods to do this in one step:

```
Dim ChosenItem as String
ChosenItem=lstMenuItem.Text(lstMenuItem.Selected)
' retrieve the text for the selection
```

Unfortunately, you can't use the Text method to set the Text of a Selected item:

```
lstMenuItem.Text(UserSelection)="Strawberry Shortcake"
' this will be flagged as an error
```

You can, however, retrieve the selected item, delete the original from the list, modify the text, then write it back using the ItemNo property. This accomplishes the same feat, although it takes a few steps:

```
Dim ChosenItem as String
Dim UserSelection as integer
'determine user's selection
UserSelection= lstMenuItem.Selected
' retrieve the text for the selection
ChosenItem=lstMenuItem.Text(UserSelection)
'delete the original
lstMenuItem.remove UserSelection
'modify the selection to capitalize it
ChosenItem=Ucase(ChosenItem)
'and write it back to its former position
lstMenuItem.Add ChosenItem,UserSelection
```

Now that you know your way around Lists, you should be able to combine the various methods with a small comparison routine to sort the items in a List. The code that follows is from the List Sorter project, and uses a simple Bubble sort to put the List in ascending order. As we'll cover in the section on sorting algorithms, the Bubble sort is not very efficient, but it's easy to understand and code, so I placed it here for demonstration purposes:

```
Dim TempString1 as String ' need to have strings for swapping
Dim TempString2 as String
Dim ListPointer1 as Integer ' pointers for sorting routine
Dim ListPointer2 as Integer
For ListPointer1 =1 to MyList.NoItems-1
    ' this is a simple bubble sort, comparing each item...
    For ListPointer2 = ListPointer1 +1 to MyList.NoItems
        ' ...to other items in the list
        MyList.selected=ListPointer1 ' select the first item...
```

```
      TempString1=MyList.text(MyList.Selected) ' and store it
      MyList.selected=ListPointer2 ' select the second item...
      TempString2= MyList.text(MyList.Selected) ' store it
      If TempString1 > TempString2 Then
          ' compare the strings (Palm OS compare, not ASCII)
          MyList.remove ListPointer1
          ' remove if it belongs later in the list...
          MyList.Add TempString2,ListPointer1
          ' and insert the earlier one.
          MyList.remove ListPointer2 ' repeat the remove...
          MyList.Add TempString1,ListPointer2
          ' and insert, and we've swapped strings
      End If
  Next
Next
MyList.Selected=0 ' clear the highlight bar after sorting
```

An interesting visual effect occurs when sorting a List "in place" like this. Since you need to use the Selected method to retrieve the text of a List item, and selecting an item highlights it, you can visually see how the list is being sorted by watching which items are being selected and removed/added. Again, this sort is a VERY INEFFICIENT sort, and should be replaced with other sorting methods (such as the Shell-Metzner sort - see the Sorting Comparison project), or the list sorting function in the NSBSystemLib (see the chapter "Extending NS Basic") if used for large Lists.

Lists are great for displaying a field from a database record, allowing you to access the rest of the record by selecting the List item. For instance, you can populate a List with the keys from a keyed database. Selecting a List item retrieves the key, which can then be used to select the corresponding record. The "dbList" project illustrates this use of Lists to hold database keys (actually, the project displays names, and uses a separate array to hold the keys).

This project uses an array to hold the key, then takes the Selected item number as the array index to retrieve the key. Alternatively, if you aren't using keyed databases, you can use the Selected item number as the record number for database access (I think I'm getting a little off the track here – we'll save the rest of the database discussion for the chapter on NS Basic databases).

> **Tip** If you are working with very large Lists, you'll find that populating the List can take a long time, even with the NoDisplay option. List performance also deteriorates with very long Lists, so you may want to use the List to only display a subset of a database or array. If, however, you always have the same information in a given List, you could create the list at design time (as previously mentioned). Why is this important? First, you can avoid the run time expense of loading the List by doing it by hand at design time (well, at least it saves your *user* the time – you still have to suffer a little!). Second, the application will appear faster in general, and more professional. Third, since you can access List items even before the List is displayed means that you can access Lists that don't *ever* get displayed. Think about that for a second, and you'll see that this is a great way to "hide" string resources for later display – you won't need to have a separate database for these strings. I often use this in my programs to hold error messages, conversion text, etc. Here's an example of a function that returns the day of the week from a day number (assumes you have a List named WeekdayList that contains the days of the week in order):

```
Function DayName(DayNumber as integer) as String
DayName=WeekdayList.text(DayNumber)
End Function
```

> Sure, you could do this with a database or array, but the database has to be created (and might be missing), and the array would need to be filled at run time, slowing down your application. But if you use a List instead, the List can be on a form that never gets displayed, or it can be a hidden List on a form in your project. As long as the List exists, you can access its elements.

But, what if the database is large, and you want to be able to modify it, yet still have rapid access to its records in a List? We already discussed that loading a List a run-time with a large number of items is very inefficient, but we can't load the List at design-time either, since the data won't be known at that time. The best approach for List use with large databases is to only use the List to display a subset of the database records at any time, and accomplish scrolling of the list by changing which records are displayed. For example, you can create a list that will hole 10 items, and by using a global variable to hold the record number, you can read and display a record and the next 9 records. Scrolling the List is accomplished by adding or subtracting 10 from the record number (making sure that you don't go below 1 or higher than the number of records in the database), then displaying the subset of records starting at that record number. The "LargeListScroll" project on the CD uses this technique to allow you to rapidly scroll through a 50-item list. Buttons are used to allow the user to go to the top and bottom of the list quickly, and Repeaters (described later) to scroll up or down the list. As an added feature, the up and down buttons on the Palm device are used to access the up/down Repeater code, so the user can scroll without having to tap the screen.

Like the Bitmap and other objects, a List's ID property can be retrieved using .ID for use with calls to API functions:

`ObjectID=lstMenuItems.ID`

Use of this ID number is described in the chapter "Extending NS Basic", and is best left to programmers knowledgeable in the use of the Palm OS API functions.

You've seen how Lists can be a powerful way to use a small area of the Palm screen to display a large amount of information. Spend the necessary time to get comfortable with Lists, and you will be rewarded with applications that are truly useful and user-friendly!

PopUp

Question: What do you get when you cross a Label with a List? No, not a "Labist", but a PopUp. Similar to a "Combo Box" in certain *other* programming languages, PopUps combine the multiple-line, scrollable capabilities of Lists with the small "footprint" of Labels. When you want your users to have a selection of many items, but don't want to consume a large chunk of form "real estate", the PopUp can be your new best friend.

On the IDE and the Palm device, the PopUp resembles a Label with a graphic "down arrow" at its left edge. Here's a PopUp in the IDE, with its default text "PopUp":

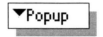

It will look the same on the Palm screen.

> **Note** Before you even ask – no, you don't have control over the graphic element used for the down arrow. What you see is what you get. Although this sounds like a restriction, it helps keep PopUps looking consistent, which results in happy, productive users. Not a bad idea after all!

What you *don't* see is what gives the PopUp its power - a List object. In fact, the PopUp really has two personalities; it acts like a Label until it gets selected, then it acts like a List, then like a Label again. Once you see it in action, you'll understand my affection for this "tiny giant".

By now you're used to creating objects in the IDE, and the PopUp follows the same rules – sort of. You place the PopUp on the form by selecting it from the IDE toolbox, and resizing it as needed. Initially, the PopUp takes up only as much horizontal room as the text you place in it, but once a PopUp is tapped, the PopUp needs enough room to display the largest item in its list, since the selected item replaces the original PopUp's text. Additionally, the PopUp, when selected, displays a bordered, shadowed list of items. So, not only should the PopUp be placed far enough to the left of your form to allow enough room for its longest item (like Lists, PopUp items are always strings), but it should be placed high enough for the number of items that will be displayed when its list "pops" down (unlike a true List object, whose vertical size depends on the number of items visible and the Font used).

> **Tip** If there isn't enough room for the "list" below the PopUp's initial label, the list will be displayed higher than the PopUp's initial position. It works fine either way, but it's more visually appealing to

have the PopUp appear to "pop down" from its original position (and POSE complains with an error message that you're trying to access an area of memory that doesn't belong to your application – see Running POSE for information on how to avoid this error message). Hmm...maybe it should have been called a "PopDown" instead of a PopUp. But, I'm not going to hold my breath waiting for Palm, Inc. to make the change just for me!

From the user's standpoint, the PopUp is intuitive. Not only does it have a label that you can use to place descriptive text, but it also has a "down arrow" at the left of the label as an indicator to your user that there are items to pick from. This screen, from a medical application I wrote using NS Basic, contains four PopUps: one used at the top of the form to allow my user to jump to any other form, and three PopUps used to select items from various visual, verbal, and motor responses for a patient:

When the user taps on the down arrow or text label for a PopUp, its associated list is dropped down; in this case my user is selecting an Eye Opening response:

Note that once a selection is made, the initial PopUp text ("Select" in this case), is replaced by the selection's text:

You can change the text of a PopUp without actually selecting one of its items. You might want to do this to re-label the PopUp's text after your user makes a selection, since otherwise the PopUp uses the text of the user's selection as its new title. Use the Text method to directly change the PopUp's label:

```
MyPopUp.Text="Pick a menu item"
```

Note Although you can change a PopUp's label, you can't do this from within the PopUp's own code. Well, you *can*, but when the PopUp code ends, the PopUp label is changed to the user's selection, even if you told it otherwise. However, you can use this code elsewhere to change the PopUp's label text.

You can see that a great deal of information can be made available in a small space. To make this information available to your user, load the PopUp as you would a List, using the Add method. From the medical application above, the following code initializes three PopUps for Eye Opening, Verbal Response, and Motor Response:

```
popEyeOpening.Clear
popEyeOpening.Add "Spontaneous: 4"
popEyeOpening.Add "To speech: 3"
popEyeOpening.Add "To pain: 2"
popEyeOpening.Add "None: 1"

popVerbalResponse.Clear
popVerbalResponse.Add "Oriented: 5"
popVerbalResponse.Add "Confused: 4"
popVerbalResponse.Add "Inappropriate words: 3"
popVerbalResponse.Add "Nonspecific sounds: 2"
popVerbalResponse.Add "None: 1"

popMotorResponse.Clear
popMotorResponse.Add "Follows commands: 6"
popMotorResponse.Add "Localizes pain: 5"
popMotorResponse.Add "Withdraws to pain: 4"
popMotorResponse.Add "Abnormal flexion: 3"
```

```
popMotorResponse.Add "Abnormal extension: 2"
popMotorResponse.Add "None: 1"
```

You'll be pleased to know that once PopUps and Lists are loaded, their contents remain even if the forms that "own" them are removed or reloaded using NextForm. This avoids the need to load PopUps and Lists each time. You can even load PopUps and Lists before their forms are even loaded. I know what you're thinking – you think it might be best to load all the PopUps/Lists in your project's StartUp code. However, if your application has many PopUp/List items, loading them in the StartUp before any forms are visible can create an unacceptable delay.

Tip You may have to do a bit of experimenting to determine the best place for the code that you use to load your PopUps. For Popups whose items are unchanging (and known at design time), consider creating them at design time (described a little later in this chapter) for the fastest performance. Lengthy item lists can take *forever* to load - or so it will seem to your users! If your PopUps are going to take so long to load that users might fear that your application is "stuck", display some sort of progress indicator, or consider modifying your code to use fewer PopUp items. Ditto for Lists. Remember the Seven Second Rule!

Like the List object, you must initialize your PopUps by using the Clear method prior to loading it with text strings (unless you want blank lines or stray characters in the first one or more PopUp strings!). Also as with the List, you can use the NoDisplay and IndexNo parameters:

```
popMotorResponse.Clear
popMotorResponse.Add "Follows commands: 6",1,NoDisplay
popMotorResponse.Add "Localizes pain: 5",1,NoDisplay
popMotorResponse.Add "Withdraws to pain: 4",1,NoDisplay
popMotorResponse.Add "Abnormal flexion: 3",1,NoDisplay
popMotorResponse.Add "Abnormal extension: 2",1,NoDisplay
popMotorResponse.Add "None: 1",1,NoDisplay
```

By using an IndexNo of 1, the PopUp will be loaded in reverse order (actually, each item will be placed at position 1, pushing the other items below it). Use the IndexNo with care, since using an IndexNo that is greater than the (number of PopUp list items +1) will cause your application to crash. Use the NoItems method to determine the number of items in the PopUp's list:

```
Dim ListSize as integer
ListSize=MyPopUp.NoItems
```

The NoDisplay parameter doesn't actually seem to *do* anything with PopUps (the PopUp items aren't displayed during the loading of the PopUp, with or without the NoDisplay parameter), but is supported by the Palm OS, so it is included with NS Basic.

Note You'll find this level of Palm OS support in other circumstances as well, such as the AnchorLeft property for objects like Buttons and Pushbuttons that are center justified, where AnchorLeft has no effect. However, by supporting these properties and Methods

according to Palm OS specifications, NS Basic is more likely to stay
upwardly compatible with future Palm OS versions.

If all this sounds confusing (and a pain), especially if you plan on having many items
in your PopUps, you're right. After all, why can't you just load the PopUps (and Lists) at
design time, avoiding the wait time altogether? Well, starting with 2.0.3, NS Basic added
a List property to PopUp and List objects. From within the IDE, you can populate the
PopUp and List objects with their initial items. You can still access these items as though
they were placed there at run time, so there's really no penalty for performing the loading
at design time.

PopUps have a wide selection of properties and methods. You've already seen a
few, so let's discuss the rest. I've mentioned that PopUps act somewhat like Labels, and
in this respect they share the ability to select the initial FontID and also the initial text in
the IDE. Additionally, you can apply the AnchorLeft property (it's set to "True" by
default), or change it to False, which means that the PopUp will be "Anchored Right" (its
right edge will stay fixed, and the left edge will move based on the length of the text
displayed). Most of the time you'll want to keep AnchorLeft by default, as it's visually
more pleasing.

You also have control over the number of PopUp items visible when the PopUp
displays its list of items. If there are fewer items than this number ("Visible Items", in
the Properties window of the IDE), blank space will show at the bottom of the list. If
there are *more* items than the Visible Items parameter, small arrows will appear at the
right edge of the list to allow your user to scroll the list. Your user can scroll this list
using these scroll arrows, or the Up and Down hard buttons, as long as no other form
code has trapped these buttons.

When the user selects an item from the drop-down list, you can retrieve the
information by using the Selected and ItemText methods (not the Text method as used
with the List object, as the Text method changes the PopUp's label):

```
Dim SelectedText as string
Dim SelectedItem as integer
SelectedItem=MyPopUp.Selected
SelectedText=MyPopUp.ItemText(Selected)
```

Like the List, you can combine these two methods for the PopUp:

```
Dim SelectedText as string
SelectedText=MyPopUp.ItemText(MyPopUp.Selected)
```

After the user makes a selection, the text of the PopUp gets replaced with the user's
selected text. Keep this in mind when you design the PopUp, leaving enough room for
the longest string that will be displayed.

There may be times that you want to change the text of the PopUp back to what it
was before your user made a selection. To do this, use the Text method as previously
mentioned:

```
MyPopUp.Text="Select a menu item"
```

Note Although this code sets the text of the Popup back to its original text, it won't work within the Popup's own code; it will have to be run at some other time. I'll get a little ahead of myself here and give you a way to solve this problem. What if we could put a button on the screen that contained code to change the PopUp's text back to what it originally was, and we wanted to programmatically "press" this button, yet hide it from our user? NS Basic doesn't contain the necessary native code to do this, but by using the NSBSystemLib shared library (available with the full, registered NS Basic package), we can issue a NSL.ControlHitControl statement (with the id of our hidden button) in the PopUp's code. The ControlHitControl statement places an event in the event queue that tells the OS that the button was pressed, and the button's code gets executed just as though the button had actually been pressed. Look at the Popup Text Changer project for an example of this sneaky (but safe and effective) technique.

You can also select an item through code, rather than having the user select it:

```
MyPopUp.Selected=5 ' fifth item in the PopUp list
```

Caution Just like we discussed regarding Lists, selecting a PopUp item through code won't run the PopUp's code. You will, however, cause the PopUp's label to change to the selected item's text, giving the *impression* that the PopUp has been selected. Actually, it's not a false impression – the PopUp item is really being selected. It's just that the PopUp's code isn't run. Confusing, I know. Probably the only time you'll use this technique for selecting a PopUp item is when you want to sort a PopUp's items (described later in this section).

In addition to selecting a PopUp item in code, you may at some point want to *remove* one or more PopUp items, and you'll need the Remove method for this:

```
MyPopUp.Remove 2 ' remove the second list item from the PopUp
```

You can combine the Remove method and the Add method with IndexNo to programmatically "change" a PopUp item:

```
MyPopUp.Remove 2
MyPopUp.Add "NewItem",2
```

Add some additional code to compare and swap two PopUp items, and you can easily sort a PopUp's items:

```
Dim TempString1 as String ' need to have strings for swapping
Dim TempString2 as String
Dim OrigPopUpLabel as string
Dim PopUpPointer1 as Integer ' pointers for sorting routine
Dim PopUpPointer2 as Integer
OrigPopUpLabel=MyPopUp.text ' save the original label
For PopUpPointer1 =1 to MyPopUp.NoItems-1
    ' this is a simple bubble sort, comparing each item...
    For PopUpPointer2 = PopUpPointer1 +1 to MyPopUp.NoItems
```

```
            ' ...to other items
        MyPopUp.selected=PopUpPointer1 ' select the first item...
        TempString1=MyPopUp.itemtext(MyPopUp.Selected)
          ' ...and store it
        MyPopUp.selected=PopUpPointer2 ' select the second item...
        TempString2= MyPopUp.itemtext(MyPopUp.Selected)
          ' ...and store it too.
        If TempString1 > TempString2 Then
            ' compare the strings (Palm OS compare, not ASCII)
            MyPopUp.remove PopUpPointer1
            ' remove if it belongs later in the popup...
            MyPopUp.Add TempString2, PopUpPointer1
            ' and insert the earlier one.
            MyPopUp.remove PopUpPointer2 ' repeat the remove...
            MyPopUp.Add TempString1, PopUpPointer2
            ' ...and insert, and we've swapped strings
        End If
     Next
Next
MyPopUp.text= OrigPopUpLabel  ' relabel after the sorting
```

As with Lists, the Bubble sort is VERY INEFFICIENT, and should be replaced with other sorting methods (such as the Shell-Metzner sort) if used for large PopUps.

> **Note** You may have noticed that this code looks an awful lot like the List sorting routine. Compare the two routines and you'll understand some of the subtle differences between PopUps and Lists.

Like the Bitmap and other objects, a Popup's ID property is retrieved using .ID for use with calls to API functions:

```
ObjectID=popMenuItems.ID
```

Use of this ID number is described in the chapter "Extending NS Basic", and is best left to programmers knowledgeable in the use of the Palm OS API functions.

PushButton

As previously mentioned in the section on CheckBoxes, you will often be faced with the need to offer your user with a choice of two or more options. Our previous example, using the CheckBox objects, looked like this:

The same functionality can be obtained using PushButton objects:

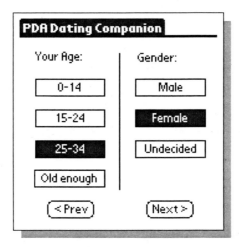

By using the PushButton you can also allow your user to use a single click to enter either discreet data or a range of data (such as age, above). By checking the status of the PushButton, you can avoid more time-consuming range checking. Compare this code, using the PushButton status:

```
If pbAge0to14.status=nsbChecked then
    'code if 0-14
ElseIf pbAge15to24.status=nsbChecked then
    'code if 15-24
ElseIf pbAge25to34.status=nsbChecked then
    'code if 25-34
Else
    'code if 35 or older
End If
```

with this code using the actual user age:

```
UserAge=val(fldAge.text) ' get age from user entry in field
If UserAge < 15 then
```

```
    'code if 0-14
ElseIf UserAge < 25 then
    'code if 15-24
ElseIf UserAge < 35 then
    'code if 25-34
Else
    'code if 35 or older
EndIf
```

The PushButton avoids having to use the conversion from text to numeric age, and is slightly faster in the comparisons (in general, equality comparisons are more efficient than comparisons using "less than" or "greater than" – but this is dependent on the compiler/interpreter used). However, the speed advantage comes at the expense of screen space – the multiple PushButtons take up far more space than a single field for user entry of age. You'll need to decide which technique suits your individual applications best.

To use PushButtons, you place them on your project's form by selecting them in the IDE, and clicking the form at the locations you wish to place the PushButtons. Like CheckBoxes, PushButtons have a default status of not selected, and labels that aren't too useful (the default label for the PushButton is "PushButton"). However, using the properties you can set their initial text, AnchorLeft status (although PushButton labels are center justified, so there won't be any visible effect), selected status (True or False, the equivalent of nsbChecked or nsbUnchecked), size, and location.

You can also set the Group ID, which is where you determine which of a number of PushButtons are grouped together in a mutually exclusive arrangement (that is, if only one value can exist at a time, only allow one choice – this eliminates the need for you *or your user* to assure that only one selection has been made). You'll notice that the default Group ID for PushButtons in the IDE is "0". This might give the false impression that all PushButtons with Group ID of "0" are mutually exclusive, but in reality a Group ID of "0" allows the PushButtons to act independently of other PushButtons and CheckBoxes on the same form. In other words, NS Basic and Palm don't assume that you want the PushButtons or CheckBoxes assigned in any specific manner, so you're given a way to allow them to act independently by default, but can easily group them together later if desired.

> **Tip** CheckBoxes act in the same manner, and can be interchanged with PushButtons for a different "look and feel" based on how you want to present feedback to your user. In fact, both PushButtons and CheckBoxes can share common Group ID's, making for some visually interesting forms! Keep your design simple, though, since a confused user isn't likely to be a happy (or productive) user.

As seen above, you can have multiple groups of PushButtons, each acting as separately mutually exclusive groups (age and gender). Just make sure that each set of PushButtons has its own non-zero Group ID. Also, make sure that each set of PushButtons has at most one PushButton marked as Selected (doing otherwise will only confuse you and your users!). You can do this at design time, or through code at run time:

```
pbAge0to14.status=nsbChecked
pbAge15to24.status=nsbUnchecked
pbAge25to34.status=nsbUnchecked
```

```
pbAgeOver34.status=nsbUnchecked
pbGenderMale.status=nsbUnchecked
pbGenderFemale.status=nsbChecked
pbGenderUnknown.status=nsbUnchecked
```

In addition to the Selected property, you can also set or retrieve a PushButton's Label property at run time:

```
pbGenderMale.label="Guy"
pbGenderFemale.label="Gal"
pbGenderUnknown.label="What? "
```

As with the CheckBoxes, you'll probably never need to use the Label or AnchorLeft properties of PushButtons, but it's nice to know about them ahead of time.

In case you're wondering, yes – you can change the font used to display the PushButton's label. Just select the FontID in the IDE that corresponds to the font you wish to use. This is a design time decision, however – you can't change the font at run time (without using the API calls, that is – but that's in the chapter on "Extending NS Basic"). Make sure you leave enough room for the largest text that you're going to place in the PushButton (especially if you plan on changing it at run time).

You might be surprised to find out that the PushButton has code associated with it. Since you will probably be checking the status of PushButtons in *other* code, it seems almost redundant to have code associated with the PushButtons themselves. However, judicious use of a PushButton's code can avoid the need for the If...Then...ElseIf...EndIf statements as shown above. Let's take the example above, with the Age and Gender choices. Since there was specific code to run based on the status of these PushButtons, why not just run the code when the PushButtons are selected or deselected, rather than wait until later? This is particularly useful if a global variable is set based on the value of mutually exclusive PushButtons.

Like most other NS Basic objects, PushButtons can be created in the IDE as visible or invisible (i.e., their Visible property is set as True or False). Similarly, the Redraw, Hide and Show methods can be used to, well, redraw, hide and show them:

```
pbGenderMale.Redraw
' in case part of the pushbutton was accidentally erased
pbGenderMale.Hide ' in case you only want non-males selected
pbGenderMale.Show ' OK, you changed your mind!
```

Keep in mind that the PushButton is inaccessible by the user when hidden, although you can still access its properties and methods in code (like other NS Basic objects).

The PushButton's ID can be retrieved at runtime as other objects:

```
ObjectID=pbGenderMale.ID
```

This ID can be used to identify the PushButton for API and shared library functions.

Repeater

By now you've seen that most of the objects perform a single action when tapped, whether it be to run some code, place the cursor into the field for user data entry, or accept a signature or other graphic being drawn. There are many times, however, that it would be useful for the user to be able to have the object continue to perform some function as long as the stylus is pressed to the screen surface, and stop when the stylus is released. It would be quite a bit of coding to call the necessary API routines for this, so thankfully there's a simpler solution – the Repeater Object.

If you think of a Repeater as a Button that keeps firing its code until the stylus is removed, you'll be right on track. In fact, I could simply refer you to the code for the Button object, rather than write anything further in this section. But, you paid good money for this book (or, at least SOMEONE did), so by George you're going to get the text here, with some examples that really wouldn't make as much sense in the section on the Button object.

To start off with, you'll place the Repeater on your NS Basic project's form the same way as any other object – select it in the IDE, and click on the form where you want to place it, and resize as needed.

Once the Repeater is in place, as with its "cousin" the Button, you can modify its Name, FontID, initial text Label, Height, Width, Left, Top, Frame properties (frame or no frame, bold or non-bold frame), and whether or not the Repeater is initially Visible when the form is drawn. All of these properties are set at design time, and cannot be modified at run time (except for the Visible property, discussed later). Also, as with Buttons, the AnchorLeft property can be set to True or False, but since the Repeater's Label text is center justified, the AnchorLeft property has no effect (but was included by NS Basic because it's supported by the Palm OS).

On the Palm device, your Repeater will look just like a Button, so how is your user going to know that it's a Repeater? I guess you could always put "I repeat if the stylus is held down" as text in the Repeater's Label, but that wouldn't be too useful:

As it turns out, if you are using the Repeater for a function the user is likely to want to repeat, the repeating function will usually be intuitive. For example, if you place repeaters to the left and right of the name of the month on a calendar, the user should be able to figure out that holding the stylus down will continue to advance the month in the desired direction, one month at a time, until the stylus is released. Similarly, in my EtchSketch project, repeaters are used in the lower right corner of the form to allow my user to continue drawing a straight line in the direction of the repeater (having arrows on the repeater helps as well). I even added frameless, blank-text repeaters for the corner directions, and users instinctively know that they're there.

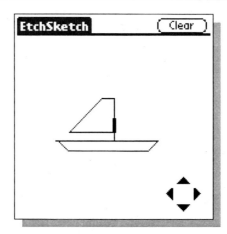

Repeaters have the same methods as Buttons, so at run time you can modify the text in the Repeater's Label (being careful not to place too much text, as strings that are too long will be truncated at both ends), Hide or Show the Repeater, and Redraw it if needed (e.g., if a graphic window was removed, and erased part of the Repeater in the process):

```
rptPixelDraw.Show ' now you see me...
rptPixelDraw.Hide ' now you don't...
rptScoreKeeper.text="Increment score"
rptPixelDraw.Redraw ' redraws the Repeater
```

Remember that Redraw will only redraw the object if it hasn't been hidden by the use of the Hide method (or creating it with a Visible property of "false" at design time, and forgetting to use the Show method to make it visible). Additionally, like other objects, the Repeater will be "immune" to stylus taps when hidden.

If you are writing games for the Palm devices, you will find many uses for the Repeater, including firing weapons, controlling thrusters, moving game objects, etc. Unfortunately, there aren't any methods or properties that allow you to control the delay or repeat speed of the Repeater object from within NS Basic, but in most cases your users won't object, as they are probably already used to the characteristics of Repeaters from other Palm Apps.

Like the Bitmap and other objects, a Repeater's ID property is retrieved using .ID for use with calls to API functions:

```
ObjectID=rptRocketThruster.ID
```

Use of this ID number is described in the chapter "Extending NS Basic", and is best left to programmers knowledgeable in the use of the Palm OS API functions.

For a little programming exercise, think of how you would create a drawing program in NS Basic using Repeater objects to perform the pixel and line drawing. Then, take a look at the EtchSketch project for my first attempt. You'll no doubt figure out different ways to achieve the same task, but it's almost always helpful to see how other programmers attack a programming problem.

ScrollBar

Since the Palm devices don't currently have physical keyboards attached (and even the best keyboards available still add considerable bulk, making the device less "portable"), alternative methods of entering data and navigating applications are welcome to most Palm users. The on-screen keyboard is a great compromise, but there are times when you don't need to enter actual data, but instead give your users a way to increment or decrement a value, or move up and down through a long section of text.

The Scrollbar Object is a versatile, graphical tool for these tasks, and when used appropriately can save you precious screen "real estate" for use by other objects. The Scrollbar only has a few properties and methods, so you'll find it fairly intuitive.

I'm getting tired of writing it, and you're getting just as tired of reading it, but you place a Scrollbar object on your project's current form as you do any other object: click it in the IDE to select it, click the place on the form to place it, and resize it as needed.

> **Tip** The IDE creates the Scrollbar as a vertical Scrollbar by default. However, if you make the width greater than the height, your scrollbar will be created in horizontal orientation. Some early versions of the Palm OS don't draw or erase the end arrows correctly, so be sure to test your applications on the target devices.

In the IDE the Scrollbar doesn't look like much of a Scrollbar at all – more like a two-headed arrow! The same would be true at run time, if you kept the default Scrollbar values, because the default values for the Scrollbar aren't very useful. At either design time or run time you can specify the minimum and maximum values for the Scrollbar, the PageSize (how far the Scrollbar indicator will move when the Scrollbar is tapped near either end), and the default value for the Scrollbar. When set up with more useful values, the Scrollbar is displayed at run time divided into two arrows (one for each end) and a gray bar along which a black slider moves (the Scrollbar doesn't get this "face lift" in the IDE, but it's not a major problem). Here's a screen shot from my Scrollbar Explorer project:

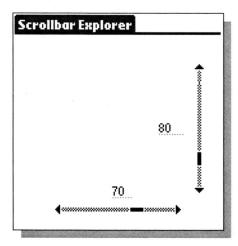

The way the Scrollbar works is like this: you select the minimum and maximum values you want for the Scrollbar, and the Palm OS divides the bar into values corresponding to these limits. Tapping the arrow at the top of a vertical Scrollbar (or left of a horizontal Scrollbar) decreases the Scrollbar value towards the low limit, while tapping the arrow at the bottom of the Scrollbar (right for horizontal Scrollbars) increases its value towards the upper limit. Tapping the Scrollbar itself in the gray areas (not the black slider) will also decrease or increase the current value of the Scrollbar, and move the slider accordingly. If the PageSize is 1, the Scrollbar value will change by 1. If it's 2, then the value changes by 2 (although it may first step to the next even value, rather than increment by 2 initially, depending on your Palm OS version). If you tap on the slider and drag it with the stylus pressed, you will change the value by 1 in the direction that you move the slider.

At design time, you have control over the following properties: Name (make it something useful, please!), Height, Width, Left, Top, Min value, Max value, Page Size, and value (the default value for the Scrollbar.

The best way to use the Scrollbar, in my humble (OK, maybe not so humble) opinion, is to decide ahead of time what you expect your minimum and maximum values to be, and set the PageSize to roughly one-tenth to one-fourth the interval:

```
Dim CurrentScrollValue as Integer
scrRecordNumber.Min=0
scrRecordNumber.Max=100
scrRecordNumber.PageSize=10
```

The value for the Scrollbar is returned and set by the "Current" method:

```
CurrentScrollValue=scrRecordNumber.Current
scrRecord.Current=CurrentScrollValue
```

You can't read them, but you can set any of the Min, Max, or PageSize values in code:

```
scrRecordNumber.Min=10
scrRecordNumber.Max=100
scrRecordNumber.PageSize=10
scrRecordNumber.Current=8
```

Like most objects, you can also change the visibility of the Scrollbar, and redraw it if needed:

```
scrRecordNumber.Hide
scrRecordNumber.Show
scrRecordNumber.Redraw
```

Unlike the Field, List, and Popup, the Scrollbar object isn't automatically "linked" to the action of the up/down buttons. In order to use the hard buttons on the Palm to control the Scrollbar, you'll have to "trap" them in the Events code, and modify the Current value of the Scrollbar based on the button pressed. This following code, from the Scrollbar Explorer project, is used in the Events section to control the vertical and horizontal Scrollbars through the use of the up, down, Address, and ToDo buttons:

```
Dim KeyPress as Integer
If GetEventType()=nsbKeyOrButton Then
    KeyPress=asc(GetKey())
```

```
   Select Case KeyPress
   Case 11 ' up arrow
       scrVert.current=scrVert.current + 1
       If scrVert.current > Ymax Then scrVert.current=Ymax
       Call object1006()
   Case 12 ' down arrow
       scrVert.current=scrVert.current - 1
       If scrVert.current < Ymin Then scrVert.current=Ymin
       Call object1006()
   Case 2 ' button 2 (address book)
       scrHoriz.current=scrHoriz.current - 1
       If scrHoriz.current < Xmin Then scrHoriz.current=Xmin
       Call object1004()
       SetEventHandled
   Case 3 ' button 3 (to do list)
       scrHoriz.current=scrHoriz.current + 1
       If scrHoriz.current > Xmax Then scrHoriz.current=Xmax
       Call object1004()
       SetEventHandled
   Case 1 ' button 1 (calendar)
       SetEventHandled
   Case 4 ' button 4 (memopad)
       SetEventHandled
   End Select
End If
```

This code increments or decrements the values of the different scrollbars based on the key pressed, and compares these values with global variables that contain the minimum and maximum values for the Scrollbars (to prevent falling out of the boundaries of the Scrollbars). To see these horizontal and vertical Scrollbars in action, load and run the Scrollbar Explorer project.

Like the Bitmap and other objects, a ScrollBar's ID property is retrieved using .ID for use with calls to API functions:

```
ObjectID=scrVolumeControl.ID
```

Use of this ID number is described in the chapter "Extending NS Basic", and is best left to programmers knowledgeable in the use of the Palm OS API functions.

Selector

The Selector object seems a bit odd, but only because it should be. That is, there's really nothing special about the Selector, but because it is typically used for specific functions (modifying the date and time, setting passwords, etc. – look at the Palm built-in Prefs app, Set Date and SetTime), that's what your users will expect.

Tip Not that you *have* to use the Selector in this way, but why complicate things? One of the most powerful aspects of Palm programming is that the user interface is so simple that users know instinctively how to use most applications, even without any written documentation. Sure, you could include the documentation in your app, but with a 160x160 pixel screen, why put your user through the torture of reading it? Keep things simple and *standard*, and you'll make your life – and the life of your users – much less complicated.

What is it about the Selector that sets it apart from the other controls? The most obvious characteristic that stands out is the Selector's border – it's the only control that has a dotted border by default, giving its contents a sort of "temporary" feel. Users come to expect that they can change the contents of a Selector just by tapping on it. They don't expect a new program to launch, databases to open, birds to sing...you get the idea.

Using a Selector in your applications starts like any other object – by selecting it in the IDE, placing it on a form, resizing it as needed. Once you have the Selector in the IDE, you have the ability to set the same properties at design time as you do for Buttons: Left, Top, Width, Height, Label, FontID, AnchorLeft, and whether or not it's initially visible. However, the Selector differs from Buttons in a couple of interesting ways that you need to be aware of.

First, the AnchorLeft property actually does something – it controls which end of the Selector remains fixed in place on the form when the Selector's Label (text) changes. With AnchorLeft set as True, the left side of the Selector remains in place, and the right side moves based on the width of the text in the Selector. The reverse is true if AnchorLeft is set to False.

Second, the Selector is resized to the width of its text (Buttons can be much larger or smaller than their text), up to the limits of the screen, rather than truncating the text if it's too long, or right/left padding the text with "white space" if the new text is shorter than what was previously in the Selector.

Third, you can't remove the border of a Selector as you can a Button, nor can you make it thick or thin. The Selector border comes in one "flavor" only – dotted. You'll get used to it.

Since the most common use of a Selector is to allow the selection (gee, how clever) of time or date, here's some code to demonstrate setting a date (place this in the code section of your Selector):

```
Dim theDate as date
Dim Result as integer
```

```
TheDate=Today()
Result=PopupDate(theDate, "Select Date")
if Result = 1 then
    selDate.text=DateMMDDYY(theDate)
End If
```

The PopupDate function is described elsewhere in this book, but here's the abbreviated version: given a valid date (theDate, in this example), PopupDate presents the standard Palm OS Calendar to your user, and allows the selection of a date. If the date selected is different than the initial date, the Result variable will be "1". Note that this doesn't automatically set the text of the Selector to the new date – you'll have to do that yourself. If the user doesn't select a new date, the Result variable will be "0", and your code can process it accordingly.

Caution Make sure you have a valid date prior to calling PopupDate. Failing to do so can produce some unusual results. The same warning concerns the PopupTime statement as well. Don't say I didn't warn you!

As with other objects, the Selector can be made visible or invisible by using Hide or Show:

```
selDate.Hide
selDate.Show
```

You can also redraw the Selector if part or all of it was inadvertently erased during other screen operations:

```
selDate.Redraw
```

You have full control over the text shown in the Selector, and can read or write this at runtime using the Text method:

```
selDate.text= DateMMDDYY(theDate)
selDate.text="invalid date selected"
Dim DateDisplay as String
```

```
DateDisplay=selDate.text
```

Like the Bitmap and other objects, a Selector's ID property is retrieved using .ID for use with calls to API functions:

```
ObjectID=selStartingDate.ID
```

Use of this ID number is described in the chapter "Extending NS Basic", and is best left to programmers knowledgeable in the use of the Palm OS API functions.

Try not to get too fancy with the Selector. Although it can be used like a Button, you'll only confuse your users if your Selector doesn't do what it's expected to do. Not only will this make your users wonder about the Selector, but they'll start to mistrust your Buttons, Gadgets, Fields, and pretty much every other object as well. *And confused users don't come back.*

Shift Indicator

The Shift Indicator is an unusual object in that the user doesn't interact with it at all. It's really just a "one-way discussion" about the Shift status of the current Field object. As mentioned in the section on Field objects, the Shift Indicator is a small arrow, usually placed on the form at the lower right corner (it can be placed anywhere, but your users will expect it in its usual position and its usual size, so try not to get too creative here).

The Shift Indicator is placed on the form like any other object in the IDE, and positioned by direct manipulation on the IDE screen, or by accessing the Left and Top properties. Note that you have no other properties or methods available with the Shift Indicator – it merely reflects the shift state of the current field on the same form.

So, to use the Shift Indicator after you place it on your form, you'll need to set the "AutoShift" property for at least one of the Fields on the form containing the Shift Indicator. If you have multiple forms on which you wish to use the Shift Indicator, each form must have its own Shift Indicator.

Fields that have AutoShift set to "True" will automatically capitalize the first letter following "terminal" punctuation (period, question mark, exclamation point). If there is a Shift Indicator on the form containing this Field, the Shift Indicator will show a solid arrow at the beginning of a new sentence (Shift Indicator at bottom right):

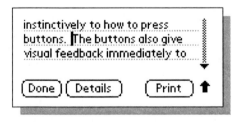

and an arrow with a broken bottom if the shift status is set for all capital letters (as though a "Caps Lock" key were pressed, or you enter two "upward" Graffiti strokes consecutively in the Field"):

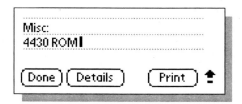

The Shift Indicator isn't necessary (AutoShift will work for any Field regardless of whether a Shift Indicator is available or not), but it's hard to justify not using it. As a simple visual reminder of the shift status of a Field, the Shift Indicator says a mouthful while only taking up a small amount of a form's "real estate." Leave it out, and your users have to guess what the shift state is for any given Field, aND THAT CAN BE AGGRAVATING!

Table

As previously mentioned, NS Basic doesn't currently support the Palm OS Table object. I'll give you a way to work around the lack of a true Table object, and you can decide if it fits your needs.

Emulating a Table object involves emulating both the function and the appearance of a Table. You might expect otherwise, but it turns out that it's easier to get the function working well than it is to produce a realistic looking table. So, we'll start with the function, then present the visual component later.

If you think of tables as rows and columns (a spreadsheet analogy comes to mind), it's easy to make the transition to a two-dimension array, where the first subscript refers to rows, and the second columns:

```
Dim TableArray(20,50) ' create 20 x 50 table array
```

The rest should be simple – create 20 rows of 50 columns of fields, where each field corresponds to a single array element. There's just a little problem – the screen! A 20x50 array (1000 array elements) on a 160x160 pixel screen (25,600 pixels) results in an average of 25.6 pixels per element. If you make each table cell 5 pixels wide and 5 pixels high, the entire array will fit. You won't be able to display anything *useful*, but it will fit.

So, what we need to do is decide how much information we want to display – that will determine how many rows and columns we will display at one time. Since we may want to allow our user to enter information directly into our table, we'll use fields for each table cell. We'll also want row and column identifiers, so we'll use labels (with AutoShift, Dynamic Size, Editable, Single Line, Left Justified true. Better still, let's use buttons (they're center justified, and they give visual feedback if our users tap them). My Table Demo project uses 6 rows and 4 columns, with an additional row of buttons for column headers, and a column of buttons for row headers. That's already 34 objects on the screen, and we still need to add some navigation controls, so we'll also add buttons to scroll in each of the four directions (up, down, left, and right). I like my users to know what's happening, so I'll add a status field.

You can create this project and screen for yourself, but make things easy for yourself, and load the Table Demo project. If you do, you'll notice that I use a 26x26 element array, but you can use whatever size you wish. I chose 26 elements to make labeling easy (26 letters in the English alphabet). I also use separate arrays for the row and column headers, each array also containing 26 elements.

Regardless of the size of the arrays, the concept is the same. The screen fields represent a subset of the actual array. When displaying the array, all that's needed is to maintain control of where we are in the array, and display the 6 rows and 4 columns at that array position. We don't need to keep track of each element, only the top left cell's row and column numbers. Each additional row and column is offset from the top left according to its position on the screen. Row and column headers get displayed according to the same numbers. Here's part of my subroutine to display the screen fields from any initial top left (row, column) pairing:

```
Sub DisplayTableInfo()
fldA1.text=TableDataArray(CurrentRow, CurrentCol)
fldA2.text=TableDataArray(CurrentRow+1, CurrentCol)
fldA3.text=TableDataArray(CurrentRow+2, CurrentCol)
fldA4.text=TableDataArray(CurrentRow+3, CurrentCol)
fldA5.text=TableDataArray(CurrentRow+4, CurrentCol)
fldA6.text=TableDataArray(CurrentRow+5, CurrentCol)
fldB1.text=TableDataArray(CurrentRow, CurrentCol+1)
fldB2.text=TableDataArray(CurrentRow+1, CurrentCol+1)
fldB3.text=TableDataArray(CurrentRow+2, CurrentCol+1)
fldB4.text=TableDataArray(CurrentRow+3, CurrentCol+1)
fldB5.text=TableDataArray(CurrentRow+4, CurrentCol+1)
fldB6.text=TableDataArray(CurrentRow+5, CurrentCol+1)
'... and so on...
End Sub
```

Scrolling the table involves incrementing or decrementing the current top and left (row and column) values, then calling the display routine. Updating the table array with each field's contents is performed when the user leaves the field. The following line, from the code for the fldB3 (3rd row, 2nd column) is:

```
TableDataArray(CurrentRow+2, CurrentCol+1)=fldB3.text
```

Clearing the table array is performed easily, looping through the rows and columns:

```
Sub ClearTable()
For CurrentRow=1 to MaxRow
    For CurrentCol=1 to MaxCol
        TableDataArray(CurrentRow,CurrentCol)=""
    Next
```

```
Next
CurrentRow=1
CurrentCol=1
End Sub
```

For more ideas on how to construct a functional table, see the Table Demo project, and feel free to modify the code for your own projects.

Chapter X - Numeric functions

NS Basic contains the usual mathematic functions found in most dialects of Basic, and, with the help of MathLib, a number of functions that you would otherwise have had to build yourself. Not that it's all that difficult in NS Basic to build additional functions, as we've seen time and time again. But why reinvent the wheel?

Standard Mathematical Functions

The usual simple mathematical functions – addition, subtraction, multiplication, division, and exponentiation (raising one number to the power of another) – in NS Basic use the common symbols:

```
Dim x as float
Dim y as float
Dim z as float
z=x+y ' simple addition
z=x-y ' subtraction
z=x*y ' multiplication
z=x/y ' division - be sure not to use the back slash
'z=x\y won't work
z=x^y ' exponentiation
```

If you have a complex expression:

```
z=x+3/y-x^2*y
```

NS Basic follows the usual convention of exponentiation first, multiplication and division next, followed by addition and subtraction. The equation would have been evaluated as though parentheses had been added:

```
z=x+(3/y)-((x^2)*y)
```

Since parentheses group calculations to determine the order that they are performed, you can use them to force NS Basic to perform calculations in a different order:

```
z=(x+3)/((y-x)^(2*y))
```

Caution Be careful with the complexity of your expressions. It's very easy to build expressions that are mathematically correct, but so complex that NS Basic can't evaluate them. If you receive the "expression too complex" error during the compile step, break your expression down to smaller, intermediate expressions.

In addition to the simple mathematical calculations shown above, the following table gives the arithmetic functions supported by NS Basic:

NS Basic arithmetic functions

Function	Description
Abs	Returns the absolute value of an arithmetic expression
Cbrt	Returns the cube root of a number**
Ceiling	Returns the next higher integer number than a given arithmetic expression
Exp	Returns the value e^ number**
Floor	Returns the next lower integer number than a given arithmetic expression
Int	Returns the integer value of an arithmetic expression
Log	Returns the natural log of a number**
Log10	Returns the base 10 log of a number**
Mod	Returns the remainder of one arithmetic expression divided by another
Pow	Returns the result of one number raised to the power of a second number**
Power10	Returns the result of raising a number to the specified power of 10 **
Rand	Returns a floating point value between 0 and 1.0 (NS Basic includes this in their list of Miscellaneous functions, but I include it here as an arithmetic function instead)
Rem	Returns the remainder of dividing one number by another number**
Round	Rounds the results of an arithmetic expression up to the nearest fractional digit
Sign	Returns an indicator of the sign (positive or negative) of an arithmetic expression
Sqrt	Returns the square root of an arithmetic expression**
Trunc	Returns a float with decimal places truncated

** Require MathLib to be installed

Although we won't go into many of them here, NS Basic and MathLib also support a wide variety of trigonometric functions as well:

NS Basic trigonometric functions

Function	Description
Acos	Returns the arc-cosine of an angle. **
Asin	Returns the arc-sine of an angle. **
Atan	Returns the arc-tangent of an angle. **
Atan2	Returns the arc-tangent of an angle expressed as the division of two numbers**
Cos	Returns the cosine of an angle. **
Sin	Returns the sine of an angle. **
Tan	Returns the tangent of an angle. **
Acosh	Returns the hyperbolic arc-cosine of an angle. **
Asinh	Returns the hyperbolic arc-sine of an angle. **
Atanh	Returns the hyperbolic arc-tangent of an angle. **
Cosh	Returns the hyperbolic cosine of an angle. **
Sinh	Returns the hyperbolic sine of an angle. **
Tanh	Returns the hyperbolic tangent of an angle **
DegToRadians	Returns the radians of angle input in degrees
RadToDegrees	Returns the degrees of an angle input in radians

** Require MathLib to be installed

Before we go into too much detail, there are a few nuances to floating point arithmetic that you need to know, or you will be caught off guard, and will have a tough time debugging code that is 100% accurate, yet still doesn't give you the results expected.

As I mentioned in the chapter on variables and constants, NS Basic supports many different numeric types: integer, short, single, double, and float. These variable types and how they are dimensioned only make a difference during database input and output, and display or string conversion. Internally, all numeric variables are represented as 64-bit, double-precision floating point. "Good," you think, "all my calculations will be as accurate as possible." Unfortunately, life isn't that kind.

The problem is that it's not possible to accurately represent all numbers with 100% accuracy in binary format, so during calculations tiny errors may be introduced. A calculation that is supposed to return the value 12.5 might actually return 12.500000001 or 12.499999999. There *is* a solution (isn't there always?), but the solution may prove to be more of a problem if you aren't careful.

Round

Syntax:

Round(FloatVal,NumDecDigits)

Description:

Used to round a value to the nearest value with the specified number of digits past the decimal point

This solution, the Round statement, allows you to take any numeric value and return a floating point number rounded to the closest value with the desired number of decimal point precision. Here are some examples:

```
Dim x as Float
Dim y as Float
x=2/7 ' returns 0.2857142857142857.....
y=Round(x,3) ' 0.286 x rounded to 3 decimal places
x=100/3 ' 33.333333333...
y=Round(x,0) ' 33 x rounded to 0 decimal places
```

So, where's the problem? There isn't any, unless you round every result in multiple step calculations, as the error introduced by rounding (you are changing the number, you know) will get amplified at each subsequent step. The same problem occurs if you round a result too early in a series of equations. You might actually need a number like 0.000003 for a calculation, and if you decide to round everything to 2 decimal points, this number would be 0, possibly making your answer invalid (or worse, you could end up dividing by zero, which most compilers don't care about, but it'll crash most computers):

```
'Determine time in minutes it takes for light to reach the Earth_
from the sun
Dim SpeedLight as Float ' 186,000 miles per second
Dim SunDistance as Float ' 93 million miles
Dim TransitTime as Float
Dim IntermediateValue as Float ' use to store partial answer
SpeedLight=186000
SunDistance=93000000
IntermediateValue=SpeedLight/SunDistance
IntermediateValue=1/IntermediateValue
IntermediateValue=IntermediateValue/60
TransitTime=round(IntermediateValue,2) ' round to 2 decimal points
MsgBox "Light from the sun reaches the Earth in "_
+str(TransitTime)+" minutes"
```

This returns the correct value (8.33 minutes). But, if we attempt to round at each step:

```
'Determine time in minutes it takes for light to reach the Earth_
from the sun
Dim SpeedLight as Float ' 186,000 miles per second
Dim SunDistance as Float ' 93 million miles
Dim TransitTime as Float
```

```
Dim IntermediateValue as Float ' use to store partial answer
SpeedLight=186000
SunDistance=93000000
IntermediateValue=round(SpeedLight/SunDistance,2)
IntermediateValue=round(1/IntermediateValue,2)
IntermediateValue=round(IntermediateValue/60,2)
TransitTime=round(IntermediateValue,2) ' round to 2 decimal points
MsgBox "Light from the sun reaches the Earth in "_
+str(TransitTime)+" minutes"
```

This produces the dreaded "divide by zero" error on the line:

```
IntermediateValue=round(1/IntermediateValue,2)
```

The IntermediateValue obtained by 186000/93000000 (actual value 0.002), rounded to 2 decimal positions gives 0.00, and 1 divided by 0.00 isn't valid. NS Basic is nice enough not to crash on you, but instead gives a message box alerting you to the problem:

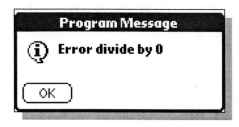

However, since this doesn't crash the app, it continues with the calculation as though nothing happened, eventually giving the wrong answer:

Your user might not think twice about the "divide by 0" error, but instead will rely on the program to produce the correct answer. So, use Round carefully, and only on the final result, to avoid this kind of error.

Let

Syntax:

> **Let var1=var2**
> **or**
> **Let var1=expression**

Description:

Assigns the value of a variable or expression to a variable.

Before we go too far, I'll introduce you to "Let" - but I'd like you to forget about it (I'll explain why later).

"Let" is a keyword that used to be required in Basic for the assignment of a variable or expression to a variable. It's included in NS Basic's list of arithmetic functions, although it can be used with any variable type.

Although Let isn't required, NS Basic includes it for compatibility with versions of Basic that require it. Since it's not needed, consumes space, doesn't improve the readability of your code, and only increases the likelihood that you will introduce typographical errors, I suggest that you omit Let altogether.

If you look at the previous table of "NS Basic arithmetic functions" - ignoring those that require MathLib - you'll see a common theme:

NS Basic built-in functions not requiring MathLib

Function	Description
Abs	Returns the absolute value of an arithmetic expression
Ceiling	Returns the next higher integer number than a given arithmetic expression
Floor	Returns the next lower integer number than a given arithmetic expression
Int	Returns the integer value of an arithmetic expression
Mod	Returns the remainder of one arithmetic expression divided by another
Round	Rounds the results of an arithmetic expression up to the nearest fractional digit
Sign	Returns an indicator of the sign (positive or negative) of an arithmetic expression
Trunc	Returns a float with decimal places truncated

Many of these functions either return a value by rounding or otherwise removing all or part of the decimal portion of a floating point value (Ceiling, Floor, Int, Round, Trunc). We've already covered Round, so we'll look at the subtle differences between the other four functions.

Trunc and Int

Syntax:

Trunc(FloatVal, NumDecDigits)
Int(FloatVal)

Description:

Returns a value by removing some (Trunc) or all (Int) of the digits to the right of the decimal point

Trunc is similar to Round, but instead of rounding the last digit, it simply removes the unwanted digits, without rounding:

```
Dim x as Float
Dim y as Float
x=3.14159
y=Trunc(x,3)
```

Note that the returned value, 3.141, is close to what the Round-ed value would be (Round(x,3)=3.142), and may be close enough for many purposes. But, how about this:

```
Dim YourPay as float
Dim YourRaise as float
Dim FinalPay as float
YourPay=50000 ' dollars this month - not bad!
YourRaise=0.49 ' raise based on performance
FinalPay=YourPay+YourPay*Round(YourRaise,1)
Msgbox "Final pay using Round = "+str(FinalPay) ' 75000 dollars
FinalPay=YourPay+YourPay*Trunc(YourRaise,1)
Msgbox "Final pay using Trunc = "+str(FinalPay) ' only 70000_
dollars
```

Which would you rather have? Although there may be times that you will want to use Trunc, for the most part it's best avoided, since the value returned may not be truly representative of the actual value.

NS Basic is very literal when it comes to Int – what you ask for is what you get. Int merely returns the integer portion of a value, without rounding (as though you used Trunc(val,0)):

```
Dim x as Float
Dim y as Integer
x=12.02
y=Int(x) ' y=12
x=-34.3
y=Int(x) ' y=-34
x=99.9999999999
y=Int(x) ' y=99
```

When you only want the integer portion of a value, use Int. When the rounded value is more appropriate, use Round. So, when would Int be more appropriate? In the chapter on date and time functions, we had functions that would add hours, minutes, or seconds to any given time, and return the new time. These functions used Int to determine the closest whole number of hours, then took the remaining number of seconds and used Int to determine the closest whole number of minutes. Here's the AddHours function:

```
Function AddHours(tStart as Time, UserHours as Integer) as Time
Dim SecStart as Integer
```

```
Dim EndSeconds as Integer
Dim NewHours as Integer
Dim NewMinutes as Integer
SecStart=second(tStart)+60*(minute(tStart)+60*Hour(tStart))
EndSeconds=SecStart+UserHours*3600 ' get the new number of seconds
EndSeconds=rem(EndSeconds, 86400) ' this eliminates any excessive_
days (86400 secs/day)
NewHours=int(EndSeconds/3600) ' get number of hours
EndSeconds=EndSeconds-NewHours*3600 ' remove hours
NewMinutes=int(EndSeconds/60)
EndSeconds=EndSeconds-NewMinutes*60 ' remove minutes
AddHours=TimeVal(NewHours,NewMinutes,EndSeconds)
End Function
```

Ceiling and Floor

Syntax:

> **Ceiling(FloatVal)**
> **Floor(FloatVal)**

Description:

> **Returns the closest integer value greater than (Ceiling), less than (Floor) or equal to the current value.**

Ceiling and Floor do exactly what their names suggest: Ceiling returns an integer that is the closest integer greater than or equal to the current value, and Floor returns the closest integer less than or equal to the current value. For example:

```
Dim x as Float
Dim y as Integer
x=3.14159
y=Ceiling(x) ' gives the result 4
y=Floor(x) ' gives the result 3
x=-3.14159 ' now, with a negative value
y=Ceiling(x) ' gives the result -3
MsgBox "Ceiling(-3.14159)="+str(y)
y=Floor(x) ' gives the result -4
MsgBox "Floor(-3.14159)="+str(y)
```

Rem and Mod

Syntax:

> **Rem(FloatVal, Divisor)**
> **Mod(IntVal,Divisor)**

Description:

> **Returns the value that remains after dividing one number by another**

Now that you've seen the various ways to return an integer or truncated decimal value, it's time to deal with the rest of NS Basic's built-in simple arithmetic functions. You previously saw in the AddHours function how I used Int to determine the whole number of hours and minutes from a number of seconds, and used Rem to return the remainder:

```
EndSeconds=SecStart+UserHours*3600
' get the new number of seconds
EndSeconds=rem(EndSeconds, 86400)
' eliminate excess days (86400 secs/day)
NewHours=int(EndSeconds/3600)
' get number of hours
EndSeconds=EndSeconds-NewHours*3600
' remove hours
NewMinutes=int(EndSeconds/60)
EndSeconds=EndSeconds-NewMinutes*60
' remove minutes
```

During a division that returns a non-integer value (like 12/7), Rem returns a floating point number that left over after a division. The best way to understand this is to take a simple example. Let's determine the average number of days per month in a year, and the number of days left over, if we decided to divide the year into equal-length months:

```
Dim DaysInYear as Integer
Dim MonthsInYear as Integer
Dim DaysInMonth as Integer
Dim DaysRemaining as Integer
DaysInYear=365 ' a non-leap year
MonthsInYear=12 ' at least here on Earth!
DaysInMonth=Int(DaysInYear/MonthsInYear) ' should be 30
MsgBox "Days in month: "+str(DaysInMonth)
DaysRemaining=Rem(DaysInYear,MonthsInYear) ' should be 5
MsgBox "Days remaining: "+str(DaysRemaining)
```

Rem isn't available in most other versions of Basic (or, if included, usually means "Remark", like our ' character). You can emulate the Rem function using other functions:

```
DaysRemaining=DaysInYear-MonthsInYear*Int(DaysInYear/MonthsInYear)
```

but it's not as easy to read, and takes a lot more typing (which translates into more chances for typographical errors)! However, you need to balance this with the fact that non-NS Basic (or new NS Basic programmers) may not be familiar with Rem, and may not grasp what you are trying to do with it, and they may be more familiar with longer statement above.

With Rem, we can rewrite the AddHours function to be a bit simpler:

```
Function AddHours(tStart as Time, UserHours as Integer) as Time
Dim SecStart as Integer
Dim EndSeconds as Integer
Dim NewHours as Integer
Dim NewMinutes as Integer
SecStart=second(tStart)+60*(minute(tStart)+60*Hour(tStart))
```

```
EndSeconds=SecStart+UserHours*3600
' get the new number of seconds
EndSeconds=rem(EndSeconds, 86400)
'eliminate excess days (86400 secs/day)
NewHours=int(EndSeconds/3600) ' get number of hours
EndSeconds=rem(EndSeconds,3600) ' remove hours
NewMinutes=int(EndSeconds/60)
EndSeconds=rem(EndSeconds,60) ' remove minutes
AddHours=TimeVal(NewHours,NewMinutes,EndSeconds)
End Function
```

Similar to Rem, the function Mod also returns the remainder after division, but Mod only works using integers. So, the AddHours function could be rewritten as:

```
Function AddHours(tStart as Time, UserHours as integer) as Time
Dim SecStart as Integer
Dim EndSeconds as Integer
Dim NewHours as Integer
Dim NewMinutes as Integer
SecStart=second(tStart)+60*(minute(tStart)+60*Hour(tStart))
EndSeconds=SecStart+UserHours*3600
' get the new number of seconds
EndSeconds=rem(EndSeconds, 86400)
' eliminate excess days (86400 secs/day)
NewHours=int(EndSeconds/3600) ' get number of hours
EndSeconds=Mod(EndSeconds,3600) ' remove hours
NewMinutes=int(EndSeconds/60)
EndSeconds=Mod(EndSeconds,60) ' remove minutes
AddHours=TimeVal(NewHours,NewMinutes,EndSeconds)
End Function
```

Since the time functions deal with integers, this is not much of a problem. Also, since NS Basic currently represents all numbers as double-precision floating point, the Rem and Mod functions are interchangeable for integers. However, stick with convention, and use Mod with integer arithmetic, and Rem for floating point.

Rand

Syntax:

  Rand()

Description:

  Returns a random floating point value between 0 and 1.0.

The Rand function is used when you need a floating point random number between 0 and 1.0:

```
Dim RandNum as float
RandNum=Rand()
```

This will give you a different number between 0 and 1.0 each time the function is run. However, what if you don't need a number between 0 and 1, but between two other numbers? For example, what if you are writing a program that simulates the roll of a six-sided die, with sides numbered one through six? If we simply multiply the result of our Rand() statement, that won't quite get us there:

```
Dim RandNum as float
RandNum=Rand()*6
```

Now we will get random floating point number between 0 and 6. Close, but two problems – we need an integer, and it has to be between 1 and 6. So, a little modification:

```
Dim RandNum as integer
RandNum=round(1+Rand()*5,0)
```

This will now give us a random floating point number from 0 to 5, so we'll add 1 to get us from 1 to 6, and round the result to the nearest integer.

Abs and Sign

Syntax:

> **Abs(arg1)**
> **Sign(arg1)**

Description:

> **Returns either the absolute value (Abs) of a number, or returns a value indicating whether the number is positive or negative (Sign)**

Abs returns the absolute value of a number (the distance from 0, regardless of positive or negative), and you'll use it when the amount is important, not whether a number is negative or positive, or when negative numbers would be acceptable mathematically, but not conceptually (e.g., speed, weight, volume):

```
Dim VehicleSpeed as Float
Dim StartPoint as float
Dim EndPoint as float
Dim tStart as float
Dim EndTime as float
Dim DistanceTraveled as float
Dim TimeTaken as Float
'
'code here to obtain values from user
'
DistanceTraveled=EndPoint-StartPoint
TimeTaken=EndTime-tStart
VehicleSpeed=Abs(DistanceTraveled/TimeTaken)
```

The use of Abs here is needed in case the user entered the starting and ending point or time values in reverse order. Although a negative speed could mean the vehicle was moving backwards, the vehicle's speed is still a positive number – only the direction changes (now we're starting to talk about velocity and vector arithmetic, and that's beyond the scope of this book).

You could always have your user merely enter the DistanceTraveled and TimeTaken values directly, but there's always the possibility that they would enter negative numbers, and the conversion would still need to be made using Abs – unless we wrote some code to deal with both positive and negative numbers:

```
VehicleSpeed=DistanceTraveled/TimeTaken
If VehicleSpeed < 0 then
VehicleSpeed=(0-VehicleSpeed)
End if
```

Another way to achieve this is to use the Sign function. Sign returns 1 if the value being checked is positive, or −1 if the value is negative. So, Abs(x) could be rewritten as x*Sign(x). Using our speed example above:

```
VehicleSpeed=DistanceTraveled/TimeTaken
VehicleSpeed=VehicleSpeed*Sign(VehicleSpeed)
```

If VehicleSpeed is positive, then VehicleSpeed*Sign(VehicleSpeed) would be the same as VehicleSpeed*1, resulting in a positive number. If VehicleSpeed is negative, then VehicleSpeed*Sign(VehicleSpeed) would be VehicleSpeed*(-1), which would be a negative number multiplied by a negative number, or a positive number.

> **Note** Don't worry if you feel a little confused. If your programs are mathematically intensive enough to require these functions, you'll most likely already have the mathematical background to use them properly. If you don't need these functions, don't worry about them. I would bet that less than 1% of all NS Basic programs (and programs in general) use these functions.

If you never need to use exponents, powers, roots, and trigonometric functions, feel free to skip the rest of this chapter.

Exponents, Powers and Logs

Many scientific and financial calculations require the use of exponents and logarithms. Without writing a "Mathematics 101" textbook, the following explanation of exponents and logarithms should help you understand the NS Basic and MathLib functions that deal with them.

Pow, Log, and Log10

Syntax:

Pow(arg1,exponent)
Log(arg1)
Log10(arg1)

Description:

Returns a natural log (Log), base 10 log (Log10), or a value obtained by raising one number to the power of another (pow)

In the expression below, "y" is the exponent:

```
z=x^y
```

In other words, an exponent is the power that another number is raised to. NS Basic has two ways to perform this function:

```
z=x^y
z=pow(x,y)
```

Actually, there's another way to perform this function as well. If y is an integer, you can multiply x by itself y times:

```
y=3
'all the following forms are equivalent
z=x^y
z=x^3
z=x*x*x
z=pow(x,y)
z=pow(x,3)
```

However, since z=x*x*x, z=x^3, and z=pow(x,3) are only useful if you know the value for y ahead of time, you'll still need to know how to use the Pow function or the use of the caret ("^") for exponentiation.

Keeping with the NS Basic tradition, if there's a function such as Pow, there must be a reverse function. This is where logarithms come in. If an exponent is a number (power) to which another number is raised, a logarithm is the number that must be raised to a power to determine another number. Too many words, so let's give an example using:

```
z=x^y
```

If x=10 and y=2:

```
z=10^2
z=100
```

In this expression, y is the logarithm, and x is the base. Mathematically speaking, y is the log of z in base x:

```
y=Logx(z)
```

So, using the previous example:

```
2=log10(100)
```

Mathematicians, scientists, and others who frequently use the functions often work with logs of two common bases. One, the natural (or Naperian) log uses e (approximately 2.718) as its base. NS Basic represents natural logarithms using Log:

```
y=Log(z) ' if z=7, y=1.946
2.718^y=z ' e is approximately 2.718
```

Since most dialects of Basic (and other languages as well) represent natural logs as Ln rather than Log, it's a good idea to create our own function for natural logs:

```
Function Ln(UserValue as float) as float
Ln=Log(UserValue)
End Function
```

The natural log is used in many financial functions, but they are beyond the scope of this book.

> **SideBar** It always surprised me when I studied COBOL that it didn't have natural logs built in. You'd think a function that's commonly used in financial applications would be a priority of COBOL (COmmon Business-Oriented Language)!

Scientific Notation

The other log function in NS Basic uses base 10, and is represented as Log10:

```
y=Log10(z) ' if z=100, y=2, 10^y=z
```

If you've ever worked with scientific notation, you are used to seeing numbers represented like "1.34 E02", which is equivalent to "1.34 * 10^2", or 134. Since "134" is easier to write than "1.34 E02", why bother? Well, let's say you wanted to represent an extremely large or small number, like "0.000000000000123456", or "9870000000000000". The large number of zeroes makes it difficult to comprehend the actual number, and increases the chance for error when transcribing the number. However, convert these numbers into scientific notation, and "0.000000000000123456" becomes "1.23 E-13", and "9870000000000000" converts to "9.87 E15". NS Basic doesn't have a function to convert numbers into scientific notation format, but using the Log10 function, combined with a few other functions, we can create our own (from the SciNot project on the CD):

```
Function SciNot(UserNum as Float,DecDigits as Integer) as String
'Given any floating point number and the desired number
'   of digits of precision, the SciNot function creates
'   a string containing the number in scientific notation
Dim exponent as Integer
Dim WorkNum as Float
Dim FinalNum as Float
WorkNum=abs(UserNum) ' log10 chokes on negative numbers
exponent=int(log10(WorkNum)) ' get exponent
FinalNum=round((WorkNum/(10^exponent)),DecDigits)
' format the number
```

```
If FinalNum < 1 Then ' adjust if < 1
    Exponent=Exponent-1
    FinalNum=Round((WorkNum/(10^exponent)),DecDigits)
End If
FinalNum=FinalNum*sign(UserNum) ' correct for negative number
SciNot=str(FinalNum)+" E"+str(Exponent) ' and return number
End Function
```

A little trigonometry

We won't cover the trigonometric functions that NS Basic supports, other than to state that in order to use them, the angles used as their arguments need to be converter from degrees to radians. You'll probably need to convert radians back to degrees, so NS Basic allows you to make this conversion in both directions:

DegToRadians, RadToDegrees

Syntax:

DegToRadians(DegreeVal)
RadToDegrees(RadianVal)

Description:

Converts degree values to and from radians

The trigonometric functions supported by NS Basic won't be covered in this book, with the exception of DegToRadians and RadToDegrees. All of the trigonometric functions expect their arguments to be in radians. You can do the math yourself (there are 2*Pi radians in 360 degrees), but NS Basic provides the functions for you. The following code, modified from the Clock Hands project, is used to draw a line at any angle:

```
Dim x as Integer ' x and y used for screen coordinates
Dim y as Integer
Dim theta as Float ' theta is the angle
Dim LineLength as Integer ' length of the line to draw
Dim OffsetX as Float ' offsets determine endpoints for the line
Dim OffsetY as Float
x=val(fldX.text) ' get the user's values
y=val(fldY.text)
LineLength=val(fldLength.text)
theta=val(fldTheta.text)
fldThetaRads.text=str(degtoradians(theta))
' show user the angle in radians
OffsetX=LineLength*(cos(degtoradians(theta))) ' calc. endpoints
OffsetY=LineLength*(sin(degtoradians(theta)))
fldOffsetX.text=str(OffsetX) ' display endpoints
fldOffsetY.text=str(OffsetY)
DrawLine x,y,X+OffsetX, Y-OffsetY ' draw the line
```

Further discussion of these functions is beyond the scope of this book, but to see these functions in action, see the Analog Clock project.

SideBar Interestingly, although the trigonometric functions that require the use of radians also require MathLib, NS Basic supports the DegToRadians and RadToDegrees functions without it. That's actually pretty easy to see, since converting from degrees to radians and back again only requires multiplying or dividing by Pi (approximately 3.14159265...), so a circle (360 degrees) is equal to 2*3.14159265 radians, or nearly 57.29578 radians, so 1 degree equals 0.159155 radians. The reverse calculation, 360/57.29578 = 6.2831852, the number of degrees per radian. Using these values in calculations, rather than using the DegToRadians and RadToDegrees functions, may speed up your applications slightly without decreasing their accuracy.

Chapter XI - String Handling

If you've programmed in Basic before, you'll be familiar with most of the NS Basic string manipulation functions. There are also a few functions missing, but knowing NS Basic's track record, they probably won't be missing for long. We'll discover work-arounds for the missing functions, though, so you won't have to wait (how's THAT for service!).

Before we discuss string manipulation, you need to remember a few things about NS Basic strings:

-    String literals can be up to 255 characters long
-    String variables can be up to 32767 characters long
-    Strings can contain any ASCII character from chr(1) – chr(255)
-    The Palm OS uses the ASCII character chr(10) as a line feed/carriage return pair(most other systems use chr(10) as line feed, and chr(13) as carriage return)
-    NS Basic strings are null-terminated (stored with a chr(0) after the string)
-    NS Basic strings are null-terminated (stored with a chr(0) after the string)

Nope – that wasn't a mistake. I need to reinforce that last statement, since it's the source of many problems that can be extremely difficult to debug. You'll understand why when we get to string concatenation (adding strings together).

Strings are important. They're the main form of variable storage and display for information that you obtain from, and display to, your users. NS Basic gives you many functions for converting back and forth between strings and other variable types, changing the case (capitalization) of strings, extracting portions of a string, searching for a string within another string, adding or removing leading and trailing spaces, concatenating strings, and a few other miscellaneous functions.

Conversions

We'll start off with the conversion functions, as you'll need these for numeric data obtained from or displayed in Fields. But you've already looked at the Field information in the manual (you HAVE, haven't you?), and you can set the Field for numeric data, so what's the problem? Setting a Field's property to numeric merely tells the Palm OS to accept only numeric data (and only *positive* data – the negative sign can't be entered!).

Val, Str, and Format

Syntax:

> **Val(StringVar)**
> **Str(NumericVar)**
> **Format(NumericVar,FormatMask)**

Description:

Used to convert between string and numeric values

In order to access the value of a Field's text (or any other string, for that matter), and convert it to a numeric value, we need to use the Val statement:

```
Dim UserWeight as Float
Dim WeightString as string
WeightString=fldWeight.text ' from a field on the form
UserWeight=val(WeightString)
UserWeight=val(fldWeight.text) ' convert field text directly
```

As you've learned in the other chapters, if a conversion works in one direction, there must be a conversion in the opposite direction. To paraphrase Sir Isaac Newton, "For every conversion there is an equal and opposite conversion" – so here's the numeric-to-string conversion:

```
Dim UserWeight as Float
Dim WeightString as string
WeightString=str(UserWeight)
```

Note that UserWeight could have been an integer, short, or any other numeric variable – they all get converted to strings easily by the Str statement. Note also that NS Basic uses the Dim and Str statements without a "$" symbol, as in most dialects of Basic:

```
'this is NOT NS Basic code!
Dim WeightString$ as String
Dim UserWeight as Float
WeightString$=Str$(UserWeight)
```

If you're used to Visual Basic or Quick Basic, Str in NS Basic operates a bit differently. It's a very subtle difference that has produced its own share of debugging nightmares. Look at the following code, and try to predict the string that Str will produce:

```
Dim UserWeight as Float
Dim WeightString as String
UserWeight=72.5
WeightString=Str(UserWeight)
```

If you said "72.5" you would have been correct. Some versions of Basic will produce the string " 72.5" with a leading space before the number (as a place-holder, since a negative number would have included the negative sign "-" before the number. If you need to include a positive or negative sign, you can do that by using the Format statement – but we'll cover that later. We're still not done with Str yet. What do you think the following will produce:

```
Dim UserWeight as Float*16,2
Dim WeightString as String
UserWeight=72.5
WeightString=Str(UserWeight)
```

Now the WeightString would equal "   72.50", since UserWeight was dimensioned with 16 digits, 2 to the right of the decimal point. If the field used to display the WeightString isn't large enough to accommodate this larger string, the displayed value will be truncated on the right, possibly displaying 72 or 7. Imagine the difficulty debugging mathematic routines to find why a displayed value didn't agree with the expected value, when the problem wasn't in the calculations after all! When in doubt, remove any leading and trailing spaces with the Trim statement:

```
Dim UserWeight as Float*16,2
Dim WeightString as String
UserWeight=72.5
WeightString=Trim(Str(UserWeight))
```

Trim produces a string that is identical to the original string, but without any leading or trailing spaces. Any spaces that are within the string are left alone, however, so don't expect Trim to compress out any internal spaces.

For the most control over the string produced by converting a numeric value, you'll need to use the Format statement. The following table shows the different characters used in the Format mask, and how they are interpreted:

Format Mask Table.

Mask Character	Output
0	replaced by a digit from the number if available, zero if not
n	replaced by a digit from the number if available, space if not
#	replaced by a digit from the number if available, nothing if not
.	places a decimal point in the output text
+	Replaced by a minus sign if the number is negative, nothing if positive
-	Replaced by a minus sign if negative, space if positive
,	places a comma in the output string if a leading digit has been encountered, a space if not
any other char	copied into the output string

The complete syntax of the statement is:

```
OutputString=Format(n,mask)
```

where OutputString is the string produced by Format, n is the numeric variable, and mask is a string that determines how each character in the OutputString is created. Well, if you haven't used Format yet, the table above might be as clear as mud, so let's see Format in action:

```
Dim UserWeight as Float
Dim WeightString as String
UserWeight=72.5
WeightString=Format(UserWeight,"nnn0.00") ' produces " 72.50"
WeightString=Format(UserWeight,"+nnn0.00") ' produces "+ 72.50"
WeightString=Format(UserWeight,"-nnn0.00") ' produces " 72.50"
WeightString=Format(UserWeight,"0000.00") ' produces "0072.50"
WeightString=Format(UserWeight,"nnnn.nn") ' produces "  72.5 "
WeightString=Format(UserWeight,"####.##") ' produces "72.5"
WeightString=Format(UserWeight,"Weight ###0.00") ' produces_
"Weight 72.50"
```

You can see how Format gives you a great deal of power and control. As is true of life in general, power and control come with responsibility. Used correctly, Format can be your "genie in a bottle". It's important that your mask has enough characters and the proper decimal placement to yield truly useful results. Too short a mask, and your output string will be truncated. Too many characters, especially after the decimal point, and the string will contain superfluous digits. Too few digits past the decimal point and your string may omit a significant digit. For example:

```
Dim Pi as float
Dim DoublePi as float
Dim OutputString as string
Pi=3.14159
DoublePi=Pi*2
OutputString=Format(DoublePi,"0.0")
```

You might expect that OutputString would contain "6.3", which would be the appropriate string if DoublePi had been rounded to one position past the decimal point. However, Format only decides what gets place in the output string – it doesn't do any rounding of the values to make the output string valid. Instead, use the Round statement:

```
Dim Pi as float
Dim DoublePi as float
Dim OutputString as string
Pi=3.14159
DoublePi=Pi*2
OutputString=Format(Round(DoublePi,1),"0.0") ' gives the_
string "6.3"
```

The Round function is covered in the chapter on Numeric Functions, but is included here so that you know not to expect too much from Format alone.

Chr and Asc

Syntax:

> **Chr(Integer)**
> **Asc(Char)**

Description:

> **Converts between characters and their ASCII values**

Since strings can be considered groups of ASCII characters, you'd expect NS Basic to have conversions for converting characters into their ASCII codes, and vice versa. Well, NS Basic won't disappoint you here, with the Chr and Asc statements for this conversion. The only caveat is that the conversion only works on a single character:

```
Dim Char as string
Dim LF as string
Dim ASCIIcode as integer
LF=chr(10) ' assign the Line feed variable
ASCIIcode=Asc("a") ' gives the ASCII code for the letter "a"
ASCIIcode=Asc("abcde")  ' still only gives the ASCII code for "a"
```

Lcase, Ucase, and Proper

Syntax:

> **Lcase(StringVar)**
> **Ucase(StringVar)**
> **Proper(StringVar)**

Description:

> **Used to modify string capitalization**

Not only can you convert back and forth between strings and numeric, ASCII, date, and time values, but you can convert between different string formats.

What?

Maybe that last statement needs some explanation. If you remember way back when I talked about case sensitivity, the Palm OS doesn't treat upper case and lower case strings alike. Since it isn't practical (or easy) to force your users to use only upper case or lower case when they work with strings, you'll appreciate these functions to convert between different cases. The NS Basic built-in functions include Lcase, Ucase, and Proper, which convert a string to lower, upper, and proper (the first letter of each word capitalized) case:

```
Dim UserString as string
Dim NewString as string
UserString="The quick brown fox"
NewString=Lcase(UserString) ' now it's "the quick brown fox"
NewString=Ucase(UserString) ' and now "THE QUICK BROWN FOX"
```

```
NewString=Proper(UserString) ' finally, "The Quick Brown Fox"
```

These conversions are very useful for comparing two strings, since they limit the number of different cases that you need to compare:

```
Dim UserString as string
UserString=Lcase(fldUserInput.text) ' convert text to lower case
Select Case UserString
Case "meat"
'code to respond to meat
Case "vegetable"
'code to respond to vegetable
Case "dessert"
'code for dessert
Case Else
'code for other entries
End Select
```

Imagine having to compare the user's input against all possibilities for each string, and you'll see how useful this can be. I'm sure you'll find other uses for these case conversions.

Concatenation, Extraction and Truncation

Since a large amount of information is textual, it should come as no surprise that NS Basic supports virtually all the usual Basic string functions. As I mentioned before, there are a few functions missing, but we'll make our own to make up for what's missing.

Concatenation, or the adding together of two strings, is one of the most common string functions. Simply put, concatenating two strings creates a single, longer string:

```
Dim UserString1 as string
Dim UserString2 as string
Dim NewString as string
UserString1="The quick brown fox"
UserString2="jumps over the lazy dog"
NewString=UserString1+" "+UserString2
```

The new string becomes "The quick brown fox jumps over the lazy dog".

Caution Note the extra space added between the two strings. You'll make the mistake, from time to time, of forgetting the space. Remember, the computer does exactly what you tell it to – no more, no less!

You might be thinking, "Why perform the concatenation? Why not just make NewString equal to the longer string?" Well, in most cases, you can. However, what if you want to include a quotation mark in your string? This won't work:

```
Dim UserString as string
UserString="He said, "How about a date, beautiful?"" ' compiler_
complains here
```

But, concatenation, using the quote character chr(34), makes it easy:

```
Dim UserString as string
UserString="He said, "+chr(34) +"How about a date,_
beautiful? "+chr(34)
```

Also, if you want to create a string that's longer than 255 characters, you'll need to use concatenation if you're going to build the string from literals:

```
Dim UserString as string
UserString="abcdefghijklmnopqrstuvwxyzabcdefghijklmnopqrstuvwxyz_
abcdefghijklmnopqrstuvwxyzabcdefghijklmnopqrstuvwxyzabcdefghijkl_
mnopqrstuvwxyzabcdefghijklmnopqrstuvwxyzabcdefghijklmnopqrstuvwx_
yzabcdefghijklmnopqrstuvwxyzabcdefghijklmnopqrstuvwxyzabcdefghij_
klmnopqrstuvwxyz" ' too long, compiler will complain
```

But, you can use smaller strings, and concatenate them:

```
Dim UserString as string
UserString="abcdefghijklmnopqrstuvwxyzabcdefghijklmnopqrstuvwxyz_
abcdefghijklmnopqrstuvwxyzabcdefghijklmnopqrstuvwxyzabcdefghijkl_
mnopqrstuvwxyz"+"abcdefghijklmnopqrstuvwxyzabcdefghijklmnopqrstu_
vwxyzabcdefghijklmnopqrstuvwxyzabcdefghijklmnopqrstuvwxyzabcdefg_
hijklmnopqrstuvwxyz" ' this will work
```

Or create the variable with the smaller string, and concatenate the variable with itself, or with successive strings:

```
Dim UserString as string
Dim HelpString as string
UserString="abcdefghijklmnopqrstuvwxyzabcdefghijklmnopqrstuvwxyz_
abcdefghijklmnopqrstuvwxyzabcdefghijklmnopqrstuvwxyzabcdefghijkl_
mnopqrstuvwxyz"
UserString=UserString+UserString
HelpString=""
HelpString=HelpString+"Assembly instructions:"
HelpString=HelpString+chr(10)+"1.  Place tab A into slot B"
HelpString=HelpString+chr(10)+"2.  Place fold C through circle D"
HelpString=HelpString+chr(10)+"3.  Put square E into rhomboid F"
HelpString=HelpString+chr(10)+"4.  Call for help!"
```

Note Instead of using the DOS convention of carriage return/line feed pair (Chr(13) followed by chr(10)) to end a line of text, the Palm OS uses chr(10) for both carriage return and line feed.

There's one case in which concatenation doesn't create a string that's equal to the two strings added together, but instead produces a shorter string. Think about it for a minute – what would cause the premature termination of a string? The string termination character! Remember that NS Basic stores strings with a null (chr(0)) terminator. If you try to add strings together that contain an embedded null character, you'll end up with a string that's shorter than expected:

```
Dim UserString as string
UserString="first string"+chr(0)+"second string"
Msgbox UserString ' will only show "first string"
```

Granted, there aren't too many cases when this might pop up, but it's better to know about this problem and avoid it from the start.

Concatenation turns out to be a fairly slow procedure – one of the slowest procedures in NS Basic. So slow, that you should avoid it whenever possible – especially in loops. For strings that aren't going to change, consider placing them in a database, then accessing the database when the string's needed. Since this would involve distributing a database along with your application, and the user might not install everything (nobody's perfect), you could always create the database from your own code. Your user will have to wait at least once during the initial creation of the database, but will appreciate the speed increase later.

> **Tip** Let your users know that this is the case – it explains the initial delay, and lets them know that the next time the program will be faster. They'll enjoy knowing that you made the extra effort for their benefit!

By the way, this is also a great way to know if your user has run the program before; if you create a database with your app the first time it's run, you will probably be checking for the presence of the database before you create it (I *hope* you do!). If the database doesn't exist, it's probably the first time the app has been run (either that, or the user beamed it to someone else, or somehow deleted the database), so you can display some introductory forms and basic information. This is a good time to create a database of user preferences, program strings for later, etc. The next time the application is run, you can bypass all this, and have a snappy application. I use this technique in several of my data-intensive applications, or when there are large blocks of information that I want to display to the user as help text, etc. By placing this in the program startup code, you can display the initial splash screen (usually a graphic image or other identifying logo), create the database and display the necessary progress indicators, and get it over with.

LeftPad and RightPad

Syntax:

LeftPad(StringVar,FinalStringSize)
RightPad(StringVar,FinalStringSize)

Description:

Returns a string by adding spaces to the left or right of an existing string

Another common string function is creating strings of fixed length. That is, as you'll see in non-keyed database access (in a later chapter), there may be times when you want to take a number of different strings and add spaces to the front or end of the shorter strings so that they're all the same length (number of characters). To add a number of spaces to the front or end of a string to create a string of specific length, the LeftPad and RightPad statements come in handy:

```
Dim UserStr as String
Dim LongStr as String
Dim LongerStr as String
UserStr="Just a little string"
LongStr=LeftPad(UserStr,40)
'LongStr = "                    Just a little string"
'padded with spaces on the left for a total of 40 characters
LongerStr=RightPad(LongStr,50)
'LongerStr = "                    Just a little string          "
'padded with spaces on the right for a total of 50 characters
```

Ltrim, Rtrim, and Trim

Syntax:

> **Ltrim(StringVar)**
> **Rtrim(StringVar)**
> **Trim(StringVar)**

Description:

> **Returns a string by removing leading and/or training spaces from an existing string**

You can remove the leading and trailing spaces (leading=in front, trailing=in back) from strings using Ltrim and Rtrim, respectively:

```
Dim UserString as string
Dim ShortString as string
Dim ShorterString as string
UserString="    Lots of padding    "
ShortString=Ltrim(UserString) ' now equals "Lots of padding    "
ShorterString=Rtrim(ShortString) ' now equals "Lots of padding"
```

You could also remove both leading and trailing spaces at the same time with the Trim statement, as mentioned previously:

```
Dim UserString as string
Dim ShorterString as string
UserString="    Lots of padding    "
ShorterString=Trim(UserString) ' now equals "Lots of padding"
```

Left, Right, Mid

Syntax:

> **Left(StringVar, Length)**
> **Right(StringVar, Length)**

Mid(StringVar,StartPos,Length)

Description:

Returns a substring from the front, end, or middle of an existing string

We previously used LeftPad and RightPad to add spaces to a string. You could produce the same effect by adding strings of spaces to the beginning or end of your original string, using the Left and Right statements:

```
Dim UserStr as String
Dim LongStr as String
Dim LongerStr as String
UserStr="Just a little string"
LongStr=Right("                         "_
+UserStr,40)
'now LongStr = "                    Just a little string"
'padded with spaces on the left for a total of 40 characters
LongerStr=Left(LongStr+_
"                                        ",50)
'now LongerStr = "                    Just_
 a little string              "
'padded with spaces on the right for a total of 50 characters
```

Left(theString, *n*) returns *n* characters from the left of theString. If theString is shorter than *n*, then the original string is returned. Similarly, Right(theString, *n*) returns *n* characters from the right of the string, returning the original string if it is shorter than *n*. Most dialects of Basic also allow you to use Left and Right to assign the *n*th-most characters to the left or right of a string:

```
'NOT NS Basic code
Dim UserString$
UserString$="Now is the time"
Left$(UserString$,3)="But"
'UserString$ would then contain "But is the time"
```

However, NS Basic doesn't have this capability – at least not built-in. However, using some clever coding (and the Len statement, which gives us the integer length of a string of characters), we can achieve the same result:

```
Function PutLeft(OrigString as String, NewChars as String)_
as String
Dim OrigLen as Integer
Dim NewLen as Integer
Dim DiffLen as Integer
OrigLen=len(OrigString)
NewLen=len(NewChars)
DiffLen=OrigLen-NewLen
If NewLen > OrigLen Then
    PutLeft=left(NewChars,OrigLen)
Else
    PutLeft=NewChars+Right(OrigString,DiffLen)
```

```
End If
End Function
```

This code would then be used as follows:

```
Dim UserString as string
Dim NewString as string
UserString="Now is the time"
NewString=PutLeft(UserString,"But")
'NewString would then contain "But is the time"
```

Similarly, we can create a function PutRight:

```
Function PutRight(OrigString as String, NewChars as String)_
as String
Dim OrigLen as Integer
Dim NewLen as Integer
Dim DiffLen as Integer
OrigLen=len(OrigString)
NewLen=len(NewChars)
DiffLen=OrigLen-NewLen
If NewLen>OrigLen Then
    PutRight=left(NewChars,OrigLen)
    ' only replace the ncessary chars, still on left
Else
    PutRight=left(OrigString,DiffLen)+NewChars
End If
End Function
```

This new function PutRight would then be used as follows:

```
Dim UserString as string
Dim NewString as string
UserString="Now is the time"
NewString=PutRight(UserString,"song")
'NewString would then contain "Now is the song"
```

So far we've looked at extracting characters from - or placing characters at – the front or end of a string. NS Basic also supports the Mid(theString, *m*, *n*) statement, which allow you to extract *n* characters from a string starting with the character at position *m* in theString:

```
Dim UserString as String
Dim NewString as String
UserString="Now is the time"
NewString=Mid(UserString,4,6) ' NewString contains "is the"
```

The string returned is limited by the number of available characters (i.e., once it hits the end of the string, MID stops, without padding the string):

```
Dim UserString as String
Dim NewString as String
UserString="Now is the time"
NewString=Mid(UserString,4,16)
```

```
' equals "is the time", even though this is shorter than 16
characters
```

Like Left and Right, NS Basic doesn't allow the use of Mid to place characters within a string:

```
'NOT NS Basic code
Dim UserString$
UserString$="Now is the time"
Mid$(UserString$,4,6)="I have"
'UserString$ will now contain "Now I have time"
```

To emulate this function in NS Basic, we'll need to do some fancy concatenation, but it's not hard logic to follow. The new string will contain the leftmost *m*-1 characters, then, starting at position *m*, add the new characters. If this string is longer than the original string, only take the leftmost characters up to the length of the original string. Otherwise, add the rightmost characters that remain from the original string.

```
Function PutMid(OrigString as String,NewChars as String,_
StartPos as Integer)as String
Dim OrigLen as Integer
Dim NewLen as Integer
Dim DiffLen as Integer
Dim TempString as String
OrigLen=len(OrigString)
NewLen=len(NewChars)
DiffLen=OrigLen-NewLen
TempString=Left(OrigString,StartPos-1)+NewChars ' put in position
If len(TempString) > OrigLen Then
    PutMid=left(TempString,OrigLen) ' keep same length as_
    OrigString
Else
    PutMid=TempString+Mid(OrigString,StartPos+NewLen,OrigLen)
End If
End Function
```

Then, to use PutMid, try this:

```
Dim userstring as String
Dim newstring as String
userstring="abcdefghij"
newstring=putmid(userstring,"xyz",2)
MsgBox newstring ' displays axyzefghij
```

Space

Another function that many dialects of Basic have that's missing from NS Basic, but easy to add, is the Space$ function:

```
"NOT NS Basic code
Dim UserString$
UserString$=Space$(12) ' produces a string of 12 spaces
```

It doesn't take too much imagination, now that you're familiar with NS Basic string manipulation, to see that Space(n) would be the same as Left(SpaceString, n), where SpaceString is a long string of spaces. If you know that n will never be longer than a given number (say, 40), then the following function will work well:

```
Function Space(n as integer) as String
Space=Left("                                        ",n)
'there are 40 spaces in the string above
End Function
```

If n might be larger than 40, you'll need a slight modification:

```
Function Space(n as Integer) as String
Dim SpaceString as String
SpaceString="                                        "
'there are 40 spaces in the string above
If n <41 Then
    Space=Left(SpaceString,n)
Else
    Dim LoopCounter as Integer
    Dim TempString as String
    TempString=""
    For LoopCounter=1 to int (n/40)
        TempString=TempString+SpaceString
    Next
    Space=TempString+left(SpaceString,rem(n,40))
End If
End Function
```

String

How about a function that will return a string of *any* character, and of *any* length?

```
Dim UserString as string
UserString=MakeString("x",50) ' not a real function...yet
```

Many dialects of Basic include this as a String$ function:

```
'NOT NS Basic
Dim UserString$
UserString$=String("x",50) ' create a string of 50 x's
```

The easiest way to create this is with a For...Next loop:

```
Function MakeString(Char as string,n as integer) as string
Dim TempString as String
Dim LoopCounter as integer
TempString=""
For LoopCounter=1 to n
    TempString=TempString+Char
Next
MakeString=TempString
End Function
```

```
Dim UserString as string
UserString=MakeString("x",50) ' now it works!
```

This will accomplish the task, but because it uses concatenation, it can be time consuming. You can cut the time considerably by doing a little division:

```
Function MakeString(Char as String,n as Integer) as String
Dim TempString as String
Dim LoopCounter as Integer
TempString=""
If n > 10 Then ' less than 10 is quick enough using the_
standard loop
    Dim QuadChar as String
    QuadChar=Char+Char
    QuadChar=QuadChar+QuadChar ' now 4 chars in a row
    For LoopCounter=1 to int(n/4)
       TempString=TempString+QuadChar
    Next
    TempString=TempString+left(char,rem(n,4))
Else
    For LoopCounter=1 to n
       TempString=TempString+Char
    Next
End If
MakeString=TempString
End Function

Dim UserString as string
UserString=MakeString("x",50) ' now it works, and fairly quickly
```

If NS Basic supported recursion, you could really speed the function up, but that's currently not possible. However, this is a good combination of speed and power, and should fit your needs.

Searching Strings – using InStr

InStr

Syntax:

InStr(StartPos,StringToSearch,StringToSearchFor,CaseSensitiveFlag)

Description:

Determines if a given string contains a substring

You will often need to search a string of characters for a specific character string. For instance, you might have a collection of recipes, and might want to search each recipe for the word "hot," in order to find all recipes that can be used to create "hot" foods (whether "hot" refers to temperature or spiciness isn't important in this example). To check for the occurrence of the word "hot" in each recipe's description, you would use the InStr statement:

```
Dim RecipeInfo as string
Dim SearchString as string
Dim StartPos as integer ' start position in string
Dim Result as integer
Dim CaseSensitive as integer
Dim CaseInsensitive as integer
RecipeInfo="Spicy hot tamale"
SearchString="hot"
StartPos=1
CaseSensitive=0
CaseInsensitive=1
Result=InStr(StartPos,RecipeInfo,SearchString,CaseInsensitive)
```

The InStr statement returns a zero if it couldn't find a match, or an integer representing the position in the string being searched where the specified string was found. Note that you can start from any point in the string, and can force InStr to only match if the capitalization (case) of the string being searched and the pattern string are equivalent. In this case Result would have returned 7, as the string "hot" was found starting at the seventh character in "Spicy hot tamale". If we wanted to start at some later part of the string, we would have used a different start position:

```
Result=InStr(8,RecipeInfo,SearchString,CaseInsensitive)
' won't find it this time
```

Caution Be sure when using InStr to specify whether you want to keep the search case sensitive or case insensitive. I have a program that runs through a drug database, looking for any occurrence of a drug name. This allows me to find any drug with that name, and drug that contains the original drug, and any antidote for overdose with the original drug. Forcing the user to enter the drug name in a specific case wouldn't be reasonable.

You can use InStr to parse a string into individual sub-strings. By looking for a character to divide the strings, you can easily break a string into smaller strings. Here's code modified from the Parser project, which breaks a quoted CSV string (quoted comma-separated values strings are in the format: "value1","value2","value3",...) into an array of sub-strings:

```
Dim InputString as String
Dim Quote as String
Dim TrimmedString as String
Dim ParsedString as String
Dim NumElements as Integer
Dim CurrentChar as String
Dim StringPointer as Integer
Dim ArrayPointer as Integer
Dim GotQuote as Integer
Dim StringArray(31) as String ' 30 fields should be enough for_
most purposes, but your needs may differ
'initialize pointers, counters, and boolean values
GotQuote = False
NumElements=0
```

```
ArrayPointer = 1
InputString=fldStringToParse.text
' retrieve String to parse from user
StringPointer=instr(1,InputString, Chr(34)+","+ Chr(34),1)
' determine if string even contains the delimiter
If Len(InputString) < 3 Then
    ' no data if shorter than the delimiter!
    MsgBox "Invalid string to parse"
    Exit Sub
ElseIf StringPointer=0 Then
    ' if instr = 0, then delimiter wasn't found
    MsgBox "Invalid delimiter, or delimiter not found"
    Exit Sub
Else
    TrimmedString = Trim(InputString)
    ' remove leading/trailing spaces
    For StringPointer = 1 To Len(TrimmedString)
        ' look for starting quote in ","
        CurrentChar = Mid(TrimmedString, StringPointer, 1)
        If CurrentChar = Chr(34) Then
            If GotQuote=true Then 'end of parsed item
                StringArray(ArrayPointer) = ParsedString
                ParsedString = ""
                GotQuote = False
                NumElements = ArrayPointer  ' number of strings
                ArrayPointer = ArrayPointer + 1
            Else
                GotQuote = True
                ParsedString = "" ' reset parsed string
            End If
        Else
            ParsedString = ParsedString + CurrentChar
            ' concatenate current parsed string
        End If
    Next
End If
```

If you always start at the beginning of the string to search, and always use case-insensitive searches, you can make a simpler function easily:

```
Function FindString(SearchString as string, Pattern as string)_
as integer
FindString=InStr(1,SearchString,Pattern,1)
End Function
```

This new function is easy to use, and helps demonstrate how easy it is in NS Basic to modify the language to fit your needs.

ReverseString

Let's end this chapter with an exercise (you didn't think you were going to get away without doing any work, did you?). Write a function that will take any string and produce a mirror-image string (one with the characters reversed from their original position, like "popcorn" -> "nrocpop"). Don't peek at my solution – try writing yours first, then compare it with mine here:

```
Function ReverseString(UserString as String) as String
Dim CharPointer as Integer
Dim TempString as String
TempString=""
For CharPointer=len(UserString) to 1 step -1
   TempString=TempString+mid(UserString,CharPointer,1)
Next
ReverseString=TempString
End Function
```

But wait – there's more!

There are a large number of functions available for working with strings in the NSBStringLib shared library, available with the full, registered version of NS Basic. Not only does this library add additional functions, they're also considerably faster than the code shown above, since they're written in C. Get comfortable with the built-in functions first, then look to the NSBStringLib for the missing functions. You won't be disappointed!

Chapter XII – Date and Time functions

It's quite possible that many (if not most) of your applications will never need to deal with time and date functions, and you can be a very successful NS Basic programmer, even without these functions – but what fun would that be? After all, you're interacting with real people who have real schedules and time constraints, so even if all you do is place a simple time and date display in your app, you'll be giving your user something extra. And the little extras mean a lot.

> **Note** In the Palm Prefs app, under the category Formats, you can tell the Palm how you want time, date, and numbers displayed, along with which day starts your week. You can use presets for various countries, or decide your own. Unfortunately (or fortunately, depending on how you look at it), the built-in NS Basic Format statement doesn't use this information. You have to decide your own formats. I personally prefer things that way, but I don't write programs that I expect this will cause much concern. However, if you're writing financial, calendar, or other apps that make heavy use of this information, you may find this a little upsetting. However, NS Basic is flexible enough to allow you to use your own formatting, so this shouldn't be too great a hurdle. Also, by using the NSBSystemLib (see the chapter "Extending NS Basic", and the NS Basic Tech Notes), you can determine the decimal and thousands separators, and use them in your apps. Eventually NS Basic will probably use the Palm Prefs to automatically format these items, but for now you're in control – like it or not!

Before you get started with NS Basic time and date manipulations, it helps to know how that the Palm OS deals with dates and times as the number of seconds lapsed since midnight (00:00) January 1, 1904. Don't ask me why – I didn't make the rules. Just accept this little fact, and move on. Besides, NS Basic doesn't store dates and times this way, which is a blessing and a curse. You'll see why later.

> **Caution** A warning about dates is important here, for those who didn't learn from the Y2K experience. Many of the NS Basic functions for date manipulation will accept either two- or four-digit years. To save space,

programmers have been in the habit of saving only two-digit dates –
with disastrous results when the year 2000 came around. No – toasters
didn't forget how to toast, refrigerators didn't forget how to refrigerate,
and planes didn't all drop from the sky. However, it's been estimated
that well over 10 million dollars (how do people estimate these things,
anyway?) was spend modifying or replacing existing software to handle
date conversions correctly. There's another similar software problem
coming in 2029, as many software packages interpret two-digit years
00-28 as indicating years 2000-2028, with the two-digit years 29-99 as
1929-1999. Be sure that you have control over which decade you refer
to if you decide to use two-digit years. Better still, I STRONGLY
suggest that you use only four-digit years, and avoid the confusion
altogether!

NS Basic has date and time variables that don't correspond exactly to any other
variable type. Instead, they are based on the following calculations:

```
'not NSBasic code, just descriptions
Date=(Year-1900)*10000+Month*100+Day
Time=Hour*10000+Minute*100+Second
```

Although NS Basic stores the date and time internally in the above formats, database
input/output uses a 64-bit value.

Confused? These concepts *can* be a bit hard to grasp at first. So, instead of mixing
the explanations for date and time, we'll discuss dates first, then time later (and you'll see
significant similarities between the two).

Date Functions

NS Basic has a large number of functions for manipulating dates – so many, in fact,
that you can easily get overwhelmed by them. However, we'll group them together so
you can get a feel for how they fit together in the grand scheme of things. Most of the
functions have "mirror" functions – allowing you to convert from dates to strings and
back again, etc.

A natural place for me to start is with the functions that convert back and forth
between NS Basic's internal date format and the more conventional string formats (for
easy display, for instance). Then we'll move on to extracting the various components of
the date (year, month, and day), see how to add or subtract dates, and last of all how to
access the built-in Palm Calendar and Time pickers.

Today

Syntax:

> **Today()**

Description:

> **Returns the current date from the Palm device**

By the way – what day is today? You can find out by looking at a calendar, of course, but why not have NS Basic tell you instead using the Today() statement:

```
Dim DateToday as date
DateToday=Today()
```

The Today() statement will return the current date from the Palm device, in NS Basic date format.

DateMMDDYY, YearMonth and MonthDay

Syntax:

> **DateMMDDYY(DateVar)**
> **YearMonth(DateVar)**
> **MonthDay(DateVar)**

Description:

> **Returns a string in MM/DD/YY, MM/DD/YYYY, YY/MM, or MM/DD format from a date value**

You can easily convert date values it into the more recognizable "MM/DD/YY" string format using the DateMMDDYY function:

```
Dim DateToday as date
Dim DisplayDate as string
DateToday=Today()
DisplayDate=DateMMDDYY(DateToday)
Msgbox "Today's date: "+DisplayDate
```

You say all you want are the year and month, or month and day? This is easy too, using YearMonth and MonthDay:

```
Dim DateToday as date
DateToday=Today()
Msgbox "Year and month: "+YearMonth(DateToday)
Msgbox "Month and day: "+MonthDay(DateToday)
```

Year, Month, and Day

Syntax:

> **Year(DateVar)**
> **Month(DateVar)**
> **Day(DateVar)**

Description:

> **Returns the year, month, or day from a date variable**

But, what if all you want is the Year, Month, or Day? The following code won't work:

```
Dim DateToday as date
DateToday=Today()
Msgbox "Current Year:"+Year(DateToday)
' compiler catches this error
Msgbox "Current Month:"+Month(DateToday) ' ...and this also...
Msgbox "Current Day:"+Day(DateToday) ' ...and this...
```

So, what's the problem? Although DateMMDDYY, YearMonth, and MonthDay return strings, the functions for Year, Month, and Day return integers (see why this can start getting a little confusing?). The proper (although not too pretty) syntax, therefore, is:

```
Dim DateToday as date
DateToday=Today()
Msgbox "Current Year:"+str(Year(DateToday))
Msgbox "Current Month:"+str(Month(DateToday))
Msgbox "Current Day:"+str(Day(DateToday))
```

Although using integers for the individual year, month, and day doesn't fit with the string conversions, it does make it easy to perform arithmetic operations, like adding to or subtracting from a date to determine a future date. However, NS Basic makes that even easier as well, with specific functions for adding or subtracting years, months, and days. But we'll cover that later...

MMDDYYtoDate and ToDate

Syntax:

> **MMDDYYtoDate("mm/dd/yyyy")**
> **or**
> **MMDDYYtoDate("mm/dd/yy")**
> **ToDate("yyyy/mm/dd")**
> **or**
> **ToDate("yy/mm/dd")**

Description:

> **Returns a date value from a date string**

To convert a string date to NS Basic date format, MMDDYYtoDate allows you to use either MM/DD/YY or MM/DD/YYYY format:

```
Dim CurDate as Date
CurDate=MMDDYYtoDate("09/08/2001")
CurDate=MMDDYYtoDate("09/08/01")
' make sure you control the century!
```

Similarly, the ToDate function allows you to generate a NS Basic date variable from a string date in YYYY/MM/DD or YY/MM/DD format:

```
Dim CurDate as Date
CurDate=ToDate("2001/09/08")
CurDate=ToDate("01/09/08")
' once again, make sure you control the century!
```

DateVal

Syntax:

DateVal(Year,Month,Day)

Description:

Returns a date value from individual year, month, and day values

I told you that we can convert back and forth between date variable and other variable types, so here are the functions to go from integer to date variable type. To generate a date from individual year, month, and day integers, use DateVal:

```
Dim CurrentDate as Date
Dim CurYear as Integer
Dim CurMonth as Integer
Dim CurDay as Integer
CurYear=2001 ' you could use 01, but avoid using 2-digit years
CurMonth=9
CurDay=8
CurrentDate=DateVal(CurYear, CurMonth, CurDay)
```

You can even directly manipulate the individual date variables, making it easy to take two dates and subtract them to get the number of years, months, and days lapsed:

```
Dim Date1 as Date
Dim Date2 as Date
Dim Lapsed as Date
Dim YearsLapsed as Integer
Dim MonthsLapsed as Integer
Dim DaysLapsed as Integer
Date2=MMDDYYtoDate(fldEndDate.text)
Date1=MMDDYYtoDate(fldStartDate.text)
Lapsed=Date2-Date1
YearsLapsed=Year(Lapsed)-1900
MonthsLapsed=Month(Lapsed)
DaysLapsed=Day(Lapsed)
fldYearsLapsed.text=str(YearsLapsed)
fldMonthsLapsed.text=str(MonthsLapsed)
fldDaysLapsed.text=str(DaysLapsed)
```

AddYears, AddMonths, AddDays, SubtractYears, SubtractMonths, and SubtractDays

Syntax:

AddYears(DateVar, YearsToAdd)
AddMonths(DateVar,MonthsToAdd)
AddDays(DateVar, DaysToAdd)
SubtractYears(DateVar, YearsToSubtract)
SubtractMonths(DateVar, MonthsToSubtract)
SubtractDays(DateVar, DaysToSubtract)

Description:

Returns a date value by adding or subtracting years, months, or days from a given date

In addition to determining the difference between two dates, you can directly add or subtract years, months, and days using – you guessed it – the NS Basic functions AddYears, AddMonths, AddDays, SubtractYears, SubtractMonths, and SubtractDays:

```
Dim CurDate as date
Dim PrevDate as date
Dim FutureDate as date
CurDate=Today()
FutureDate=AddYears(CurDate,2) ' the date 2 years from now
FutureDate=AddMonths(CurDate,3) ' or 3 months from now
FutureDate=AddDays(CurDate,14) ' or 2 weeks from now
PrevDate=SubtractYears(CurDate,10) ' what was it a decate ago?
PrevDate=SubtractMonths(CurDate,3) ' ...3 months ago?
PrevDate=SubtractDays(CurDate,7) ' ...or last week?
```

DayOfWeek, DayOfYear, FirstOfMonth, and LastOfMonth

Syntax:

DayOfWeek(DateVar)
DayOfYear(DateVar)
FirstOfMonth(DateVar)
LastOfMonth(DateVar)

Description:

Returns an integer (DayOfWeek, DayOfYear) or date value (FirstOfMonth, LastOfMonth) based on a given date

NS Basic even includes functions for determining the day of the week, day of the year, and even the first or last day of any given month:

```
Dim UserDate as Date
Dim MonthStart as Date
Dim MonthEnd as Date
Dim Weekday as Integer
Dim DayName (7) as string
DayName (1)="Sunday"
DayName (2)="Monday"
```

```
DayName (3)="Tuesday"
DayName (4)="Wednesday"
' bet you thought I was going to misspell this, right?
DayName (5)="Thursday"
DayName (6)="Friday"
DayName (7)="Saturday"
UserDate=Today()
Weekday=DayOfWeek(UserDate) ' 1=Sunday, 7=Saturday
Msgbox "Today is "+DayName(Weekday)
Msgbox "Day number: " +str(DayOfYear(UserDate)) ' from 1-365
MonthStart=FirstOfMonth(UserDate)
Msgbox "The first of the month is "+DateMMDDYY(MonthStart)
MonthEnd=LastOfMonth(UserDate)
Msgbox "and the end of the month is "+DateMMDDYY(MonthEnd)
```

You'll notice that all of these examples so far either use a "hard-coded" date, or one obtained from a field in your app. Unfortunately, if you use the "field" approach, you have to rely on your user entering the date in a particular format. You could always force your date format on the user, or write code to parse the date (very difficult to anticipate all different variations).

PopupDate

Syntax:

PopupDate(DateVar, PromptString)

Description:

Returns a user-selected date

To help you out, the Palm OS has a built-in calendar, or "date picker":

You can access this date picker from NS Basic, using the PopupDate function:

```
Dim UserDate as Date
Dim Result as Integer
UserDate=Today()
```

```
Result=PopupDate(UserDate,"Select date")
If Result=1 then
   'user has selected a different date
Else
   'user has not changed the date
End If
```

You can then take whatever action is appropriate, knowing that the date will be in a standard format.

> **Tip** Note that the PopupDate function expects a valid date as its first parameter (we mentioned this before when we looked at the Selector trigger). A common mistake is to forget to initialize the date parameter, expecting the user to select a valid date. PopupDate will not work properly unless the function is called with a valid date. You should also provide a short prompt for your user as well, like the "Select date" prompt used above.

DateDiff

One of the most requested functions in NS Basic is one that takes two dates, and determines the difference in days between them. The following code (from the NS Basic message base) performs this calculation, and returns the difference as an integer:

```
Function DateDiff(D1 as Date, D2 as Date) as Integer
' This function returns days between two dates.
' it assumes Year(D1)<=Year(D2)
Dim Y1 as Integer
Dim Y2 as Integer
Dim I as Integer
Dim NumDays as Integer
Y1 = Year(D1)
Y2 = Year(D2)
If Y1 = Y2 Then
   'If the same year, just return day difference
   DateDiff = DayOfYear(D2) - DayOfYear(D1)
Else
   'If more than one year, add all years before current year.
   For I = Y1 to Y2-1
      NumDays = NumDays + DayOfYear(DateVal(I, 12, 31) )
   Next
   DateDiff = (NumDays + DayOfYear(D2)) - DayOfYear(D1)
End If
End Function
```

Time Functions

As I mentioned earlier, NS Basic time manipulation functions are similar to the date functions, at least in concept: NS Basic stores the time in an internal format, and provides functions to convert between this format and more standard string and integer formats. Many of the functions dealing with hours, minutes, and seconds are similar to those for years, months, and days, although there are no functions to add or subtract hours, minutes, or seconds. But, what kind of programming book would this be if I didn't give you a way to work around this? I'll give you functions that you can use for this very purpose.

Delay

Syntax:

Delay Seconds

Description:

Delays program execution for a given number of seconds

NS Basic allows you to specify a delay of any number of seconds, including fractional seconds, through the use of the Delay statement. Use Delay with a floating point number to tell NS Basic to suspend processing for the desired length of time in seconds:

```
Delay 5 ' 5 seconds
Delay 1 ' 1 second
Delay 0.01 ' 1/100 second
```

There is a limit to how precise the Delay will be, and it varies with the speed of the device, and the number of ticks per second the device generates. In addition, the processing of the Delay statement itself takes time, so the following code:

```
For Interval=1 to 100
    Delay 0.01
Next
```

Will produce a delay longer than 1 second, although it appears that it shouldn't. Delay is fine for short pauses, but not ideal for a true "stopwatch" application, or anything else that requires split-second timing.

Now, HourMinAMPM and HourMin

Syntax:

Now()
HourMinAMPM(TimeVar)
HourMin(TimeVar)

Description:

Returns the current time (Now), or formatted time string

To start off with, let's look at the various functions for converting from NS Basic time format to strings. If you want an easy way to display the current time, look no further than the functions Now() and HourMinAMPM:

```
Dim CurTime as time
```

```
CurTime=Now() ' get the current time
Msgbox "The current time is "+HourMinAMPM(CurTime)
Msgbox "The current time is "+HourMinAMPM(Now()) ' combine them
```

Note that this doesn't give us the time with seconds displayed, and there's no HourMinSecAMPM function...so let's build one:

```
Function HourMinSecAMPM(UserTime as Time) as string
HourMinSecAMPM=left(HourMinAMPM(UserTime),5)+":"_
+format(Second(UserTime),"00")+right(HourMinAMPM(UserTime),3)
End Function
```

Of course, if the programmers at NS Basic read this book and create this new function, I'll have to write another book! For now, let's get back to the time conversion functions. There aren't as many of them as there are date conversions, so we'll finish these, and then create the rest of our functions to add to NS Basic.

If you want to use 24-hour time, rather than 12-hour am/pm time, then the HourMin function is for you:

```
Dim CurTime as time
CurTime=Now() ' get the current time
Msgbox "The current time is "+HourMin(CurTime)
Msgbox "The current time is "+HourMin(Now()) ' combine if you want
```

ToTime

Syntax:

> **ToTime("HH:MM")**
> **Or**
> **ToTime("HH:MM:SS")**

Description:

> **Returns a time value from a formatted time string**

Converting from a string in the form HH:MM or HH:MM:SS to the NS Basic internal time format is straightforward using ToTime:

```
Dim UserTime as time
UserTime=ToTime("15:30") ' set the time to 15:30, or 3:30pm
UserTime= ToTime("15:30:15") ' set to 15:30:15, or 3:30:15pm
```

Hour, Minute, and Second

Syntax:

> **Hour(TimeVar)**
> **Minute(TimeVar)**
> **Second(TimeVar)**

Description:

Returns the hour, minute, or second from a given time value

Just as you can extract the Year, Month, and Day using the Date functions, you have access to the Hour, Minute, and Second – also as integers, similar to the Date functions:

```
Dim UserHour as integer
Dim UserMinute as integer
Dim UserSecond as integer
Dim UserTime as time
UserTime=Now()
UserHour=Hour(UserTime)
UserMinute=Minute(UserTime)
UserSecond=Second(UserTime)
```

TimeVal

Syntax:

TimeVal(Hours, Minutes, Seconds)

Description:

Returns a time value from hour, minute, and second values

Going the opposite direction (from integers to time) is just as easy:

```
Dim UserHour as integer
Dim UserMinute as integer
Dim UserSecond as integer
Dim UserTime as time
UserHour=12
UserMinute=30
UserSecond=15
UserTime=TimeVal(UserHour,UserMinute,UserSecond)
```

PopupTime

Syntax:

PopupTime(tStart,EndTime,PromptString)

Description:

Returns user-selected time values

The Palm OS had a date picker (calendar) to make your life easier, so why not a time picker as well? You even get to determine both starting AND ending times!

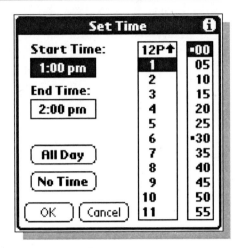

Here's the PopupTime function in action:

```
Dim tStart as time
Dim EndTime as time
Dim Result as integer
tStart=now()
EndTime=now() ' need to have valid times for the next statement
Result=PopupTime(tStart,EndTime,"Select Appointment Times")
If Result=0 then
    'user made no changes, tStart and EndTime remain the same
Else
    'user selected different times
End If
```

AddHours, AddMinutes, AddSeconds, SubtractHours, SubtractMinutes, and SubtractSeconds

As you can see, NS Basic and the Palm OS have a wealth of time and date functions. However, unlike the functions for adding and subtracting date values, there aren't any functions for adding or subtracting hours, minutes, and seconds. For good programming experience you should try to come up with your own routines, but for now here are mine (you'll find these functions in the Time Adjust Demo project and code module "timedate.cod" on the included CD):

```
Function AddHours(tStart as time, UserHours as integer) as Time
Dim SecStart as Integer
Dim EndSeconds as Integer
Dim NewHours as Integer
Dim NewMinutes as Integer
SecStart=second(tStart)+60*(minute(tStart)+60*Hour(tStart))
EndSeconds=SecStart+UserHours*3600
 ' get the new number of seconds
EndSeconds=rem(EndSeconds, 86400)
' this eliminates any excessive days (86400 secs/day)
NewHours=int(EndSeconds/3600) ' get number of hours
EndSeconds=EndSeconds-NewHours*3600 ' remove hours
NewMinutes=int(EndSeconds/60)
EndSeconds=EndSeconds-NewMinutes*60 ' remove minutes
```

```
AddHours=TimeVal(NewHours,NewMinutes,EndSeconds)
End Function


Function AddMinutes(tStart as time, UserMinutes as integer)_
as Time
Dim SecStart as Integer
Dim EndSeconds as Integer
Dim NewHours as Integer
Dim NewMinutes as Integer
SecStart=second(tStart)+60*(minute(tStart)+60*Hour(tStart))
EndSeconds=SecStart+UserMinutes*60
' get the new number of seconds
EndSeconds=rem(EndSeconds, 86400)
' this eliminates any excessive days (86400 secs/day)
NewHours=int(EndSeconds/3600) ' get number of hours
EndSeconds=EndSeconds-NewHours*3600 ' remove hours
NewMinutes=int(EndSeconds/60)
EndSeconds=EndSeconds-NewMinutes*60 ' remove minutes
AddMinutes=TimeVal(NewHours,NewMinutes,EndSeconds)
End Function


Function AddSeconds(tStart as time, UserSeconds as integer)_
as Time
Dim SecStart as Integer
Dim EndSeconds as Integer
Dim NewHours as Integer
Dim NewMinutes as Integer
SecStart=second(tStart)+60*(minute(tStart)+60*Hour(tStart))
EndSeconds=SecStart+UserSeconds ' get the new number of seconds
EndSeconds=rem(EndSeconds, 86400)
' this eliminates any excessive days (86400 secs/day)
NewHours=int(EndSeconds/3600) ' get number of hours
EndSeconds=EndSeconds-NewHours*3600 ' remove hours
NewMinutes=int(EndSeconds/60)
EndSeconds=EndSeconds-NewMinutes*60 ' remove minutes
AddSeconds =TimeVal(NewHours,NewMinutes,EndSeconds)
End Function


Function SubtractHours(tStart as time, UserHours as integer)_
as Time
Dim SecStart as Integer
Dim EndSeconds as Integer
Dim NewHours as Integer
Dim NewMinutes as Integer
SecStart=second(tStart)+60*(minute(tStart)+60*Hour(tStart))
EndSeconds=SecStart-UserHours*3600
' get the new number of seconds
Do while EndSeconds<0 ' correct for negative numbers
   EndSeconds=EndSeconds+86400 ' add one day, check in loop
Loop
If EndSeconds > 86400 then
   EndSeconds=rem(EndSeconds, 86400)
   ' this eliminates any excessive days (86400 secs/day)
End If
NewHours=int(EndSeconds/3600) ' get number of hours
EndSeconds=EndSeconds-NewHours*3600 ' remove hours
```

```
NewMinutes=int(EndSeconds/60)
EndSeconds=EndSeconds-NewMinutes*60 ' remove minutes
SubtractHours=TimeVal(NewHours,NewMinutes,EndSeconds)
End Function

Function SubtractMinutes(tStart as time, UserMinutes as integer)_
as Time
Dim SecStart as Integer
Dim EndSeconds as Integer
Dim NewHours as Integer
Dim NewMinutes as Integer
SecStart=second(tStart)+60*(minute(tStart)+60*Hour(tStart))
EndSeconds=SecStart-UserMinutes*60
' get the new number of seconds
Do while EndSeconds<0 ' correct for negative numbers
   EndSeconds=EndSeconds+86400 ' add one day, check in loop
Loop
If EndSeconds > 86400 then
   EndSeconds=rem(EndSeconds, 86400)
    ' eliminate extra days (86400 secs/day)
End If
NewHours=int(EndSeconds/3600) ' get number of hours
EndSeconds=EndSeconds-NewHours*3600 ' remove hours
NewMinutes=int(EndSeconds/60)
EndSeconds=EndSeconds-NewMinutes*60 ' remove minutes
SubtractMinutes=TimeVal(NewHours,NewMinutes,EndSeconds)
End Function

Function SubtractSeconds(tStart as time, UserSeconds as integer)_
as Time
Dim SecStart as Integer
Dim EndSeconds as Integer
Dim NewHours as Integer
Dim NewMinutes as Integer
SecStart=second(tStart)+60*(minute(tStart)+60*Hour(tStart))
EndSeconds=SecStart-UserSeconds ' get the new number of seconds
Do while EndSeconds<0 ' correct for negative numbers
   EndSeconds=EndSeconds+86400 ' add one day, check in loop
Loop
If EndSeconds > 86400 then
   EndSeconds=rem(EndSeconds, 86400)
    ' this eliminates any excessive days (86400 secs/day)
End If
NewHours=int(EndSeconds/3600) ' get number of hours
EndSeconds=EndSeconds-NewHours*3600 ' remove hours
NewMinutes=int(EndSeconds/60)
EndSeconds=EndSeconds-NewMinutes*60 ' remove minutes
SubtractSeconds =TimeVal(NewHours,NewMinutes,EndSeconds)
End Function
```

Feel free to add these functions to your projects as though they were a part of NS Basic (don't forget to use the Define statement if you place the functions in locations where they will be called before the compile sees the function for the first time).

Chapter XIII - Database Management

Our daily lives are cluttered with data – little bits and pieces of information that we "can't live without." Take a look at the applications that come with the Palm OS devices and you'll see what I mean: a calendar, phone book, memo pad, "to do" list, and more. Add to that the huge number of other data organization programs available, and you'll see why the ability to remain "connected" to our data is what made the Palm devices so popular, and continues to fuel their appeal. Before we discuss the NS Basic database functions, you need to have a firm grasp on the format of Palm databases. It's not that they're terribly complex. It's actually their simplicity that stumps most beginning NS Basic programmers. If you've ever done database programming before, try to forget everything you've ever learned. We'll come back later and see how we can apply the old concepts to Palm databases.

As I mentioned previously, Palm databases are quite simple. They begin with a database header that you don't really need to know a thing about, except that it's there. There are some special areas of the database header that deal with application and sorting information, but NS Basic doesn't currently use this information, so you're isolated from it anyway.

Following the header are the database's records, with each record composed of one or more fields. The Palm OS doesn't care what's in these records and fields – as far as Palm is concerned, databases are simply *groups of bytes* separated into records and fields. In fact, when you read the data, there's no way to know what each byte in each field stands for. That's not *really* true, because in many cases string data will be easy to spot. What I'm trying to stress is that you don't need to have a preset format for the fields in each record. In fact, any record in any database can contain any type of data – string, data, integer, float, array, UDT, date/time – any type at all. We'll start with string data, since it's easier to picture, and it's handled somewhat differently than the other data types.

I said before that Palm databases were simply groups of bytes. While that's true, it's important to remember that strings are stored and written with a chr(0) as a null terminator. Whether in memory or as fields in databases, strings retain this format. So, the string "NS Basic" would be represented as:

NS Basic/

Each character takes one byte, with "/" representing the extra null byte at the end (I'm using the slash to represent the null character, since using 0 might be confused with the character 0). You don't have to worry about this extra null byte when writing the data, since NS Basic writes it for you. Similarly, when you read the data as a string, NS Basic will read each character until it comes to the null character. If a record contains multiple string fields, each will be terminated with the same null character. Multiple records written to a phonebook database might contain fields of last name, first name, address, city, state, zip code, and phone number:

Doe/John/123 Main St./Anywhere/IL/61234/3125551212/
Gates/Bill/111 Microsoft Way/Silicon Valley/CA/90211/9195551212/

Although string data is written with a null terminator, numeric, date, and time values are written using the exact number of bytes necessary to represent them (the list of data types and their size used during database input and output is listed in the help file and manual under the Dim statement). Since NS Basic knows the length that these various data types use, when reading the data you'll need to tell NS Basic what type of data to expect, so it can read the correct number of bytes for each field.

NS Basic provides a powerful set of database manipulation functions that allow you to access records sequentially (forwards or backwards), by record position ("non-keyed" access), and based on the contents of a data field ("keyed" access):

NS Basic Database Functions

Function	Description
DbCreate	Creates a database in the Palm OS device's memory
DbErase	Removes a database from the Palm OS device's memory
DbOpen	Opens a database and initializes it for processing
DbClose	Closes an open database
DbGetNoRecs	Returns the number of records in a database
DbPosition	Locates a database record by record number
DbGet	Reads data from the current database record
DbPut	Writes data to the current database record
DbReset	Resets a database to the beginning record
DbFind	Finds a database record by key
DbInsert	Inserts a new record in a database by key
DbDelete	Deletes a database record by key
DbRead	Reads a database record by key
DbReadNext	Reads the next database record
DbReadPrev	Reads the previous database record

DbUpdate	Updates the contents of a database record by key

Before you actually write data to a database, you must create it. That is, before the Palm OS let's you write data to the database, you need to tell it to allocate some space. At this point, neither you nor the Palm OS need to know how much data is going to be written, or what format it's going to be. However, the Palm OS *does* need to know the Creator ID of the program that writes the data, and the memory card that you are writing the database on.

> **Note** Initially the Palm OS only supported a single memory card – card 0, which refers to the main system memory. Many applications assume that this will always be so, and use the card number of 0 as a hard-coded literal value, rather than a variable. Palm advises against this, and suggests that programmers use a variable for the card number. Since we want out apps to be as compatible as possible with future versions of the Palm OS, we'll use variables for the card number.

Why does the Palm OS need to know what program uses the data? Does that mean that only one application can read a database? We'll see later that the answer to the second question is "no", so we'll answer the first question: the Palm OS uses the Creator ID to associate databases with their applications when showing how much memory (and how many records) are used by the application. Additionally, when you delete an application using the Palm OS launcher, databases that have the same Creator ID as the application being deleted are removed from memory as well. This help avoid leaving "orphaned" databases when applications are no longer needed, leaving as much memory for remaining applications as possible.

Creating Databases

So, let's create our first database, and I'll discuss each step as we go. Using the KeyedDBPhone, a keyed phonebook app that was one of my first projects, here's code that I use to create the phonebook database (slightly modified for this chapter):

```
Global testdb as Database
Global result as Integer
Global dbPhoneBook as String
Global CreatorID as String
CreatorID="NKPb"
dbPhoneBook="phonebook"
result=dbcreate(testdb,dbPhonebook,0,CreatorID)    ' create_
the database
If result Not= 0 Then
    MsgBox "Error "+str(result)+ " creating phonebook database"
    Exit Sub ' can't continue without database
End If
```

The first line - Dim testdb as Database - is used to create a variable that will be used to refer to the database during subsequent statements. The **testdb** variable is a "handle" that the Palm OS links to the actual database, rather than referring to the database by name. You'll use this handle with every database function – there are no native NS Basic functions for database manipulation that don't require the use of handles.

The other variables are created for returning error codes, and setting up the Creator ID and phonebook names. I could have used the literal values "Kphb" and "phonebook" for the Creator ID and database names, but these variables are used elsewhere in the application, so creating them as Global variables makes them available in the entire app. Using literals in multiple locations increases the likelihood of typing errors.

DbCreate

Syntax:

DbCreate(DatabaseVar,Name,CardNo,CreatorID)

Description:

Creates a database in the Palm OS device's memory

With NS Basic's DbCreate statement, DatabaseVar is a variable of type "database" (often referred to as a database *handle* – see below), Name is the string name for the database (no longer than 31 characters), CardNo is an integer used for the memory card (usually 0), and CreatorID is the 4-character Creator ID of the application that creates the database.

> **Tip** Three important points: 1) the database "handle" is used to refer to the database once it's created and opened, rather than use the name each time, 2) the Creator ID should match the Creator ID of the app, and 3) the database name and Creator ID are case-sensitive. The first point is optional – you could make the Creator ID any 4 characters that you want (between ASCII 33-127), but for consistency it's best to have the databases and applications use the same Creator ID, as mentioned previously. Point 3 is something you should etch into your brain. You'd be surprised how easy it is to forget this simple principle!

So, the line:

```
result=dbcreate(testdb,dbPhonebook,0,CreatorID)
```

creates the "phonebook" database with CreatorID of "Kphb" in memory card 0. Actually, all that's created is the header – there's no data yet. Once the database is created, you can't change the Creator ID without completely removing the database and creating it again with a different Creator ID. Note that the next few lines check to see if the result is successful (as with most of the database statements, dbCreate returns a code of 0 if successful. There are only a couple exceptions to this rule, which we'll discuss when we get to them). There's not a lot of incredible error-checking here, simply a message telling my user that there's an error, what the error number is, and then the subroutine exits. Since the program can't continue without a database, we might as well leave if we can't create one.

> **Tip** Yes, even simple programs like this need error-checking. In fact, make it a point to check the result of every database statement, at

least during your initial programming and debugging. Little errors can always creep into any app, and some users delight in crashing applications! Trapping errors and responding to them will not only make your programs more robust (able to handle errors gracefully), but you can avoid a lot of wasted time debugging your apps when you can pinpoint the problem spots.

Of course, there's at least one good reason why the dbCreate could fail, yet you'd still want to continue – when the database already exists! So, maybe it's not a good idea to ignore all errors. If you look at the common results (errors?) returned in database operations, you'll see that result 537 occurs when the database already exists (a more comprehensive list is included in the ehlp file and manual - these are the codes you're most likely to see):

Common result codes returned from database functions

Code	Description
-1	EOF on DbGet
0	Operation Successful
1	Operation Failed
2	Key not found - next higher key returned
3	Database open in read-only mode
513	Memory Error
514	Index Out Of Range
517	Database Open
519	Can't Find
532	Write Out Of Bounds
534	Already Open For Writes
537	Already Exists
538	Invalid Database Name

Perhaps a better way to handle the code would be:

```
Global testdb as Database
Global result as Integer
Global dbPhoneBook as String
Global CreatorID as String
CreatorID="NKPb"
dbPhoneBook="phonebook"
result=dbcreate(testdb,dbPhonebook,0,CreatorID)   ' create_
the database
If (result Not= 0) and (result Not= 537) Then
    MsgBox "Error "+str(result)+ " creating phonebook database"
```

```
    Exit Sub ' can't continue without database
End If
```

Another approach, and one I used in the phonebook app, is to attempt to open the database first (we'll cover opening next, but I wanted to discuss this logic now). If you can open it, then it exists (OK, so that's a little obvious!). If you can't open the database, the next step would be to try to create it. If creating the database fails as well, there's not much else you can do about the situation, so it's safest to bail out at that time. This code is part of the routine that writes data to the phonebook. If the phonebook database exists, it's opened. If it doesn't exist, it's created, then opened. If the phonebook can't be opened (or created, then opened) the routine exits with a message to the user:

```
result=dbOpen(testdb,Phonebook,CardNo)  ' open database
If result Not= 0 Then ' Phonebook not found, so we'll...
    result=dbcreate(testdb,Phonebook,CardNo,CreatorID)
    ' ...create the database
    If result Not= 0 Then
        MsgBox "Error "+str(result)+ " creating phonebook database"
        Exit Sub ' can't continue without database
    End If
    result=dbOpen(testdb,Phonebook,CardNo) ' open database
End If
```

Other common errors that can occur with database creation include attempting to create a database with an invalid Creator ID (one that doesn't contain 4 characters in the range of ASCII 33-127), an invalid name (greater that 31 alphanumeric characters), an invalid memory card number, or insufficient memory.

Now that you know what these errors are, you'll avoid them, right?

Opening Databases

Once the database has been created, you need to open it successfully before you can do anything else with it. In the examples above, I introduced the dbOpen command.

DbOpen

Syntax:

DbOpen(DatabaseVar,Name,CardNo)

Description:

Opens a database in the Palm's memory

As we've previously seen, the DatabaseVar handle is a variable of type "database" that's used to identify the database, name is a case-sensitive alphanumeric string no longer than 31 characters long, and CardNo is the memory card number that the database is located on. Each of these variables can be previously declared using the Global statement, so you can access the database anywhere in your application without having to specify the name and card number each time.

But, wait a minute! Where's the Creator ID?

Well, it turns out that you only specify the Creator ID when the database is created, since it's assumed that the application that creates the database will be the one using the data, and therefore should logically be associated with it. You can't read it or modify it later, and none of the other database management commands use it, so once the database is written, you can forget about the Creator ID in the rest of your application.

When you attempt to open a database using dbOpen, there are a number of possible return codes (see above). In general, as with dbCreate, there are only a couple codes that you can accept in your application. The first code – 0 – indicates that the database open was successful. Other possibly acceptable codes would be those in which you had previously opened the database.

> **Note** I say that these are *possibly* acceptable, since you might have already opened the database in a previous section of code, and accidentally tried to open it again. However, in my opinion you *must* always maintain control over your databases – no exceptions! Careful attention to when databases are opened and closed will help you avoid these situations. Some programmers open all databases in the program startup code, and close them in the termination code, which for most applications will be the safest bet. However, there will be cases when you will want to close and reopen a database. As usual, we'll cover those situations as we get to them.

Attempting to access a database without having successfully opened it can cause unpredictable results, and by now you know how I feel about unpredictable applications! Protect yourself and your users by taking control of all aspects of database management.

Closing and Erasing Databases

I know what you're probably thinking – "We haven't done anything with the database, and he wants to close it already!" Well, since there are multiple ways to access the data for reading and writing (sequential, non-keyed, and keyed), I thought I'd finish the two database operations left that remain constant – closing and erasing databases.

DbClose

Syntax:

DbClose(DatabaseVar)

Description:

Closes a previously opened database

As with all other database operations, closing and erasing databases require the use of a database handle, and return a result code:

```
Dim result as integer
Dim dbFH as database
'code here that opens the database, performs some actions...
result=dbClose(dbFH)
```

It's highly unlikely that you'll ever need to check the result of the dbClose command – but that doesn't mean that you shouldn't. Even if you've followed my previous advice on always maintaining control over database operations, there's always the chance that some stray code gets introduced (especially if you decide to try copying code from one project to another, or you have database functions in code modules). The most likely error would occur if you tried to close a database that hadn't been opened yet (if at all). But, that's not going to happen, is it???

DbErase

Syntax:

> **DbErase(DatabaseVar)**

Description:

> **Removes a database from Palm memory**

Erasing a database is just as simple:

```
Dim result as integer
Dim dbFH as database
'code here that opens the database, performs some actions...
result=dbClose(dbFH)   ' must close it before we erase it
result=dbErase(dbFH)
```

Erasing a database doesn't simply erase the database's contents – it removes it from memory. Note that the database must be closed before it can be erased. Oddly enough, you also can't erase a database unless it has been opened at least once. Of course, it must also actually exist to be erased as well. Neither of these last two conditions are likely to be much of a problem if you've maintained appropriate database control.

With dbErase you can erase any database (except those in ROM). Any database at all. *Any database*.

Why am I repeating myself? Have I been drinking too much coffee? Have I been writing so long that I'm losing my grip on reality?

Remember when we discussed the fact that Palm applications are, in fact, a special type of database? Well, with respect to dbErase, Palm applications are handled the same as standard databases. Since dbErase requires a handle for the application/database, you'll need to use dbOpen followed by dbClose, the dbErase. For example, to remove the application with the name "test":

```
Dim dbFH as database
Dim result as integer
result=dbOpen(dbFH,"test",0)
result=dbClose(dbFH)
result=dbErase(dbFH)
```

Note that in order for this to work, the application must have an internal name of "test", which is usually the same as the name in the Launcher (but not always). I can't think of too many instances where this would be useful, but if you are writing a utility like ZarfCatalog, the ability to delete any Palm database may come in handy. This power has a price, though, so use it wisely!

Caution Before we move on, a word or two on opening and closing databases. With the current Palm devices, leaving databases open throughout an application can help speed up program operation, but I personally think it's a bad idea. My experience has shown that applications are most likely to crash when users enter bad (or unexpected) data, so I usually try to close databases while waiting for user input, then open them only as needed. Although this increases program complexity and size, it can save data from being lost if a program crashes before a disk cache writes data. Since the Palm devices don't currently use hard disks or caching systems, this may be a little paranoia on my part. I'd still rather be safe than sorry.

Data Access – a Parting of the Ways

I mentioned earlier that Palm databases could be accessed sequentially, by record position, and by the use of a "key" field. I'll cover access by record position, since it's the easiest to implement (in theory, at least), and because it has the fewest commands. This form of access is known as "non-keyed" access in NS Basic circles, where access by key is referred to as "keyed" access. Sequential access can be performed with either method.

Non-keyed Database Access

If you look at databases as containing tables of information, and divide the tables into horizontal rows and vertical columns, you've got non-keyed access (direct access by position) half-way understood. Let's explore writing the data that we used previously by creating a simple phonebook application. You can load the application into NS Basic, and read along, or create a new project, and type along with me to create the application one line at a time. It's your choice, but if this is your first app (the "Hello, World!" app doesn't really count!), I suggest creating the app from scratch. Start the IDE, create a new project, and give it whatever name and Creator ID you like – I use "Non-Keyed Phonebook" for the name, and "NKPb" as the Creator ID. We'll give our application a suitable bitmap to use as an icon, so right click on the Bitmaps folder in the Project Explorer, select "Add Bitmap", and select a bitmap from the NS Basic Bitmap directory – I selected the "crdfle05.bmp" bitmap, since it looks like cards from a card file. Place the ID for this bitmap in the "ID, Large Icon" property for the project.

Tip Tip #1: Don't remember what each bitmap looks like? You could use a program like Print Shop Pro (one of the accessory programs on the CD) to print a "catalog" of graphic images. However, if you have the Windows "Quick View" installed, you can right click on a bitmap, choose "Quick View", and preview the bitmap from within the "Open Bitmap" dialog. You can also right click on the bitmap and choose "Open" to open the bitmap with the system's default viewer for that type of bitmap. Some versions of Windows allow you to preview the bitmaps while you're browsing, which is even better. A graphic preview would be a great addition to NS Basic, but until then, try the options mentioned above.

Tip ▌ **Tip #2**: Now would be a good time to copy all of the bitmaps from the CD to the NS Basic Bitmaps subdirectory, if you haven't done so already. I've included all of the default bitmaps, plus some of my own, and you don't want to have to search everywhere for them, or get the "bitmap not found" error during compilation!

Not too clever or imaginative, but to the point. We'll place the following code in the project's Startup Code section to declare our global variables and perform the initial database creation and opening process. Error-checking has been left out for now, to keep things simple, but we'll add it later:

```
Global dbFH as Database
' use global variables, since the app will need to access
' these variables from any form
Global result as Integer
Global CardNo as Integer
Global dbName as String
CardNo=0
dbName="NKphonebook"
result=dbCreate(dbFH,dbName, CardNo," NKPb")
result=dbOpen(dbFH,dbName,CardNo)
```

Writing Data

Now that we have the database open, we need to write our data. Since this is non-keyed access, we need to tell the Palm OS where we want the data written. Although you might think that it's pretty obvious that we want to start at the beginning, the Palm OS doesn't know this, so we have to be explicit.

DbPosition

Syntax:

DbPosition(DatabaseVar,RecordNum,Offset)

Description:

Sets the record pointer for subsequent database access

The dbPosition statement has three arguments – the database handle, record number, and offset. Although the handle and record number should be pretty straightforward to you by now, the offset is a new concept. Offset is the number of bytes into the record that we want to go to write our data, starting at the beginning of the record. The first field in the record is at offset 0, so our data starts there.

```
result=dbPosition(dbFH,RecordNumber,0)
```

Caution ▌ You might wonder what happens if you attempt to use dbPosition with invalid record number or offset. If the *record* number you wish to write to refers to a non-existent record, the Palm OS creates empty records for the missing, or "skipped" records, and goes happily on its way. However, use an *offset* that's invalid, and you'll get a fatal error, since the offset would be pointing into a different record – and that's not allowed!

DbPut

Syntax:

DbPut(DatabaseVar,arg1[,arg2][,arg3][...])

Description:

Writes a record to a database

Once we've decided where we want our data, we'll write it using dbPut. Data will be written with the appropriate number of bytes according to the data type (see Dim for details). If the data is a string, it will be written with a null-terminator. So, to write "Doe" for the first field of the first record:

```
result=dbPut(dbFH,"Doe")
```

Once you've written the first field, subsequent fields can be written without explicitly using the dbPosition statement:

```
result=dbPut(dbFH,"John")
result=dbPut(dbFH,"123 Main St.")
result=dbPut(dbFH,"Anywhere")
result=dbPut(dbFH,"IL")
result=dbPut(dbFH,"61234")
result=dbPut(dbFH,"3125551212")
```

I know what you're thinking, and you're right! You shouldn't have to write each field separately, should you? Luckily, dbPut allows you to write all fields at once:

```
result=dbPut(dbFH, "Doe","John","123 Main St.", "Anywhere", "IL",
"61234", "3125551212")
```

Similarly, you could put the data into variables, and write them instead of using the literal values:

```
Global LastName as String
Global FirstName as String
Global Address as String
Global City as String
Global State as String
Global Zip as String
Global Phone as String
LastName="Doe"
```

```
FirstName="John"
Address="123 Main St."
City="Anywhere"
State="IL"
Zip="61234"
Phone="3125551212"
result=dbPut(dbFH,LastName,FirstName,Address,City,State,Zip,Phone)
```

> **Tip** Although this phonebook application only uses string data, any of the other variable types can be written – and read – using NS Basic non-keyed or keyed access methods. Since the Palm OS doesn't care what gets put in any field of any record, you need to be sure that you read database information using the same variable types as were used during writing. If you write integers, read integers. If you write floating point numbers, read them back as floating point. UDT's, arrays, and any other variable type can be written and read using NS Basic.

You could then repeat this code for each additional phonebook entry that you wish to enter, incrementing the record number used in the dbPosition statement.

> **Caution** You may have noticed that you can write multiple fields without having to use dbPosition to tell NS Basic where each field gets written. In NS Basic, all data written using dbPut will be considered part of the current record until you change the record number using dbPosition. Twenty records, each containing twenty fields would then be written as one 400 field record! There are times you might want to do this (transferring one record of 400 fields during a HotSync operation is considerably faster than transferring twenty records of twenty fields), but be sure this is what you had in mind!

We'll use a variable to hold the record number, since we'll need this later. After the StartUp code writes the first three entries to the phonebook, we'll close the database. Since the application is going to be used more than once, we'll check to see if we can open the database first, and if not, then create it and write the first three items. The completed code for this portion of the phonebook, placed in the application's StartUp code:

```
Global dbFH as Database ' use global to access from any form
Global result as Integer
Global CardNo as Integer
Global dbName as String
Global RecordNumber as Integer
Global NumRecs as Integer
Global LastName as String
Global FirstName as String
Global Address as String
Global City as String
Global State as String
Global Zip as String
Global Phone as String
CardNo=0
dbName="NKphonebook"
Result=dbOpen(dbFH,dbName,CardNo)
```

```
If result<>0 Then
    result=dbCreate(dbFH,dbName, CardNo,"NKPb").
    result=dbOpen(dbFH,dbName,CardNo)
    RecordNumber=1
    result=dbPosition(dbFH,RecordNumber,0)
    result=dbPut(dbFH, "Doe","John",_
    "123 Main St.","Anywhere","IL","61234","3125551212")
    RecordNumber=2
    result=dbPosition(dbFH,RecordNumber,0)
    result=dbPut(dbFH,"McDonald","Ronald",_
    "555 Hamburger Ln.","Milwaukee","WI","54333","9205551212")
    RecordNumber=3
    result=dbPosition(dbFH,RecordNumber,0)
    result=dbPut(dbFH,"Gates","Bill",_
    "111 Microsoft Way","Silicon Valley","CA",_
    "90211","9195551212")
End If
result=dbClose(dbFH)
```

Since we're going to allow our users to add their own data, let's create fields on the main form to accept the data. We'll name these fields fldLastName, fldFirstName, fldAddress, fldCity, fldState, fldZip, and fldPhone. Since the data in the fields might be longer than the physical fields, we'll set the Dynamic Size properties to True. Also, since most of the data will be capitalized, we'll set the AutoShift property to True for the fields (except for the ZIP and Phone fields). We'll put labels on the form in front of the fields so the user knows where everything goes. Add a useful form title, and a Shift Indicator to the form, and we're almost ready. Place a Button on the form with the label "Write New" to allow your users to save the data. The code for the button will start like this:

```
result=dbOpen(dbFH,dbName,CardNo)
NumRecs=dbGetNoRecs(dbFH)
RecordNumber=NumRecs+1
```

DbGetNoRecs

Syntax:

DbGetNoRecs(DatabaseVar)

Description:

Returns the number of records in a Palm database

This introduces the dbGetNoRecs statement. After a database has been opened, dbGetNoRecs will return the number of records in the database. Since we'll be adding new records to the phonebook, the next record number will be one greater than the number of records currently in the database. Once we have the new record number, writing the data is a simple matter of setting the database record pointer using dbPosition, then writing the data directly from the form's fields:

```
result=dbPosition(dbFH,RecordNumber,0)
```

```
result=dbPut(dbFH, fldLastName.text, fldFirstName.text,_
fldAddress.text, fldCity.text, fldState.text, fldZip.text,_
fldPhone.text)
```

We'll then give the user some feedback, and close the database:

```
If result=0 then
    MsgBox "Phonebook entry: "+str(RecordNumber)+" written"
Else
    MsgBox "Unable to write phonebook entry"
End if
result=dbClose(dbFH)
```

It's a good idea with an interactive application such as this to give your users appropriate feedback. How else would they know that the information had actually been written to the phonebook database? Without this feedback, your users might think that the app didn't do anything, and they're likely to tap the "Write New" button again, needlessly duplicating data. Here's the completed code for the "Write New" button:

```
result=dbOpen(dbFH,dbName,CardNo)
NumRecs=dbGetNoRecs(dbFH)
RecordNumber=NumRecs+1
result=dbPosition(dbFH,RecordNumber,0)
result=dbPut(dbFH,fldLastName.text,fldFirstName.text,_
fldAddress.text,fldCity.text,fldState.text,fldZip.text,_
fldPhone.text)
If result=0 Then
    MsgBox "Phonebook entry: "+str(RecordNumber)+" written"
Else
    MsgBox "Unable to write phonebook entry"
End If
result=dbClose(dbFH)
```

Reading Data

A phonebook that you could only write to wouldn't be very useful. We need to be able to retrieve our users' data, and display it in a recognizable format. Since we already have the fields set up, all we need is a button of the form to read the data.

But, which record do we want? We could always start at the beginning of the database and "walk" through the records one at a time. Since non-keyed access allows us to specify any valid record number, we can read any record just by knowing the record number, and checking to make sure that the record number is valid. Since we can also obtain the number of records in a database, it's easy to check for a valid record number by seeing if it is between 1 and the number of records in the database.

DbGet

Syntax:

DbGet(DatabaseVar,arg1[,arg2][,arg3][...]

Description:

Reads a record from a Palm database

Once the record pointer is set using dbPosition, the data is retrieved by non-keyed access using the dbGet statement. As with dbPut, dbGet allows more than one variable to be accessed in the current statement. The dbGet statement reads data at the current position in the database, so we need to specify the record and offset. We do this using dbPosition, just as we did with dbPut. You can see how simple and direct this approach is:

```
result=dbPosition(dbFH,1,0)
result=dbGet(dbFH,LastName,FirstName,Address,City,State,Zip,Phone)
```

So, let's modify our form by adding buttons for accessing the first record, the next record, the previous record, and last record, and the user's specified record. We'll also add a label and field for the record number, since we'll need access to this later. Then, we can easily write the code for each of these buttons. In the code for the "Read First" button:

```
RecordNumber=1
fldRecordNumber.text=str(RecordNumber)
result=dbOpen(dbFH,dbName,CardNo)
result=dbPosition(dbFH,RecordNumber,0)
result=dbGet(dbFH,LastName,FirstName,Address,City,State,Zip,Phone)
fldLastName.text=LastName
fldFirstName.text=FirstName
fldAddress.text=Address
fldCity.text=City
fldState.text=State
fldZip.text=Zip
fldPhone.text=Phone
result=dbClose(dbFH)
```

Note Although writing the records can be done in the dbPut statement by using the field contents directly, you can't do the same with dbGet. This is a common theme in NS Basic – you can't use object properties in function calls that result in changing the properties. You must use variables for the functions, then change the object properties later, based on the variables returned.

If retrieving the first record is easy, using 1 as the record number, then retrieving the last record should be just as simple, since we can easily retrieve the number of records in the database, using dbGetNoRecs as before. The code for the "Read Last" button will look very similar to the "Read First" button:

```
result=dbOpen(dbFH,dbName,CardNo)
RecordNumber=dbGetNoRecs(dbFH)
fldRecordNumber.text=str(RecordNumber)
result=dbPosition(dbFH,RecordNumber,0)
result=dbGet(dbFH,LastName,FirstName,Address,City,State,Zip,Phone)
fldLastName.text=LastName
fldFirstName.text=FirstName
fldAddress.text=Address
```

```
fldCity.text=City
fldState.text=State
fldZip.text=Zip
fldPhone.text=Phone
result=dbClose(dbFH)
```

Other than the code for determining the record number, the code is exactly the same as that for the "Read First" button. We can use this to our advantage by placing the common code in a code module. Create a code module, and enter the following:

```
Sub ReadRecord(DataRecord as integer)
result=dbOpen(dbFH,dbName,CardNo)
result=dbPosition(dbFH, DataRecord,0)
result=dbGet(dbFH,LastName,FirstName,Address,City,State,Zip,Phone)
fldLastName.text=LastName
fldFirstName.text=FirstName
fldAddress.text=Address
fldCity.text=City
fldState.text=State
fldZip.text=Zip
fldPhone.text=Phone
fldRecordNumber.text=str(DataRecord)
result=dbClose(dbFH)
End Sub
```

Save this code module with the name "Non-Keyed Phonebook". Now, when we want to read a specific record, all we need to do is issue call the subroutine with the desired record number.

Let's use this to read the next record in the phonebook. Place a button on the form, label it "Read Next", and enter this code:

```
Result=dbOpen(dbFH,dbName,CardNo)
NumRecs=dbGetNoRecs(dbFH)
Result=dbClose(dbFH)
RecordNumber=RecordNumber+1
If RecordNumber > NumRecs Then
    RecordNumber=NumRecs
    MsgBox "Already at last record"
End If
Call ReadRecord(RecordNumber)
```

Since the next number is one greater than the previous record, we have to have some way of knowing if we're going past the end of the database. We could always have the program crash when it can't read anymore, but I think you'll agree that controlling the record number is a better method. Since we can't know what the record number is before the user presses this button, we have to make sure that we have a valid record number to start with. In the form's After Code, we'll place this line:

```
RecordNumber=0
```

This will assure that there's always a valid record number. NS Basic will actually initialize numeric variables with a value of zero anyway, but it's good programming practice to initialize your variables yourself.

Now that we're assured of a valid RecordNumber, we can easily create code to read the previous record. As before, create a button on your form, and label it "Read Prev". The code should be self-explanatory (but we'll discuss it anyway):

```
RecordNumber=RecordNumber-1
If RecordNumber < 1 then
    RecordNumber=1
    MsgBox "Already at beginning record"
End If
Call ReadRecord(RecordNumber)
```

This code simply decreases the current RecordNumber, and doesn't allow values less than one. Combine the error checking for upper and lower limits of record numbers, and we can then retrieve any record by its RecordNumber. Create a button, label it "Read Record", and insert this code:

```
Result=dbOpen(dbFH,dbName,CardNo)
NumRecs=dbGetNoRecs(dbFH)
Result=dbClose(dbFH)
RecordNumber=val(fldRecordNumber.text)
If RecordNumber > NumRecs Then
    RecordNumber=NumRecs
    MsgBox "Already at last record"
Elseif RecordNumber < 1 then
    RecordNumber=1
    MsgBox "Already at beginning record"
End If
Call ReadRecord(RecordNumber)
```

If we can read any record, we should be able to write any record as well, which we'll use to update a record. We can easily do this by using the code to write a record, with code to check first to make sure that our user doesn't attempt to update a non-existent record. Create a button with the label "Update", and include this code:

```
Result=dbOpen(dbFH,dbName,CardNo)
NumRecs=dbGetNoRecs(dbFH)
RecordNumber=val(fldRecordNumber.text)
If (RecordNumber > NumRecs) Or (RecordNumber < 1) Then
    MsgBox "Invalid Record Number"
Else
    result=dbPosition(dbFH,RecordNumber,0)
    result=dbPut(dbFH,fldLastName.text,fldFirstName.text,fldAddress.text,_
    fldCity.text,fldState.text,fldZip.text,fldPhone.text)
    If result=0 Then
        MsgBox "Phonebook entry: "+str(RecordNumber)+" updated"
    Else
        MsgBox "Unable to update phonebook entry"
    End If
End If
result=dbClose(dbFH)
```

If you've been creating this phonebook from scratch, you'll notice that the form is getting a little cluttered. Now that most of the code has been written, we can make the buttons smaller by using graphical buttons instead of text. Although we can use some of the different fonts for graphical characters, we'll keep things simple by using one and two-character labels for the buttons. My choices:

Read First <<
Read Prev <
Read Next >
Read Last >>

Let's add a little code to clear the form (to allow a new entry, for instance), and put it in the code section of a new button, labeled "Clear":

```
fldLastName.text=""
fldFirstName.text=""
fldAddress.text=""
fldCity.text=""
fldState.text=""
fldZip.text=""
fldPhone.text=""
fldRecordNumber.text=""
```

That's it! You've created a full-fledged phonebook. Although your app may look somewhat different, here's my Non-Keyed Phonebook app in action:

We're missing a few functions, like the ability to search by name (might be useful in a phonebook, don't you think?), but we'll tackle that problem in the next section when we discuss keyed access. Other functions that are missing are the ability to keep the data sorted, and the ability to delete records – also easily handled using keyed access.

Keyed Database Access

If you play around with the Non-Keyed Phonebook application, you'll notice after a while that there's something seriously lacking – the database isn't in alphabetic order. Heck, it's not in any order at all! Records are written one after another, with no regard for where they *should* be. Searching a large amount of data like this will be extremely frustrating, and your users won't put up with it. Sure, we could always sort the database every time we changed it, but this could add considerable overhead to our application,

and Palm devices aren't particularly quick. What if we could keep the ability to read and
write data sequentially, yet keep the data automatically sorted, and access records by the
field used to sort them?

Keyed access gives us this functionality, and more. Databases managed by keyed
access remain in sorted order based on their first field, which is used as the key field. In
order for keyed access to be available for a database, it must follow these rules, with no
exceptions:

-   The first field of the database is the key

-   Keys can be any standard data type other than arrays and user-defined
    types (UDT's)

-   Keys must be all the same data type

-   Keys must be unique

-   Records must be in key-sorted order

At first glance these rules seem pretty restrictive, but the rules are actually pretty
easy to follow. In fact, if you use NS Basic exclusively to perform keyed access on these
databases, and don't manipulate the databases using non-keyed methods, NS Basic
enforces these rules, so you can't violate them even if you try. However, if you also use
non-keyed methods on these databases, it's easy to write records with duplicate keys, or
in non-sorted order. For now we'll stick with using NS Basic's keyed methods, and
explain what each does (and how the Palm OS accomplishes the various tasks).

> **Caution** The Palm sorting order is straightforward for databases using
> numeric keys, but string keys are a bit trickier. You might expect Palm
> to use ASCII values for sorting strings, but in fact the actual sort order is
> only loosely based on ASCII codes. This sort order is given in the back
> of this book in the Appendices, and I strongly recommend that you
> review this before using string keys.

Reading and Writing Data with Keyed Access Methods

With non-keyed access, you had to explicitly position the database record pointer
before writing data. If you wanted to put new data in alphabetic order, you'd have to
determine the correct position in the file, move the existing data to open up a blank
record, then write the data. With keyed access, all you need to do is write the record, and
it will automatically be placed in its correct position. OK, it's a little more involved than
that, but not much.

When you manipulate a database using keyed access methods, NS Basic and the
Palm OS work together to keep records in key-sorted order. These methods use a binary
search algorithm to find, insert, update, and delete records, which results in extremely
quick access. You could always write these routines yourself, but why bother? Actually,
you may need to write your own sorting and searching routines if your database isn't in
key-sorted order, or you want to use a field other than the first field as your key (or want
to do multi-level sorting based on several keys). For the vast majority of NS Basic

programming you won't need to get involved in the details – just knowing how the underlying code works may help you understand when a keyed access method is needed.

Nothing helps understand a technique like an example, so should we write another phonebook application? No? I didn't think so, either. Not that it wouldn't be a good exercise, but there's already a good phonebook that comes with the Palm PDA's (plus, one of my keyed phonebook apps is distributed with NS Basic anyway). Instead, let's create a "Daily Diary" that will allow us to keep track of thoughts that pop up during the day. Using the date as the key, we can easily call up any day's thoughts and edit them as needed. Since we can select dates in the future, we can even write notes to remind us of upcoming events. We'll even add the ability to print using NS Basic and PalmPrint, and even save our daily notes to the MemoPad app. And all explained, every step of the way.

> **Tip** As we did with the non-keyed phonebook app, we'll walk through the code together. The finished app is already available on the CD as "Daily Diary.prj", but you should type along with me to really get the most out of this chapter.

Start the IDE and start with a new project. Call this project "Daily Diary", and give it a useful Creator ID (I chose "DaDi"). Select a suitable bitmap for the main icon, and place its ID number in the "ID, Large Icon" property for the project. The app will need a few global variables for the database name, handle, card number, etc. placed in the startup code (most of this should look familiar to you):

```
Global dbFH as Database
Global dbName as String
Global CardNo as Integer
Global key as Date
Global CurrentDate as Date
Global Result as Integer
Global DiaryText as String
```

Our database design will be pretty simple – the key date as the first field, and the diary text as the second. Not a very complicated format, to say the least, but it's simplicity is its strength. Similarly, we'll make the diary as easy to use as possible, with only the necessary controls on our form. If we make our users jump through too many hoops to get to their daily information, they won't come back.

So we'll keep it simple. Our form will have a multiline field (fldDiary) and a selector (selDate). The field will hold our diary text, and the selector will be used to choose the date. Create the field with a scrollbar, AutoShift true, and a maximum of 4000 characters (to keep within MemoPad's 4k char limit). To keep your users happy, place a shift indicator on the form in the lower right corner as well.

DbFind and DbRead

Syntax:

> **DbFind(DatabaseVar,dbKey)**
> **DbRead(DatabaseVar,dbKey[,field2][,field3][,...])**

Description:

Determines if a record exists with a given key (DbFind), or reads a record with a given key (DbRead)

When our form loads, we'll check to see if we can open the database. If we can't, it must not exist, so we'll create it. If we can't create it, then we'll let the user know about the problem and exit. Otherwise, we'll set the current date, and if we have a valid database, we'll try to read the data for the current date, using the date as the key. If the record exists, we'll display the data on the form for the user to read, modify, delete, print, send to MemoPad – but the actual form code will be simple:

```
dbName="DailyDiary"
CardNo=0
CurrentDate=Today()
selDate.text=DateMMDDYY(CurrentDate)
Result=dbOpen(dbFH,dbName,CardNo)
If Result=0 Then ' open ok, so read data
   Result=dbRead(dbFH,CurrentDate,DiaryText)
   If Result=0 Then ' read ok, so show text
      fldDiary.text=DiaryText
      Result=dbClose(dbFH)
   End If
Else ' open didn't work, so try to create database
   Result=dbCreate(dbFH,dbName,CardNo,"DaDi")
   If Result<>0 Then
      MsgBox "Unable to create diary database"
      Stop
   End If
End If
```

Note the use of dbRead – we attempt to read the record using the date as the key. We could have used dbFind (to see if the record existed), but there's no real time or code saved – we actually end up with *more* code:

```
Result=dbFind(dbFH,CurrentDate)
If Result=0 Then ' read ok, so read and show text
   Result=dbRead(dbFH,CurrentDate,DiaryText)
   fldDiary.text=DiaryText
   Result=dbClose(dbFH)
End If
```

> **Tip** Using dbRead instead of dbFind to determine if a record exists with a given key has an additional benefit – if the read is unsuccessful, but there is a record with a key that follows the "search" key, dbRead will return a result of 2, the next key, and the data for the record. In this diary app we could ask our user if he wants to see this record, but for now we'll keep it simple. However, it's still nice to know the power behind dbRead.

If all has gone well, our user either has a record displayed for the current date, or a blank field for the daily diary. So far, though, we haven't even written any data to the database. We'll want to make it as easy as possible for our user to save his data. To put

it another way, we want to make it impossible for our user to lose (forget to save) his
data.

> **Tip** I can't stress how important this is! You can have the most
> amazing application ever created, but if your users can easily,
> irreplaceably lose their data, your app is about as useful as a toaster in
> the ocean. Protect your users from themselves, do it invisibly, and you
> will win their loyalty.

We could always put a button on the form and force our user to press the button, but
that's not very "friendly". What we need to do is save the data whenever the user decides
to do something – anything – that would take him away from our diary's current data.
There are two ways this can happen: 1) he decides to select a different date, and 2) he
decides to run a different application. Putting data writing routines in the date selector's
code, and in the project's "termination" code would accomplish this protection.

DbInsert and DbUpdate

Syntax:

> **DbInsert(DatabaseVar,dbKey[,field2][,field3][,…])**
> **DbUpdate(DatabaseVar,dbKey[,field2][,field3][,…])**

Description:

> **Writes a new (DbInsert) or modified (DbUpdate) record to a database, based on
> a given key**

We already have the current date in a global variable, and the data in the fldDiary
field, so the following will write the data (if any exists):

```
If fldDiary.text="" then
    Exit sub
End If
Result=dbOpen(dbFH,dbName,CardNo)
Result=dbFind(dbFH,CurrentDate)
If Result=0 Then
    Result=dbUpdate(dbFH,CurrentDate,fldDiary.text)
Else
    Result=dbInsert(dbFH,CurrentDate,fldDiary.text)
End If
result=dbClose(dbFH)
```

This routine will use dbUpdate to write over the previous data if a record already
exists for today's date, or use dbInsert if the record doesn't exist. Here dbFind is more
useful, since we only need to determine if a record exists prior to writing it.

We'll put this routine in both locations, so the current data gets saved if the user
changes dates, or moves to a different app. Putting the actual code in both locations isn't
the best programming practice, since any modifications to code would have to made in
both locations, increasing the chance for error. Instead, we'll create a code module and
create a subroutine called SaveCurrentData:

```
Sub SaveCurrentData()
If fldDiary.text="" then
    Exit sub
End If
Result=dbOpen(dbFH,dbName,CardNo)
Result=dbFind(dbFH,CurrentDate)
If Result=0 Then
    Result=dbUpdate(dbFH,CurrentDate,fldDiary.text)
Else
    Result=dbInsert(dbFH,CurrentDate,fldDiary.text)
End If
result=dbClose(dbFH)
End Sub
```

This way, we can issue a simple subroutine call in each location:

```
Call SaveCurrentData()
```

This keeps our code clean and more readable, and makes future code maintenance easier. If you haven't already done so, create the code module with the SaveCurrentData subroutine, save the code module, and put the subroutine call in the project's termination and date selector code.

Before we leave the selector code, we also need to write code to allow our user to pick a new date, then read the diary entry if one exists for the new date. Using PopupDate makes it easy to get the new date, and we can then use the new date as a key to search the database:

```
Result=PopupDate(CurrentDate, "New Diary Date")
selDate.text=DateMMDDYY(CurrentDate)
Result=dbOpen(dbFH,dbName,CardNo)
Result=dbRead(dbFH,CurrentDate,DiaryText)
If Result=0 Then ' read ok, so show text
    fldDiary.text=DiaryText
Else
    fldDiary.text=""
End If
Result=dbClose(dbFH)
```

We should also allow our user to "thumb through" the dates, backwards and forwards. We can do this one day at a time, or by actual database records. To move the date one day forward or backward, all we need to do is use the AddDays and SubtractDays functions to adjust the current date, and read any records with matching keys. We'll perform that code first, then look at moving sequentially back and forth through the database records by key.

Place four small buttons on the form, labeled "Prev", "<", ">", and "Next". We'll use the ">" and "<" buttons to move up and down by date, respectively. The code for reading a diary entry based on the date is identical to the code used in the selector after the date is changed – and we'll also save the current data (if there's any data to save) before changing the date. For the "<" button:

```
Call SaveCurrentData()
CurrentDate=SubtractDays(CurrentDate,1)
```

```
selDate.text=DateMMDDYY(CurrentDate)
Result=dbOpen(dbFH,dbName,CardNo)
Result=dbFind(dbFH,CurrentDate)
If Result=0 Then ' read ok, so show text
    Result=dbRead(dbFH,CurrentDate,DiaryText)
    fldDiary.text=DiaryText
Else
    fldDiary.text=""
End IfResult=dbClose(dbFH)
```

The code for the ">" button is created by a minor modification of the above code, using AddDays instead of SubtractDays:

```
Call SaveCurrentData()
CurrentDate=AddDays(CurrentDate,1)
selDate.text=DateMMDDYY(CurrentDate)
Result=dbOpen(dbFH,dbName,CardNo)
Result=dbFind(dbFH,CurrentDate)
If Result=0 Then ' read ok, so show text
    Result=dbRead(dbFH,CurrentDate,DiaryText)
    fldDiary.text=DiaryText
Else
    fldDiary.text=""
End If
Result=dbClose(dbFH)
```

DbReadPrev and DbReadNext

Syntax:

> **DbReadPrev(DatabaseVar,dbKey[,field2][,field3][,...])**
> **DbReadNext(DatabaseVar,dbKey[,field2][,field3][,...])**

Description:

> **Reads the previous or next record in a database, based on a given key returned by a previously successful read**

Code for retrieving the previous or next record requires that the Palm OS already knows where the database record pointer is. Once we have retrieved a valid key, dbReadPrev and dbReadNext are based on reading backward or forward from the current record. So, all we need to do is read the key for a valid record, then use dbReadPrev and dbReadNext. First, the code for the "Prev" button:

```
Call SaveCurrentData()
dim NumRecs as integer ' number of records in database
Result=dbOpen(dbFH,dbName,CardNo)
NumRecs=dbGetNoRecs(dbFH)
if NumRecs=0 then
    msgbox "No diary entries"
    exit sub
endif
```

```
Result=dbRead(dbFH,CurrentDate,DiaryText) ' get current data
If (result=0) or (Result=2) then
    Result=dbReadPrev(dbFH,CurrentDate,DiaryText) ' get previous
     if Result=0 then
        fldDiary.text=DiaryText
        selDate.text=DateMMDDYY(CurrentDate)
    else
        msgbox "Already at first record"
    end if
Else ' must have a date past the last record
    result=dbClose(dbFH)
    result=dbOpen(dbFH,dbName,CardNo)
    result=dbPosition(dbFH,NumRecs,0) ' position to last record
    result=dbGet(dbFH,CurrentDate,DiaryText)
    fldDiary.text=DiaryText
    selDate.text=DateMMDDYY(CurrentDate)
End If
Result=dbClose(dbFH)
```

Since we might be past the last record, we have to do some non-keyed work to find the last record and key (the first field, remember?). We have to do the opposite reasoning when we look for the "Next" button, although the coding is a bit simpler:

```
Call SaveCurrentData()
dim NumRecs as integer ' number of records in database
Result=dbOpen(dbFH,dbName,CardNo)
NumRecs=dbGetNoRecs(dbFH)
if NumRecs=0 then
    msgbox "No diary entries"
    exit sub
endif
Result=dbRead(dbFH,CurrentDate,DiaryText)
If result=0 then
Result=dbReadNext(dbFH,CurrentDate,DiaryText)
    if Result=0 then
        fldDiary.text=DiaryText
        selDate.text=DateMMDDYY(CurrentDate)
    else
        msgbox "Already at last diary entry"
    end if
Elseif Result=2 then ' we have the data already
    fldDiary.text=DiaryText
    selDate.text=DateMMDDYY(CurrentDate)
else
    msgbox "Already at last diary entry"
End If
Result=dbClose(dbFH)
```

DbReset

Syntax:

DbReset(DatabaseVar)

Description:

Resets the record pointer to the first record in preparation for a DbReadNext statement

We didn't cover DbReset in this diary application, but it's extremely important to understand. In non-keyed database access, we used the actual record number with dbPosition to set the record pointer. With keyed access, we don't know the record number, so if we decide to start at the first record and "ReadNext" through to the end, how can we accomplish this? The following code won't work:

```
Result=DbOpen(DatabaseVar,DatabaseName,CardNo)
Result=DbReadNext(DatabaseVar,dbKey,dbInfo)
```

If you try this on a valid database, the DbReadNext skips the first record, and returns the second record instead! Remember, DbReadNext and DbReadPrev require that a record with a valid key had previously been read, and no such record has been read yet. So, when used on a freshly opened database, DbReadNext *acts as though the first record had already been read*, and it retrieves the next record.

DbReset acts as though you read the first record successfully, *but then resets the record pointer to the beginning of the database*, so that DbReadNext returns the first record.

(now, back to our diary application...)

We could stop here and have a fully functional diary, but our user's data is "captive" – he can't do anything with it other than read it. Let's give him the ability to print his daily thoughts (using PalmPrint, on the enclosed CD), or write them to MemoPad. For this we'll add a button labeled "Print".

Printing to PalmPrint in NS Basic is performed through the use of AppLaunch, an NS Basic function that we covered before. Writing to MemoPad is a bit more complicated (we'll cover it in the next section). To make things simple for now (and you know how I like to keep things as simple as possible) I've written two code modules – txt2memo.cod and PalmPrint.cod. Add them to your project, and add the following code to the "Print" button:

```
result=alert("Daily Diary","Print to MemoPad or PalmPrint?",_
2, "MemoPad", "PalmPrint", "Cancel")
Dim PrintText as String
PrintText=DateMMDDYY(CurrentDate) + " - "+fldDiary.text
If result=0 Then
    TextToMemo PrintText
    result=alert("Daily Diary","Daily diary saved to Memo Pad",_
    1, "OK")
ElseIf result=1 Then
    PalmPrint PrintText
End If
```

This section of code asks the user if he wants to save the diary data to MemoPad (with a small header using the current date), print to a printer connected using PalmPrint, or cancel the operation completely.

DbDelete

Syntax:

>   **DbDelete(DatabaseVar,dbKey)**

Description:

>   **Deletes a database record, based on a given key**

Since we're being so nice to our user, let's add one last button to the form, and label it "Clear". This gives our user an easy way to clear the current day's diary, both on the screen, and from the database with the dbDelete statement. Using an alert box like the one in the Print button, we'll ask the user if he wants to delete the current day's diary, or cancel to preserve his data:

```
result=alert("Daily Diary","Delete current day's_
diary?",2,"OK","Cancel")
If result=0 Then
    result=dbOpen(dbFH,dbName,CardNo)
    result=dbDelete(dbFH,CurrentDate)
    result=dbClose(dbFH)
    fldDiary.text="" ' clear the screen as well
End If
```

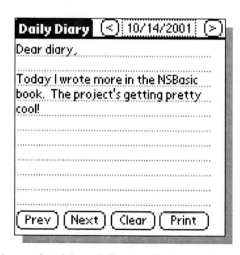

There you have it! A completed, keyed diary application, using every keyed access technique, plus a few extras thrown in for free. Using these techniques, you should be well on your way to create your own keyed database management applications.

Safely mixing keyed and non-keyed methods

Non-keyed access is very simple, and if you need to retrieve records by record number, is the only way to go. However, keyed access is much more powerful, allows you to delete records, and keeps the database sorted automatically. How can we use the two methods together, to get the best of both worlds?

Since the main advantage that non-keyed access gives you over keyed access is the ability to access records by record number, if we can come up with a way to determine the record number for a record based on its key, we can mix the methods safely. Or at least it's a good start.

Binary Searches

Since databases must be in ascending, key-sorted order for keyed access to work, we can use a binary search method on these databases to determine the record number for any given key.

Binary searching gets its name from the fact that the search starts by dividing the data to be sorted into two groups, one above and the other below a middle record. The search starts by determining the start, end, and middle records, then compares the middle record with the record being searched for. If the records match, the search ends successfully.

If the record being searched for is located above the middle record, then the search starts again, with the new start record equal to the record immediately following the previous middle record, and the new middle record halfway between the new start record and the last record.

On the other hand, if the record being searched for is located below the middle record, then we know that the record (if it exists) must be in the first half, so the record immediately below the previous middle record will be the new "end" record, with a new middle record halfway between the start and new ending record.

The binary search then continues until a match is found, or until the search list cannot be divided any further. By breaking the list down to half its previous size each time, the routine is extremely efficient. A list of 256 items can be searched in 8 or less comparisons (2^8=256). As each additional power of 2 only requires 1 additional comparison, the following table gives the number of comparisons needed for various database sizes:

Binary search statistics

Database size (records)	Maximum number of comparisons
256	8
512	9
1024	10
2048	11
4096	12
8192	13
16384	14

Referring to the table above, a database with 10000 different records (very large, by Palm standards) can be searched using a maximum of 14 comparisons. Since not every search is likely to require this number of comparisons, the average number of comparisons needed will fall below this number.

   Code routines for retrieving the record of a number by key are given below (and in the code module "recnumbykey.cod" in the projects directory on the CD). The first routine assumes that you have already retrieved a valid key, and just need to find the record number, while the other search starts with no assumptions about whether or not the key exists. Both routines are functions that return either that actual record number (which would be from 1 to the number of records), or -1, to indicate that the search was unsuccessful.

```
Function GetRecNumByKeyFound(DatabaseName as String,StringKey_
as String) as Integer
'
'Written for use in NS Basic 2.0 by Mike Verive
'
'This routine performs a binary search to determine record number
'for a record based on its key (database must be available
'for keyed access).
'To use this routine, a record with the given key must already
'exist. If you want to use a routine without first verifying that
'the key is valid, use the GetRecNumByKey function.
'
'With this and the GetRecNumByKey routine, the function will
'return either a valid record number, or -1 if no record with the
'given key is found.
'
Dim result as Integer
Dim dbfh as Database
Dim LowRec as Integer
Dim HighRec as Integer
Dim SearchRec as Integer
Dim KeyFound as String
result=dbOpen(dbfh,DatabaseName,0)
LowRec=1
HighRec=dbGetNoRecs(dbfh)
KeyFound=""
Do Until HighRec=LowRec
   SearchRec=int((HighRec+LowRec)/2)'look in middle of range
   result=dbPosition(dbfh,SearchRec,0)
   result=dbGet(dbfh,KeyFound)
   If KeyFound=StringKey Then
     GetRecNumByKeyFound=SearchRec
     Exit Do
   ElseIf KeyFound > StringKey Then
     HighRec=SearchRec-1
   ElseIf KeyFound < StringKey Then
     LowRec=SearchRec+1
   End If
   GetRecNumByKeyFound=-1
Loop
result=dbClose(dbfh)
End Function

Function GetRecNumByKey(DatabaseName as String,StringKey_
as String) as Integer
'
'Written for use in NS Basic 2.0 by Mike Verive
```

```
'
'This routine performs a binary search to determine record number
'for a record based on its key (database must be available for
'keyed access). To use this routine, a record with the given key
'must already exist. If you want to use a routine with a key that
'you know exists, use the GetRecNumByKeyFound function.
'
'With this and the GetRecNumByKeyFound routine, the function will
'return either a valid record number, or -1 if no record with the
'given key is found.
'
Dim result as Integer
Dim dbfh as Database
Dim LowRec as Integer
Dim HighRec as Integer
Dim SearchRec as Integer
Dim KeyFound as String
result=dbOpen(dbfh,DatabaseName,0)
result=dbFind(dbfh,StringKey)
If result<>0 Then
    GetRecNumByKey=-1
Else
    LowRec=1
    HighRec=dbGetNoRecs(dbfh)
    KeyFound=""
    Do Until HighRec=LowRec
        SearchRec=int((HighRec+LowRec)/2)'look in middle of range
        result=dbPosition(dbfh,SearchRec,0)
        result=dbGet(dbfh,KeyFound)
        If KeyFound=StringKey Then
          GetRecNumByKey=SearchRec
          Exit Do
        ElseIf KeyFound > StringKey Then
          HighRec=SearchRec-1
        ElseIf KeyFound < StringKey Then
          LowRec=SearchRec+1
        End If
        GetRecNumByKey=-1
    Loop
End If
result=dbClose(dbfh)
End Function
```

Once you have the record number for a record by key, you can then use dbPosition to set the record pointer (and optional offset), then use dbGet or dbPut. Remember that you are accessing a record that needs to stay in its current location within the database, so avoid changing the first field (used by keyed access as the key). If you change the first field, and the records end up out of key-sorted order (or you end up duplicating a key), your database may not be accessible later using keyed methods.

Writing to MemoPad

We've created our applications now, and I introduced you earlier to writing data to the Palm MemoPad application. Let's look at MemoPad in a little more depth, since you should really understand it if you're going to write to it.

Like any other database, MemoPad's database "MemoDB" can be written to using non-keyed techniques. As long as we're careful to keep our keys unique, we can write to MemoPad using keyed methods as well. I prefer keyed access, partly because it keeps data sorted (assuming it's sorted in the first place), but also because keyed access allows us to delete records, something that can't be done using non-keyed methods.

> **Note** Since MemoPad isn't one of our own applications, I often wonder if we should be deleting its records at all. I'm not sure that I would want another application altering *my* databases, so I have to admit that I think it's a bad idea. Besides, Palm reserves the right to modify their database structure at any time (and has announce that they will in Palm OS 5). However, many programmers want to know how to access data stored by the current tandard Palm applications, so I'll help you out a little. But I still think it's a bad idea, at least until Palm creates API's specifically for manipulating their built-in databases.

From what you now know about accessing Palm databases with NS Basic, you realize that for keyed access the first field in each MemoPad record will be the key, and this key must be a standard variable type. And, unless the key field is the entire MemoPad record, there must be at least one more field. Let's examine the code in the "txt2memo.cod" code module, which I adapted from Jeff Debrosse's "Take-a-Memo" project. His original project used both keyed access (with date and time as keys), and non-keyed access methods. To keep the routine simple, I decided to use only the non-keyed method. We'll discuss that method first, then show you how to use keyed access.

Like most of our routines, we have to set up the variables that we'll use. Since this is going to be a subroutine, we'll use Dim to set up our variables, rather than Global. You *could* use Globals, but why would you want to? Subroutines should be self-contained, so declaring variables as Global in a subroutine is a bad, bad idea. If you need to pass values from a subroutine, put them in the arguments that get passed to and from the subroutine. Our variables, since we're talking database access here, are:

```
Dim dbFH as Database
Dim result as Integer
Dim RecCount as Integer
Dim CardNo as integer
Dim dbName as string
```

Wait a minute! Aren't most of these the same variables that we already declared as Global variables? Isn't it a bad idea to declare the variables in two locations?

Actually, since we're creating a subroutine, we want our variables to be local variables – used only for the subroutine – as opposed to Global variables that are used throughout. That's where Dim comes in; variables declared with Dim are local to the routine that they're declared in, even if they share the same name as variables declared elsewhere. We can safely use any variable name here, confident that we won't change the value of a variable somewhere else in the program.

Since we'll be using non-keyed access, we need to determine the number of records that exist in MemoPad's database, so we'll open the database and use dbGetNoRecs:

```
CardNo=0
dbName="MemoDB"
result = dbopen(dbFH,dbName,CardNo)
```

```
RecCount = dbgetnorecs(dbFH)
```

Now that we have the number of records in the database, we can add 1 to get the next higher position, write our new record there, then close the database:

```
RecCount=RecCount+1
result = dbPosition(dbFH, RecCount ,0)
result = dbPut(dbFH,Message)
result = dbclose(dbFH)
```

If you've looked at this closely, you'll see that we never declared the Message variable that we used in the dbPut statement. That's because this is a subroutine, with Message passed as a string in the subroutine call. The complete subroutine looks like this:

```
Sub TextToMemo(Message as String)
Dim dbFH as Database
Dim result as Integer
Dim RecCount as Integer
Dim CardNo as integer
Dim dbName as string
CardNo=0
dbName="MemoDB"
result = dbopen(dbFH,dbName,CardNo)
RecCount = dbgetnorecs(dbFH)
RecCount=RecCount+1
result = dbPosition(dbFH, RecCount ,0)
result = dbPut(dbFH,Message)
result = dbclose(dbFH)
End Sub
```

Note that there's no error-checking. We should actually check for errors at each database access, and pass the status back to the calling program. A little re-writing, and we're all set:

```
Sub TextToMemo2(Message as String, ErrStatus as integer)
Dim dbFH as Database
Dim result as Integer
Dim RecCount as Integer
Dim CardNo as integer
Dim dbName as string
CardNo=0
dbName="MemoDB"
result = dbopen(dbFH,dbName,CardNo)
If Result<>0 then
   ErrStatus=Result
   exit sub
end if
RecCount = dbgetnorecs(dbFH)
RecCount=RecCount+1
result = dbPosition(dbFH, RecCount ,0)
if result <>0 then
   ErrStatus=Result
   Result=dbClose(dbFH)
```

```
Else
    result = dbPut(dbFH,Message)
    if result<>0 then
        ErrStatus=Result
        Result=dbClose(dbFH)
    Else
        result = dbclose(dbFH)
        ErrCode=Result
    End If
End If
End Sub
```

Since we're returning a value, we could have turned this into a function instead (this code is from the WriteTextToMemo.cod code module):

```
Function WriteTextToMemo(Message as String) as Integer
Dim dbFH as Database
Dim result as Integer
Dim RecCount as Integer
Dim CardNo as Integer
Dim dbName as String
CardNo=0
dbName="MemoDB"
result = dbopen(dbFH,dbName,CardNo)
If Result<>0 Then
    WriteTextToMemo =Result
    Exit Function
End If
RecCount = dbgetnorecs(dbFH)
RecCount=RecCount+1
result = dbPosition(dbFH, RecCount ,0)
If result <>0 Then
    WriteTextToMemo =Result
    Result=dbClose(dbFH)
    Exit Function
End If
result = dbPut(dbFH,Message)
If result<>0 Then
    WriteTextToMemo =Result
    Result=dbClose(dbFH)
    Exit Function
End If
result = dbclose(dbFH)
WriteTextToMemo =Result
End Function
```

We can then use this function to send a record to MemoPad, and then check the result of the function:

```
Dim result as integer
result=WriteTextToMemo("Hello, World!")
If result<>0 then
    msgbox "Error writing to MemoPad"
end if
```

To write to MemoPad using keyed access, instead of determining the number of
records and adding 1, we'll generate a key using the date and time, append our message
to the key, then write it to MemoPad's database. Using the previous function as our
template, our modification (based on the WriteKeyedTextToMemo.cod code module)
looks like this:

```
Function WriteKeyedTextToMemo(Message as String) as Integer
Dim dbFH as Database
Dim result as Integer
Dim RecCount as Integer
Dim CardNo as Integer
Dim dbName as String
Dim dbkey as String
CardNo=0
dbName="MemoDB"
result = dbopen(dbFH,dbName,CardNo)
If Result<>0 Then
   WriteKeyedTextToMemo =Result
Else
   dbKey=DateMMDDYY(Today())+" - "+HourMinAMPM(Now()) + Message
   result = dbFind(dbFH,Message)
   If result=0 Then
      result=dbUpdate(dbFH,dbKey,"")
      If result<>0 Then
         WriteKeyedTextToMemo =Result
         result=dbClose(dbFH)
         Exit Function
      End If
   Else
      result=dbInsert(dbFH,dbKey,"")
      If result<>0 Then
         WriteKeyedTextToMemo =Result
         result=dbClose(dbFH)
         Exit Function
      End If
   End If
   result = dbclose(dbFH)
   WriteKeyedTextToMemo =Result
End If
End Function
```

To delete a memo from MemoPad, you have to use dbDelete, which is a keyed
method. However, it's possible that the first field (the key) in the memo you want to
delete is the same as the first field or a different record, written with non-keyed access
methods. There's no function to determine if there are duplicate keys, since they're not
supposed to exist. The ONLY way you can safely delete a memo from MemoPad is to
assure that the key is unique, and that the record can actually be found (keyed access
depends on a binary search, which gives unpredictable results if the records aren't in key-
sorted order, which is likely if records are written using non-keyed methods). You can
then issue the dbDelete statement:

```
result=dbDelete(dbFH,dbKey)
```

and check to be sure the statement worked as expected (returns a code of 0). Unfortunately, the likelihood that this statement will work is quite low, since we don't have control over how other users write information to MemoPad.

| Caution | See what I mean about deleting data from another application's database? Don't get in over your head on this. If you do, at least don't say I didn't warn you!

Chapter XIV – Menus

Unless you live in a vacuum, your users are likely to expect your apps to act like other Palm apps. Buttons should do something when you press them, PopUps should bring up (down) a list of items to choose from, etc. Menus are no exception. If you have them, they should appear when the user taps on the menu area of the Palm silkscreen.

And, if your apps don't have menus, why not? If you think that menus aren't worth the effort, I hope you'll change your mind.

Look at your apps – are there options that could/should be present on more that one form? Are there buttons on your forms that are infrequently used, but should be available? Remember, the Palm OS screen is so small that the available screen space should be used wisely. That's not to say that every button needs to be turned into a menu item – navigating several levels of a menu for a commonly used function may not be the best solution. On the other hand, functions that are commonly called from menus (cut, copy, and paste, to name a few) probably should remain in menus. If your apps have these functions, your menus should give your users these functions in their usual places. Remember that everything your application does is aimed at helping your user. Anything else is wasted code.

There are two templates (Basic and General) on the CD that should help you get started with menus. The "General Template" uses some of the functions in the NSBSystemLib shared library (see "Extending NS Basic") for clipboard functions, but the "Basic Template" has a general-purpose menu already set up for many most common programming functions.

Creating Menus

There are two steps in using menus from within your NS Basic apps. The first step is to create the menu; later we'll learn the second step - how to activate the menu.

Once again, I lied. There are more that just two steps in using menus. Before you create your menus, you should decide what the menu contents will be, then you'll decide what the hierarchy of the menus will be. Each menu level should have a logical reason to exist, with sublevels organized by function. This takes considerable thought; you don't want to start designing a menu off the top of your head, since you're more likely to have the make major modifications later.

You don't know what you want in your menus? Look at the existing Palm apps, and other apps you use from day to day. Take a look at your desktop programs as well, and you're bound to see common themes. Even if they're just there as a way to add "About" screens, having menus makes your apps more professional and user-friendly. Trust me on this.

In NS Basic your menu has a hierarchical, tree-like structure. OK, so it's an upside-down tree, with the root on the top, with branches moving down the screen – but it's still a tree. These menus, like other Palm programming elements, contain code, so they're created with names. The NS Basic IDE makes it easy to create menus and their submenus, and additional submenus as needed.

> **Tip** It's all too easy to go crazy with menus, and end up with menus that are longer than the screen is wide – and this can cause unpredictable behavior. Keep your menus simple, and their text short, to avoid this potential pitfall.

To start the menu creation process, start up the IDE with a new or existing project, and create a new menu by selecting Project > Add Menu from the IDE menu, right click on the Menu folder in Project Explorer, and select Add Menu, or double-click the area on the IDE screen that corresponds to the silkscreen menu button. You will be presented with the Add New Menu box that asks you to enter a menu name. This will be the name that your menu will be called by, so a descriptive name like "mnuMain" will help identify it later.

Clicking OK brings up the Menu Editor, which will give you the opportunity to create the caption for your menu, which will be displayed on the screen in the top left corner when the menu is activated (menus must be drawn on the screen using the MenuDraw statement in order to be accessible – more on that later).

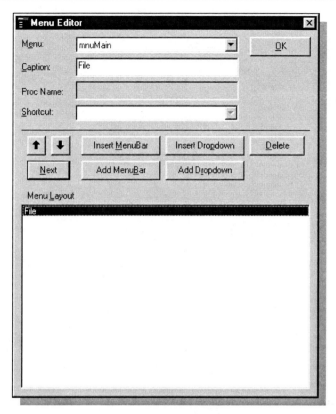

Since "File" is the usual first menu item, we'll use that as our first menu as well. For now we'll create a submenu called "About". However, there's no "create sub menu" button, so where do we go from here? Clicking the "Next" button give us a new menu, but at the same level as "File", and we want a submenu instead. For this we'll instead click the "Insert Dropdown" button, which creates a sub-level in the menu, and creates this sublevel with the name "...untitled". The ellipsis (...) is used to set the level apart from the next higher level. This submenus is what we'll use for our "About" form. Change the Caption from "...untitled" to something more useful, like "...About". This will change the name of the submenu. Notice that you can't change the "..." – NS Basic uses it for the level, so it's not really part of the name. We'll add another menu item at this same level – this time using the "Next" button, and change the caption to "Exit".

> **Tip** Use a single hyphen as the name of a menu dropdown, and you will create a dividing line (or separator bar, as it's commonly called in Visual Basic) between the other dropdown items, which is great for separating dropdowns into logical groups. Unlike Visual Basic, however, you don't have to give your separator bars different names; a single hyphen is all you need.

Click the OK button to exit from the Menu Editor and return to the IDE. You'll notice that, unlike Windows applications, the menu doesn't automatically appear at the top of the Palm screen. The reason for this is that the menu isn't part of the form – any form can display any menu.

Caution Just because you *can* display any menu on any form, doesn't mean that you *should*. Menus should have a logical reason for being there, and should contain functions relative to that form. Take care to avoid referring to form objects in menus; if a menu attempts to read or modify a form-specific object property (a Label's text, a Scrollbar's Current value, etc) that isn't currently available, it will generate a fatal crash.

As mentioned before, we'll discuss the display of menus in a while, but for now you can see your menu by going to the Project Explorer, and looking in the Menus folder. To see all of the submenus, click on each [+] in front of each menu.

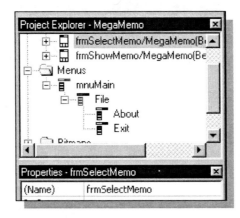

OK, now we have the menu started. Somewhere we'll need to place the code for our menu items. For the "About" menu, we'll simply use the MsgBox statement. Since I'm currently using my MegaMemo project, my code will be:

```
MsgBox "MegaMemo Copyright 2001 by Michael J. Verive"+chr(10)_
+"All Rights Reserved"
'Using chr(10) forces the OS to start a new line
```

For the "Exit" menu, the following code is all that's needed:

```
Stop
```

But, where do we place this code? Like other programming elements, code can be added to menus by right-clicking the menu item in the Project Explorer, and selecting "View Code". This will open up the code editor for the given menu item. You'll notice that only the final level of any menu can have code associated with it. Right-clicking on a higher (lower?) level menu doesn't bring up the option for viewing code, but allows you to add a new dropdown menu.

Note When discussing lower and higher levels in menus, the common nomenclature is to refer to levels closer to the root as lower levels, and those of the branches higher levels. Since our menu hierarchy is more like an upside-down tree, the highest level menus are

> actually further down on the screen than lower levels. I'll try to avoid the use of these terms as much as possible.

You'll notice that the code window doesn't use your menu names, but subroutine names instead. This is both good news and bad news. First, the bad news: this can make it a little difficult to remember which menu you happen to be writing code for. The good news outweighs the bad, however – you can call the menu code like any other subroutine. This makes it easy for you to perform the menu's functions without the user having to explicitly select the menu item. The same rules apply to the menu routines as other subroutines, including the inability to access form items other than Lists or PopUps unless the form with its objects is available.

MenuDraw

Syntax:

MenuDraw "MenuName"

Description:

Displays a menu at the top of the current form

Once the code is in the appropriate menus, it still won't be displayed until we issue the MenuDraw statement. The best place to put this statement is in the Form's MenuCode section. Unfortunately, no such section exists, so we need to rely on the Palm OS telling us that the user tapped on the silkscreen Menu area. To do this, we'll put program statements in the Events Code section of our form to respond to this screen tap, and only display the menu if the silkscreen button is tapped (also works with tapping the upper left "form name" with OS 3.5 and above):

```
Dim EventType as Integer
Dim key as String
EventType=GetEventType()
If EventType=nsbKeyOrButton Then
    key=GetKey()
    If asc(key)=5 Then
        MenuDraw "mnuMain"
    End If
End If
```

Note that for each form, this is only needed to display the menu – each submenu is part of the main menu, and gets displayed when tapped. Note also that we have to give the menu name, since menus aren't associated with any specific form.

> **Note** But, wouldn't it make more sense to have the menu already assigned to the form? Well, it would simplify things, but you'd need to have separate menus for each form, even if you had multiple forms that used the exact same menu. Since the Palm devices are relatively short on memory, this savings can add up!

MenuErase

Syntax:

MenuErase

Description:

Erases the current menu from the top of the current form

Erasing menus is easier than displaying them; in most cases you don't need to erase them – this is taken care of "behind the scenes". However, should you need to erase a menu, you'll use the MenuErase statement:

```
MenuErase
```

MenuErase erases the current menu from the top of the Palm screen, regardless of the level of the menu, or what form is active. As previously mentioned, you normally won't have any reason to use MenuErase – NS Basic takes care of the erasing of menus after the End Sub of the menu subroutine that your user selects, or if the user taps outside of the menu (as a way of not selecting anything). However, if you want to completely control the display of menus from code, you can always use MenuErase to maintain complete control.

MenuReset

Syntax:

MenuReset

Description:

Cancels the current dropdown menu

If you don't want to erase the entire menu, but instead just remove the "popdown" menus (and leave the main menu line displayed), you can use MenuReset. Like MenuErase, you simply issue the MenuReset statement without any additional parameters:

```
MenuReset
```

Also like MenuErase, you're not likely to need to use MenuReset, since the user's actions normally dictate how the menu will act, and NS Basic shields you from having to deal with these background details. But it's nice to know that its there, in case you decide to do some fancy menu footwork. In the interest of not confusing your users, however, keep things simple.

Chapter XV - Interacting with your user

Your Palm apps, like any other programs, would be pretty useless if your user couldn't interact with them. Sure, we've seen how we can use fields, labels, and other objects to get user input and display out results – but we want more, don't we? How about those instances when we need to alert the user to an action, or display something temporarily, and don't want to waste screen space just for the occasional error? We could always use screen graphics commands, but then we need to erase them, and redraw the underlying objects. There's got to be another way.

Interacting Visually - Message and Alert Boxes

MsgBox, Alert

Syntax:

> **MsgBox MessageString**
> **Alert(TitleMsg,PromptMsg,AlertType,Option1[,Option2][,Option3][,...])**

Description:

> **Displays a message on a small box on the screen (MsgBox), and allows the selection of one or more options (Alert)**

As you've come to know by now, if I tell you something is possible, I'll show you how to do it. Even if it's impossible, we've sometimes been able to accomplish that as well. Temporary message display is no exception.

NS Basic and the Palm OS give us two simple messaging boxes (and I'm sure more are yet to come). For now, we have the Message Box and Alert. We'll discuss Message Boxes first, since they're pretty simple and easy to use. Next, we'll show you what you were missing with the Message Box.

As its name implies, the Message Box is an easy way to present a box with a message in it to your user. Not too impressive, to be sure, but useful none the less. To use it, decide what message you want to display to your user (up to 185 characters), and issue the MsgBox statement:

```
dim msg as string
msg="This application copyright Michael Verive"
MsgBox msg
```

This statement displays a simple message box with your message, a border with title "Program Message", and an "OK" button.

As I said – not too impressive. However, there are times when a simple message like this is enough. Especially when you're programming and using Message boxes to display the results of a variable, you may not need to alter the Message box title, and won't necessarily need more than one option ("OK"). When it comes time to present information to your user, you'll want something with a little more pizzazz, a little more "oomph" – the Alert.

The Alert function allows you to provide a title for your box, a message to display (also up to 185 characters, like the Message box), multiple options, and returns an integer that corresponds to your user's choice. Here's an example:

```
dim titlemsg as string
dim msg as string
dim result as integer
dim AlertType as integer
AlertType=0 ' information message
'AlertType=1 ' confirmation message
'AlertType=2 ' warning message
'AlertType=3 ' error message
titlemsg="Program Message"
msg="This application copyright Michael Verive"
result=Alert(titlemsg,msg,0,"OK")
```

OK, so all I did was emulate the Message Box. But I *did* include the different Alert types, so don't be too hard on me! For a more useful example, let's use the Alert function to ask our user if he wants to send a string to the MemoPad application, or to PalmPrint (modified from my MegaMemo project):

```
result=alert("MegaMemo","Print to Memo Pad or PalmPrint?",_
1, "MemoPad", "PalmPrint", "Cancel")
If result=0 Then
    TextToMemo dbRecord ' send the memo to MemoPad
    result=alert("MegaMemo","Memo saved to Memo Pad",1,"OK")
ElseIf result=1 Then
    PalmPrint dbRecord ' print it using PalmPrint
End If
```

The first Alert gives the user three options: "MemoPad", "PalmPrint", and "Cancel". The second Alert is used like a Message box with a title (I really don't like the "Program Message" default Message box title).

The integer returned by the Alert function tells you which option your user selected. A result of 0 indicates the first option, a result of 1 for the second option, and so on. This allows you to branch off based on the selection your user makes, erasing the Alert box afterwards, redrawing the underlying screen contents automatically.

> **Tip** Always give your user a way out! If I had forced the choice of "MemoPad" or "PalmPrint" without the option to "Cancel", I could easily lose my user if he didn't really want to choose either one. Make your applications forgiving, and you'll have happier users every time.

Note that the Alert function gives you control over the title, and even allows you to use a "null" title if desired, to create an Alert without a title:

```
result=Alert("","This Alert has no title",0,"OK")
```

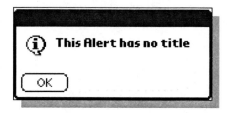

Also, maybe not so useful, since the title bar still takes up some space, even if you omit the title. So make good use of the space with an informative title.

A few more words about space. As we've seen many times, the Palm screen is pretty skimpy on room, so everything needs to be as compact as possible. You may have noticed that the different options are displayed as buttons, all in a single horizontal line. Not only does having all the text on one line limit the total text length, but the buttons take up additional room as well. You need to be careful not to use too many buttons, or too much text on the buttons. Each button displayed will attempt to use as much space as it would if used alone, with subsequent buttons having less "white space" around the button text. The following screen shots from the Alert Function Explorer project demonstrate this phenomenon:

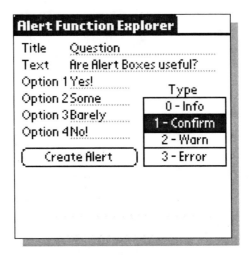

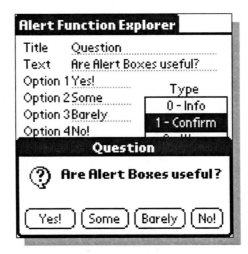

As mentioned in the NS Basic manual, you can use as many buttons as will fit, but more than three buttons will make your Alerts too cluttered.

Let's end this section with a custom Alert. I've already said that I don't like the default Message box title, and we've seen that we can use Alert to give the same visual effect as a Message box, so we'll combine the best of both methods, and generate a custom Message box:

```
Sub CustomMessageBox(MsgBoxTitle as string, msg as string)
dim result as integer
result=Alert(MsgBoxTitle,msg,0,"OK")
end sub
```

To use this subroutine, simply call it with the title and message that you wish to use:

```
Call CustomMessageBox("This is the Title","and this is the_
  message")
```

You can use string variables for the title and message. Additionally, as we've seen before with subroutines, if the subroutine is placed in a code module, you can call the subroutine without the use of the Call keyword and parentheses, so the previous call could be rewritten as:

```
CustomMessageBox "This is the Title","and this is the message"
```

A little creativity and you can easily come up with other variations on this theme to make your programming life easier.

Interacting Audibly - Beep and Sound

Beep, Sound

Syntax:

> **Beep**
> **Sound Freq,Duration,Amplitude[,nsbWait|nsbNoWait]**

Description:

> **Creates a sound of fixed duration and frequency (Beep), or of variable frequency, duration, and amplitude**

So far our applications have relied on the user looking at the screen for our output. Although most of the time we'll communicate with our users with screen text and other visual methods (bitmaps, progress bars, etc.), there are special instances where sound is more useful.

Take an alarm clock, for instance. Could you imagine having to read the time on the clock to rely on an alarm? The vast majority of your users would certainly question your sanity if you created an alarm clock that didn't use an audible alarm (can you think of someone who might want a visual alarm instead?). So, we'll explore the NS Basic statements that create sounds. As we did with Message boxes and Alerts, we'll show the simpler statement first, then move on to the more flexible statement later.

Well, nothing is simpler than the Beep statement. Issue the Beep statement, and your application will beep:

```
Beep
```

If all you need is a simple audible indicator, Beep might be good enough. You might want to use it to signal the end of a long procedure, or use it at intervals during a long procedure, so that your user doesn't need to stare at the Palm screen to know when the app is ready. Beep is easy to use, has a simple syntax (none!), and there's elegance in its simplicity.

But that's about as good as it gets for Beep. Since you have no control over the pitch, duration, or volume, Beep is really limited.

Enter Sound to the rescue! With the Sound statement, you can decide what pitch to use, how long to play it, and what volume to use, and whether the Palm OS should wait to for the sound to play before resuming operation (although we'll see that it probably won't matter whether you ask Sound to wait or not). This is what your Sound statement will look like:

```
Dim freq as integer ' in Hertz
Dim duration as integer ' in milliseconds
Dim amplitude as integer ' 1 or any number greater than 1
freq=880
duration=500
amplitude=1
Sound freq, duration, amplitude
' plays 880 Hz tone for 500 milliseconds at low amplitude (volume)
Sound 14000,1000,2
' plays 14000 Hz tone for one second at louder amplitude
Sound 25000,2000,2
' only your dog and Superman can hear this 25000Hz, 2 second tone
Sound 60,5000,2
' this is 5 seconds of 60 Hz tone, the "line hum" in the USA
```

> **Note** You may notice that the volume parameter doesn't seem to make much of a difference, or that the sound isn't audible at all. If so, check out the setting for "Game Sound" in the Prefs application. Sound plays tones whose volume is dependent on this parameter, not "System Sound" (Note – this may be OS version dependent).

You can also add the optional wait parameter, but as of Palm OS 3.5, the wait parameter isn't used:

```
Sound 14000,1000,2,nsbWait
' plays a 14000 Hz tone for one second, waits until tone_
is finished playing to continue
```

You can create interesting sound effects by using various tones and durations in loops. In the TicTacToe project, different sounds are used for a win or draw:

```
'win - loops with rising then falling tones
Dim freq as Integer
For freq = 60 to 400 step 40
   Sound freq,50,2
Next
For freq = 400 to 60 step -40
   Sound freq,50,2
Next
Sound 60,500,2
'draw, or "cat's game", just some low frequency buzzes
Sound 400,200,2
Sound 200,200,2
Sound 100,800,2
```

You could use different tones for different functions. For instance, you could use a tone that continues to rise along with a value in your application, such as temperature, humidity, or other values. With a little experimentation, and a little creativity, you can come up with plans for other useful or novel applications (a guitar tuner and a simple piano come to mind).

> **SideBar** I come from a musical family. Nearly everyone in my family has either a great voice, can play many instruments, or in some other way has an inborn musical talent. Most of us are also quite mathematical, so in the interest of satisfying my musical, mathematical, programming side, I've created two small projects - tuners for Guitar and Cello (two of my favorite instruments) that play notes at the correct frequencies for each. For the typical six-string guitar, the notes E-A-D-G-B-E are represented by frequencies of 83, 110, 147, 196, 247, and 330 Hz, respectively. The cello starts lower, and its four strings are tuned C-G-D-A, at frequencies of 65, 98, 147, and 220 Hz. Orchestras are typically tuned using A at 440 Hz. The file musicnotes.txt on the CD gives a much more complete list of notes and their frequencies, including frequencies outside the range of human hearing, which is approximately 15-20,000 Hz.

Trapping user actions

Despite the large number of screen objects, you may find the need to design your own method of obtaining user input. No doubt about it – the predefined objects work well, but they're not perfect. The Field, for example, only runs its code when you exit the field (and even then not every time, only when you move to certain other controls that can receive their own focus). What if you want to perform some action when the user *enters* the field? At other times you may wish to keep the user from activating other screen objects, or may want to use the Palm's buttons for special purposes in your applications, rather than having them perform their usual functions.

We've briefly mentioned a special section of code that each form has, the *Event* code (called the Events code is earlier versions of NS Basic). Every time your application generates an event (by a screen tap, for instance), it gets placed in an "event queue". The Palm OS then responds to each event in order. However, NS Basic gives you the chance to respond to these events yourself by intercepting ("trapping") these events in your form's Event code.

GetEventType, GetPen, GetKey, and SetEventHandled

Syntax:

> **GetEventType()**
> **GetPen penX, penY, penStatus**
> **GetKey()**
> **SetEventHandled**

Description:

> **Used to determine the nature of a user action, and optionally tell the Palm OS to ignore the event (SetEventHandled)**

The first step in trapping events is determining what type of event has occurred. The NS Basic function GetEventType gives you this information:

```
Dim res as integer
res=GetEventType()
```

The possible values and return codes for the event types are given in the following table:

Event types

NS Basic Type	Description	Integer value
NsbKeyOrButton	Key or button pressed	1
NsbPenDown	PenDown event (stylus pressed on the screen)	2
NsbPenUp	PenUp event (stylus lifted from the screen)	3
NsbJogDial	Sony jog dial pressed	4
	HandEra Jog Dial	5
	Event from Shared Library	> 24832

Once you know the type of event that has occurred, you can respond to it appropriately. Let's say you wanted to determine when a user has entered a specific screen field, located at left 5, top 30, with a width of 100 and height of 12. You can trap the PenUp or PenDown event (we'll use PenDown), compare the coordinates with the location of your field, and perform an action if your user taps within the field. In the Event code of your form:

```
dim EventType as integer
dim x as integer
dim y as integer
dim PenStatus as integer
EventType=GetEventType()
If EventType=NsbPenDown then
  GetPen x,y,PenStatus
  If (x > 4) and (x < 106) and (y > 29) and (y < 43) then
    'user tapped on field, so perform the appropriate action...
  end if
endif
```

This code will allow us to perform some action when our user enters the field, rather than wait until our user exited the field. The Palm OS will then continue processing the event (showing the cursor in the field), and allow data entry/editing (unless the field was declared as non-editable). Note that we didn't use SetEventHandled:

```
dim EventType as integer
dim x as integer
dim y as integer
```

```
dim PenStatus as integer
EventType=GetEventType()
If EventType=NsbPenDown then
  GetPen x,y,PenStatus
  If (x > 4) and (x < 106) and (y > 29) and (y < 43) then
    'user tapped on field, so perform the appropriate action…
    SetEventHandled
  end if
end if
```

In this case, our action would have still been performed, but by issuing the SetEventHandled command we tell the Palm OS to ignore the event (remove it from the queue). The Palm OS would then not "know" that our user wanted to enter the field – not necessarily what we wanted.

Caution I warned you earlier that it's easy to cause your app to get stuck and not respond to any user action, and this is one demonstration of how it can happen. You could all too easily use SetEventHandled after any event, requiring a hard reset.

Note that the above code used GetPen to determine the location of the stylus tap. GetPen can also be used outside of the Event code, and will return the last screen coordinates for the stylus tap, as well as the PenStatus (which, when used out of the Event code, will virtually always be nsbPenUp).

I mentioned that you could use the Event code to give your app control over the Palm's buttons and silk-screened "soft keys" (we used this technique to trap Menu taps to display our menus). You can easily trap the buttons for use in games or other applications where you want to use the buttons for non-standard functions:

```
If GetEventType()=nsbKeyOrButton then
dim key as integer
key=asc(getKey())
select case key
case 1 ' hard button #1 on bottom of case
'
case 2 ' hard button #2 on bottom of case
'
case 3 ' hard button #3 on bottom of case
'
case 4 ' hard button #4 on bottom of case
'(misprinted in some manuals and help files as button #5)
'
case 5 ' menu key on silkscreen area
'
case 6 ' shortcut stroke in Grafitti area
'
case 7 ' find key on silkscreen area
'
case 11 ' up button
'
case 12 ' down button
'
case 14 ' power on/off button
```

```
'
case 15 ' cradle hotsync button
'
case 16 ' calculator key on silkscreen area
'
case 17 ' application launch key on silkscreen area
'
case 23 ' shortcut key in graffiti area
'
case else
'
end select
end if
```

One application I'm currently working has its own calculator, so I trap the calculator button, perform my own calculation, and return control afterwards (I'd show the code, but the app isn't ready yet, and I promised you that I'd only include tested code – but you get the idea anyway).

You'll find this useful in games, should you decide to write any. In my Mouse Race project, I trap the Calendar and MemoPad buttons to allow the players to use them rather than rely on screen taps to move their mice:

```
dim key as integer
key=asc(getKey())
Select Case key
Case 1     'hard button #1 on bottom of case
'let player 1 use the left hand button
Play1Score=Play1Score+1 ' increase score
Play1Y=100-Play1Score   ' decrease Y value to move mouse up
DisplayMice             ' display the mice
SetEventHandled         ' don't run the calendar

Case 4     'hard button #2 on bottom of case
'let player 2 use the right hand button
Play2Score=Play2Score+1 ' increase score
Play2Y=100-Play2Score   ' change y value to move mouse
DisplayMice             ' display the mice
SetEventHandled         ' don't run the memopad
End Select
```

Here I make sure to include SetEventHandled to keep the user from accidentally running the Calendar or MemoPad apps.

Although this code demonstrates the trapping of Events on a form, if you compile and run the Mouse Race project, and run it on a real Palm device, you'll notice a nasty problem – once either of the players' mice hits the finish line, a Message Box gets briefly displayed, then the Calendar or MemoPad runs! But I thought we trapped these buttons on our form – what went wrong?

Nothing is wrong, really. The problem is that although we trapped these two buttons on our Mouse Race form, when the Message Box gets displayed it's really a form of its own, with an Event handler that we don't have access to. Since we can't modify the Message Box's Event code, we can't stop it from responding appropriately to button taps. The solution is to not use Alerts or Message Boxes at all, but to display our "Game Over" message using other form objects or screen graphics.

As you can tell, trapping user actions isn't something you'll want to get too involved with until you're comfortable with the rest of what NS Basic has to offer. These techniques are powerful, though, and worth the time taken to master them.

Chapter XVI - Serial Input/Output (I/O)

Up to this point our applications have been very self-centered. Everything they've done has involved one-to-one communication with our user, without any interaction with the rest of the outside world (with the exception of the use of PalmPrint to communicate with printers – and even that has been a one-way communication). Well, the world can be a lonely place if we don't reach out to our neighbors, even if it's only through the serial port.

If you've never programmed serial I/O before, you're in for a treat. Actually, initially it's more of a headache than a treat, but once you get the communication parameters worked out, you'll see that serial I/O is very straightforward. In fact, serial communication is probably too simple. This simplicity is its greatest strength and greatest weakness, rolled into one.

Serial output involves sending single bits of data, one bit at a time and in a row, which is why it's called serial (parallel I/O involves sending a number of bits all at the same time, which has significant speed advantages, but requires that both the sending and receiving devices are prepared to handle the exact number of bits at the same time). Since these serial bits are sent in a single stream, the sending and receiving devices must both be set to know how many bits make up a discreet piece of data, how quickly the data is being sent, how many bits to use to separate discreet pieces of data, and other information to establish successful communication. If the sender is putting data out 7 bits per character, with one bit between characters, at 2400 bits per second, and the receiver is expecting 8 bits per character, 2 bits between each character, and a bit stream running at 300 bits per second, it's clear that the two devices aren't going to understand each other. Successful serial communication demands attention to these little details. Get two devices to agree, and you've got communication. Fail to control the serial parameters and you'll have about as much success as attempting to teach a pig to play chess.

In order to perform serial I/O, the basic steps to follow are:

- Open the serial port

- Set the parameters

- Send or receive data

- Close the serial port

We'll discuss each of these steps in detail, and develop a working serial communication app. Much of this will only pertain to a small percentage of programmers, so feel free to skip the rest of this chapter if you have no urge to pursue serial programming.

NS Basic provides several functions to control the serial port, listed below.

NS Basic Serial Input/Output Functions.

Function	Description
SerialOpen	Opens the serial port and prepares for input/output
SerialClose	Closes the serial port to discontinue its use
SerialReceive	Accepts input from the serial port
SerialSend	Transmits data out through the serial port
SerialSet	Sets the value of several serial port parameters to control transmission options
SerialDial	Dials a phone number through the modem
SerialHangup	Disconnects a phone line connection

Since the best way to understand any programming topic is to use it, let's prepare our app. Open the IDE, start a new project, and name it "Serial I/O Explorer". We'll declare several variables in our project's StartUp section as globals:

```
Global baudrate as Integer
Global handshake as Integer
Global Parity as Integer
Global stopbits as Integer
Global bitsperchar as Integer
Global ctstimeout as Integer
Global result as Integer
```

Most of these variables will be used to set different communications parameters with the SerialSet statement – we'll discuss it further when we get to it.

SerialOpen

Syntax:

SerialOpen(PortNum,Baudrate)

Description:

Opens the specified serial port, and sets the initial baud rate

For now, our next step will be to "open" the serial port, which tells the Palm OS that we are going to take control of the port for our uses. Once the port is opened by an application, no other application can use it. This isn't a problem with the Palm OS, since for the most part it acts like a single-threaded, non-multitasking operating system. We'll just need to be sure that we close the port when we're done. The easiest way to ascertain that we have the port open during the running of our app is to place the opening code in the StartUp section, so we'll do that now, using SerialOpen:

```
baudrate=2400 ' use a default value
result=SerialOpen(0,baudrate)
```

The SerialOpen function takes two parameters: the port number (zero in this case, which is the only port available on most devices), and the baud rate, roughly equivalent to the number of bits sent through the serial port per second. We'll give our user the chance to select a different baud rate later, but we need one for the SerialOpen function, so I decided on a reasonable value, 2400 bps (bits per second).

> **Note** The Palm OS currently supports baud rates up to 1 megabit per second, but most serial devices can't handle those speeds. The highest rate supported by most current devices is 57,600 bps, which we'll use as our peak speed. Just remember that higher speeds are possible. In the world of computers, too fast is never enough!

Since our application needs to have control of the serial port, we'll introduce error checking to allow the app to shut down peacefully if it can't open the serial port:

```
If result > 0 Then
    MsgBox "Error: "+str(result)+" during serial open, can't
continue"
    Stop
End If
```

I doubt that you will ever experience an error opening the serial port in the StartUp section of your application, since the port should be "free and clear" by other applications having closed it when they were through. Since we can't guarantee it, though, it's best to use error checking. At the very least it helps avoid having to perform a hard reset!

SerialClose

Syntax:

SerialClose()

Description:

Closes a previously opened serial port

While we're thinking about maintaining control over the serial port, let's create our Termination code to close the port:

```
result=SerialClose()
If Result > 0 then
   MsgBox "Error: "+str(result)+" closing the serial port"
end if
```

Note that SerialClose doesn't require any port number or other parameter – it assumes a port number of zero. Like SerialOpen in the StartUp section, SerialClose isn't likely to cause any errors, but we provide error checking just in case. Better safe than sorry.

Now that we have the StartUp and Termination code completed, we'll create our form's objects, and attach code. This app will allow the user to set communications parameters, then send or receive data through the serial port. To do this we'll need a multi-line field for the data, PopUps to set baud rate, parity, handshaking, the number of bits per character, the number of stop bits, and the amount of time we'll allow our app to wait for data before deciding that it isn't going to wait any longer. We'll also use three screen buttons – send, clear, and receive – to manage our text field. You can decide any layout you want, but here's what my form looks like:

One control you don't see is the Shift Indicator, placed on the screen at the lower right corner, with the field's AutoShift set to true, to automatically capitalize the first letter after a period, exclamation point, or question mark.

SerialSet

Syntax:

SerialSet("ParameterName", Value)

Description:

Used to set one of various serial communications parameters

With our objects in place, we can give them the code they require. For each of the PopUp's, we'll create lists of items for our user to choose from. This eliminates many of the chances for error, and makes our user's life easier as well. For the PopUp's, create the following lists (you could do this in code, but now that the IDE allows you to build these lists at design time, why fill these "static" lists in code and force your user to wait during the time-consuming process?):

Baud rate : 300, 600, 1200, 2400, 4800, 9600, 14400, 19200, 38400, 57600
Parity: 1 - Odd Parity, 2 - Even Parity, 3 - No Parite
Handshake: 0 - None, 1 - Handshake
BitsPerChar: 7, 8
StopBits: 1, 2
Timeout: 5 secs, 15 secs, 30 secs, 60 secs, 90 secs

The complete list of SerialSet values that can be set, along with their default values, is given in the following table:

SerialSet parameters and default values.

Parameter	Possible values	Default
Autobaud	Allows the Palm OS to determine baud rate automatically (0=off, 1=on)	1
Buffersize	Maximum characters for SerialReceive	512
Baudrate	Speed of communication in bits/second	(SerialOpen value)
BitsPerChar	Number of bits/character (5,6,7,or 8)	8
Cmdtimeout	Timeout in microseconds	500,000
CTSauto	Tells the OS whether or not to use ClearToSend (1 for on, 2 for off)	1
CTStimeout	Seconds before timeout error occurs	5
Dcdwait	Seconds to wait for connection	70
Dialtone	Use 0 for pulse dialing, 1 for tone dialing	1
DTwait	Seconds to wait for dialtone	4
Handshake	1 if Handshaking used, 0 if not	0
IR	Allows OS to redirect serial functions to IR port (0=serial port, 1=IR port)	0
Parity	1=odd parity, 2=even parity, 3=no parity	3
RTSauto	Tells OS whether or not to use RequestToSend (1 for on, 2 for off)	1
Stopbits	Number of stopbits to use (0,1, or 2)	1
Volume	Modem volume level (from 0 to 3, where 0 is off and 3 is maximum)	1
XonXoff*	Tells OS whether or not to use XonXoff (1 for on, 2 for off)	1

*some Palm OS docs state that this is not implemented.

The baud rate and timeout values can be any value you choose, but I've chosen values likely to be useful (additionally, most communications software can only handle specific baud rates, and don't allow arbitrary baud rates, such as 3481 bps).

A complete description of each of these parameters is beyond the scope of this book. However, special mention is made of the IR parameter. This was added in previous versions of NS Basic to allow serial commands to be redirected to the infrared port. Unfortunately, this redirection only makes "raw" use of the serial data, and isn't as sophisticated as any of the IrDA protocols, so its function is fairly limited. However, two Palm units set to communicate with serial I/O via the IR ports may be useful, so you should know about this option.

Once you have the PopUp's filled out with their respective lists, we can move on to creating the code that will be executed when our user taps one of the PopUp's.

> **Tip** Save your work NOW! Don't go any farther! You've just entered several lists – do you really want to enter them all over again? NS Basic offers the "Save before compile" option, but it's all too easy to crash many Windows systems. A good rule of thumb: *never leave anything unprotected that you don't want to recreate from scratch.*

You may wonder why I used the mixed numeric/text formats for some of the PopUps. All of the parameters used by the SerialSet function are expected to be integers, so by using a numeric value, or a text string that begins with a number, I can convert the string returned by the PopUp with the use of the Val function. For each of the PopUp's, we'll get the user's selection, and it to an integer, and use SerialSet to set the specific parameter. Any parameter that our user doesn't select will be filled in by the Palm OS default values:

For our BaudRate PopUp:

```
baudrate=val(popBaud.itemtext(popBaud.selected))
result=serialset("baudrate",baudrate)
```

For Parity:

```
parity=val(popParity.itemtext(popParity.selected))
result=serialset("parity",parity)
```

For Handshake:

```
Handshake=val(popHandshake.itemtext(popHandshake.selected))
result=serialset("handshake",handshake)
```

For BitsPerChar:

```
bitsperchar=val(popBitsPerChar.itemtext(popBitsPerChar.selected))
result=serialset("bitsperchar",bitsperchar)
```

For StopBits:

```
stopbits=val(popStopBits.itemtext(popStopBits.selected))
```

```
result=serialset("stopbits",stopbits)
```

For Timeout:

```
cmdtimeout=1000000*val(popTimeout.itemtext(popTimeout.selected))
'cmdtimeout is in microseconds
result=serialset("cmdtimeout",cmdtimeout)
```

Each of these functions can return one of several error codes, which are listed in the manual and help file under SerialOpen. I've included them here for your convenience.

Return codes for Serial I/O functions.

Code	Description
0	Operation successful
1	Operation failed
769	Bad Parameter
770	Bad Port
771	No Memory
772	Bad Connect ID
773	Time Out
774	Line Error
775	Already Open
776	Still Open
777	Not Open
778	Not Supported

I've arranged my PopUp's at the top of the form as a visual clue to my user that the communication parameters should be set first, before attempting to send or receive text. At this point, all we have left to do is write the code for the Send, Clear, and Receive buttons, and we're ready to give our app a test run.

SerialSend

Syntax:

> **SerialSend(StringBuffer, NumChars)**
> **or**
> **SerialSend(IntegerArrayName,NumChars)**

Description:

Used to send a string or integer array through the previously opened serial port

Sending data through the serial port is accomplished using the SerialSend function. You might guess that since we've already used SerialSet to set the various communications parameters, we shouldn't have to do much with SerialSend – and you'd be right. The SerialSend function has only two parameters – the string to send, and its length. For string data, you can easily pass the string and its length at the same time, as I do in this app's Send button:

```
If len(fldData.text)<>0 then
   result=serialsend(fldData.text,len(fldData.text))
   MsgBox "Result of send: "+str(result)
else
   Msgbox "No data to send"
end if
```

If you want to send a null character, use:

```
result=SerialSend(chr(0),1)
```

> **Note** You aren't limited to string data – NS Basic allows you to pass entire integer arrays (nope – no floats or other numeric types), with each array element transmitted as its ASCII character.

For our Clear button, all it needs to do is clear the screen field:

```
fldData.text=""
```

SerialReceive

Syntax:

SerialReceive(StringBuffer, NumChars,TimeOut)

Description:

Used to receive data transmitted through a previously opened serial communications port

Reading serial data, once the communications parameters have been set, is almost as easy as sending it. Slightly more demanding than SerialSend, the SerialReceive function has three parameters – a buffer to receive the data, a buffersize variable, and a timeout parameter.

```
result=SerialReceive(buffer as string or integer array,_
 buffsize as integer, timeout as double)
```

For our Receive button:

```
Dim buffer as String
result=serialreceive(buffer,512,(cmdtimeout/1000000))
If result < 1 Then
    flddata.text=buffer
Else
    MsgBox "Result of receive: "+str(result)
End If
```

Our buffer needs to be large enough to receive the data being sent, so the sending application doesn't "time out" waiting for us to accept the data. SerialReceive will accept up to the buffer size number of characters, and will stop after receiving the data, allowing you to call SerialReceive again later to receive additional characters after clearing your buffer. As with SerialSend, integer arrays will be transmitted with an ASCII character for each element of the array. In either case, even if the buffer isn't filled, the SerialReceive will end after the timeout in seconds (since our cmdtimeout variable is in microseconds, we need to divide by 1000000). You may have to experiment with the baud rates and timeout values for your individual applications.

To test this app, compile it, and HotSync it to your Palm device. If you have a serial cradle, you can test directly through the cable attached to your computer's serial port. You don't need to use a null modem, but you do need to make sure that HotSync isn't running, since it will try to control the serial port, and make it unavailable to our app.

If you have a standard Windows installation, you should have HyperTerminal, a simple communications application that can be used to dial up to bulletin boards and other simple communications systems. With HyperTerminal set up to communicate directly through the serial (COM) port that your cradle is connected to, set both HyperTeminal and the Serial I/O Explorer to common parameters. For testing, the following parameters should be a good starting point:

-    BaudRate 2400 bps

-    No parity

-    No Handshaking

-    8 bits per character (called data bits on most systems)

-    1 stop bit

-    30 second timeout

Make sure HyperTerminal is connected ("dialed up", even though this is a direct connection), and attempt to send the default text. If all goes well, you should see it sent to the HyperTerminal screen. (Remember my promise to not have any bad code? I'm testing this as I'm writing it, so you can rest assured that this actually works!). My screen shot from HyperTerminal:

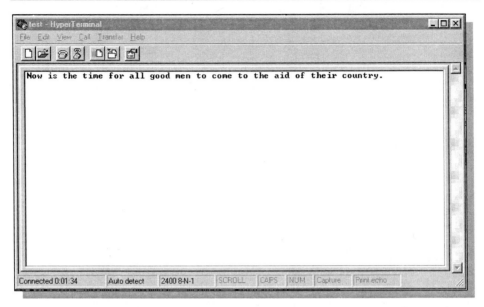

To send data in the opposite direction, tap the Clear button to clear the field on the Serial I/O Explorer, and in HyperTerminal, select Transfer, then Send Text File. Find a text file on your computer (you can use the readme.txt file that gets installed with almost any program), and prior to actually sending it, tap the Receive button in the Serial I/O Explorer. You'll see up to 512 characters of text from the file (there will probably be some strange "box" characters, since DOS and Windows use Chr(13) as a carriage return, while the Palm OS uses Chr(10)). However, this is one way to transfer files from your computer to your Palm OS device, without having to convert the file into a PDB. But that's a topic of a different chapter.

SerialDial

Syntax:

SerialDial(PhoneNumberString, ModemCommandString)

Description:

Dials the given phone number and passes an optional modem command string to a modem on a previously opened serial communications port

If you intend on writing full-fledged communications programs, you'll probably want to be able to communicate with modems for dial-up access. NS Basic supports SerialDial and SerialHangup to handle the dial-up connection.

SerialDial allows you to supply a modem setup or initialization string (without the "AT" prefix, as these are supplied automatically by the SerialDial function), and the phone number to dial. Modem commands are sent directly to the modem – NS Basic doesn't perform any interpretation of these commands.

```
result=SerialDial("9,1-555-123-4567","ATDT")
```

If there is no modem command, use the null, or empty string.

```
result=SerialDial("9,1-555-123-4567","")
```

SerialDial doesn't open the serial port, however – you still need to issue the SerialOpen function before you can begin communications.

SerialHangup

Syntax:

SerialHangup()

Description:

Hangs up the connection on a modem on a previously opened serial communications port

Like SerialClose, SerialHangup is issued without any parameters.

```
result=SerialHangup()
```

SerialHangup does exactly what its name suggests – it hangs up the phone line. SerialHangup does NOT close the serial port – you still need to use SerialClose. This is an important point, yet one that's easily overlooked.

> **Note** As this book is being written, NS Basic is adding new functionality to the serial input/output routines to reflect changes in the Palm OS. Since I promised that I would test any code that I put in this book, I won't address the new functions here other than to let you know what NS Basic has in the new release (slightly modified from NS Basic's announcement):
>
> **Changes to Serial Communications**
> --------------------------------
> Palm introduced a new Serial Manager in Palm OS 3.3. For compatibility, the old Serial Manager continued to work fine: it just mapped its calls to the new serial manager. NS Basic until now used the old serial manager version of the calls. Starting with 2.1.1, the old serial manager is only used for devices running Palm OS 3.2 and earlier. The changes should be transparent to users. Here are descriptions of the new functions:
>
> **SYSINFO(3)**
> Description - Returns the PortID that the Palm OS uses to refer to an open serial port. For pre 3.3 devices, this returns the serial library reference.
>
> Example:
>
> ```
> dim portID as integer
> portID=sysInfo(3)
> ```
>
> **SERIALOPEN(port, baudrate):**

This function is unchanged, but the Port can now have values other than zero.
Here are the choices (Palm OS 3.3 and later only)

        0 Cradle Port. USB or RS 232
    32768 Same as 0
    32769 IR: Raw IrDA, no protocol support
    32770 Debug console port
    32771 Cradle - RS 232
    32772 Cradle – USB

Physical and Virtual port numbers are OK too - check the Palm OS
documentation for more info. You can convert virtual port names such as 'rfcm'
(Bluetooth virtual plug in) to a numeric port number by using the String4ToInt
function in the NSBSystemLib.

```
SERIALSET("DTRAssert",x)
' 0=normal, 1=asserted. (Palm OS 3.3 and higher)

SERIALSET("PortID",x)
' Where x is a valid PortID. See SysInfo(3)
```

SerialReceiveWithEvent()
Description - This new function sets up the Palm to wait for data to come in,
When characters arrive, a SerialIn event is generated that you can pick up in
your Event code. This function has no parameters.

Example

```
'anywhere in your program
dim err as integer
err=SerialReceiveWithEvent()

'in your form's Event Script
Dim err as Integer
Dim received as String
If getEventType()=nsbSerialIn Then
   MsgBox "Serial In Event"
   err=serialReceive(received, 10, 0)
   If Err > 0 Then
      Beep
      error.text=str(err)
      data.text=data.text+"."+Received
   Else
      error.text=""
      data.text=data.text+received
   End If
End If
```

SERIALRECEIVE(buffer as string or integer array , noChars as integer, timeout as double)
Modified - Receives incoming data from the serial port and places it into
buffer. It can be used to wait for data to arrive, or to get data once a program
has been notified of incoming data by a SerialIn event. It stops after receiving
at least noChars characters and cancels further receipt of data. If more
characters are received than the BufferSize set with the SerialSet() function.
This function returns a result code: see SerialOpen for a list of result codes.

If SerialReceive is called as a result of a SerialIn event, it will return when all the characters are read, even if noChars has not yet been received. The timeout argument is ignored.

If SerialReceive is not called after a SerialEvent, it will return when noChars are received or no characters are received in the timeout period in seconds. Fractions of a second are allowed. In the event of a timeout, the function will return 773, along with any data that was received in buffer.

If buffer is an integer array, the ASCII value of each byte (including null) will be put into an element of the array. This allows you to receive null characters.

Example:

```
Err=SerialReceive(inputString,200,.5)'non event case
```

Testing Serial Apps using POSE

Testing applications that use serial communications can be complex and time consuming. If you are testing on a device, you need to HotSync frequently, which can interrupt the serial connection you are trying to debug.

A better solution in many cases is to use POSE. In POSE Settings, under Properties, you can set the serial port to COM1 or COM2. You will need to download the full POSE from Palm's website. The bound emulator that comes with NS Basic won't let you do this.

POSE will then use your computer's serial port, just like a Palm OS device port, so you can run your program on POSE. Now here comes the clever part: leave your Palm plugged into the serial port and use it to mimic the other end of your communications. A freeware program like "ptelnet", available on www.palmgear.com, can be used to control it.

Now you can write, download and test your serial communications on POSE, without having to Hotsync.

Chapter XVII - Extending NS Basic

We've explored almost every aspect of NS Basic programming, at least as far as the NS Basic objects, statements, and functions can get us. But we know there's more – one look at the Palm OS SDK documentation reveals a large number of API functions that aren't accessible using the standard NS Basic language.

NS Basic realizes this limitation, and has provided three methods to allow you to access the majority of these functions. If you are comfortable with C programming, the sky's the limit.

> **Note** I don't fall into that last group. If you remember, I chose NS Basic partly because I didn't *want* to learn C just to program my Palm. The good news is that you don't have to worry about doing any C programming to use the techniques in this chapter.

Accessing the Palm OS API

NS Basic includes SysTrapSub and SysTrapFunc, subroutine and function calls that allow you to call API functions from within your NS Basic app. The safe, effective use of these functions requires that you understand the Palm OS well, and that's beyond the scope of this book. If you want to use these function, but don't care to study the Palm OS, restrict yourself to using functions as they are already written in the sample projects on the CD, or projects written by other programmers who are well versed in using the Palm OS. If you already have a good understanding of the OS and API, then by all means, read on!

> **Note** To help you out, recent versions of NS Basic added the .ID method to form objects, since many of the API functions require an object's ID number as one of their parameters. If you look into the NSBSystemLib functions, you'll see that many of them use this ID number as well.

SysTrapSub

The difference between SysTrapSub and SysTrapFunc is that SysTrapFunc returns a value (as does every function). SysTrapSub calls the API function, and uses the following syntax:

```
SysTrapSub APInum, NumParms [ ,parm1][ ,parm2] ...
' up to 6 parameters
```

APInum refers to the actual number of the API call as defined in the Palm OS (the actual API numbers start with 0xA000, and this value is added by NS Basic during runtime). NumParms is the number of parameters being passed to SysTrapSub, with the parameters themselves starting at parm1. Depending on the call, you may need to use any number of these parameters.

> **Note** The last sentence isn't strictly true – you can't use *any* number of parameters. SysTrapSub can accept up to 6 parameters, while SysTrapFunc can only accept 5. While this limits the API calls that you can call, we'll see when we discuss shared libraries that there are ways around these limitations.

There are currently more than 100 API calls (also referred to as "traps" – hence the terms SysTrapSub and SysTrapFunc) that you can access with NS Basic, and this number will almost certainly be larger by the time this book gets to press. A list of these traps can be found on the NS Basic API forum (currently at http://groups.yahoo.com/group/NS Basic-palmapi).

> **Caution** Just because these API functions are syntactically correct and can be used from within NS Basic doesn't mean that you can just call them and be on your way. Many of these functions must be called in a specific order, or after fulfilling some OS prerequisites. Working with the API is a potentially dangerous undertaking, and must be approached with a complete understanding of the Palm OS. Discussed later in this section are shared libraries, which shield you from some of this danger, but they must be used with care as well. Get comfortable with NS Basic's built-in functions before "tinkering under the hood" of the Palm OS API.

Additionally, Palm has documentation on the API calls on its website at www.Palm OS.com/dev/tech/docs/. NS Basic TechNote 6 (in the IDE, under Help) discusses the use of SysTrapSub and SysTrapFunc in detail.

> **Note** As is true with many websites, it's quite possible that these sites don't exist anymore. Some people and companies change Web addresses and pages more frequently than some programmers change socks! I guaranteed no bad code – the guarantee doesn't apply to website addresses. Sorry!

Since I've whetted your appetite, though, it wouldn't be fair to leave you without some examples:

```
SysTrapSub 564, 1, 5*256 ' SndPlaySystemSound (5 is the_
alarm sound)
```

```
SysTrapSub 531, 4, 80, 0, 80, 160 ' WinDrawLine
SysTrapSub 304,0 ' reset auto off timer
SysTrapSub 939,0 ' brightness adjust
SysTrapSub 844,0 ' contrast adjust, not available on all devices
SysTrapSub 140,0 ' SysReset (be careful with this one!!!)
```

Want to programmatically show the various built-in soft keyboards? Set the focus to your field for text entry, and use of these simple routines (from the Keyboard Explorer project):

```
Sub ShowAlphaKeyboard()
   Dim KeyboardType as short
   KeyBoardType=0
SysTrapSub 738,1,KeyBoardType
End Sub

Sub ShowNumericKeyboard()
   Dim KeyboardType as short
   KeyBoardType=256
SysTrapSub 738,1,KeyBoardType
End Sub

Sub ShowInternationalKeyboard()
   Dim KeyboardType as short
   KeyBoardType=512
SysTrapSub 738,1,KeyBoardType
End Sub

'the next subroutine courtesy Douglas Handy
'(not in KeyboardExplorer project)
'shows the appropriate keyboard, depending on the field
'if numeric, only the numeric keyboard will show
Sub ShowDefaultKeyboard()
   Dim KeyboardType as short
   KeyBoardType= -256
   SysTrapSub 738,1,KeyBoardType
End Sub
```

SysTrapFunc

When you need to use an API call that returns a value, you'll use SysTrapFunc. The syntax is similar to that of SysTrapSub, except that SysTrapFunc (like all NS Basic functions) returns a value:

```
Dim Err as Integer
Err=SysTrapFunc(APInum, NumParms [ ,parm1][ ,parm2] ...)
```

Since SysTrapFunc returns information, it's easy to think of SysTrapSub and SysTrapFunc as forms of communication. In a paternalistic, authoritative tone, SysTrapSub says, "Do this - and don't tell me what happens!", while SysTrapFunc is more friendly, with "Here's something to do – what do you think?". Clearly, SysTrapFunc provides two-way communication between the Palm OS and your user. A good example is passing information between objects and the clipboard – the familiar cut, copy, and paste.

Combining SysTrapSub and SysTrapFunc gives us easy access to the Palm OS clipboard, making it easy to add cut, copy, and paste to our applications. The following code is modified slightly from various sections of my MegaMemo project, and is presented here together to show how the API traps work together:

```
Global CurrentForm as Variant ' current form
Global FieldPointer as Variant  ' field object
Global FieldIndex as Short   ' field index
'
CurrentForm = SysTrapFunc(371, 0) ' FrmGetActiveForm
FieldIndex=systrapfunc(376,1,CurrentForm) ' FrmGetFocus
If FieldIndex <> -1 then
    FieldPointer = SysTrapFunc (387, 2, CurrentForm, FieldIndex)
    'FrmGetObjectPtr - use only if valid FieldIndex
End If
'
SysTrapSub 308, 1, FieldPointer ' FldCut
SysTrapSub 307, 1, FieldPointer ' FldCopy
SysTrapSub 316, 1, FieldPointer ' FldPaste
```

You probably noticed that in the code above I introduced a new variable type that we haven't used before: variant.   The variant type is officially supported only for passing values to API calls – especially pointers and other variable types that may not correlate exactly with NS Basic's standard variable types.

C and NS Basic variable types

C Type	NS Basic Type	Comments
Boolean	Short	1=true, 0=false
Char*	String	
UInt	Short	
Double	Float, Double	NS Basic floats and doubles are 64-bit floating point
enum	Byte, Short, Integer	Smallest size required to hold the largest enumerated variable
float	Single	
null	Integer	
pointer/Null	Integer, short	
pointers	Variant	

In fact, if you've worked with C or other languages, you may notice that NS Basic's variables don't necessarily agree with what you're used to. The table above lists common C variable types, their NS Basic equivalents, and some comments.

> **Tip** The variable types used in the API calls must match exactly
> with what the Palm OS expects, or unexpected results (crashes, burnt
> toast, etc.) are likely. When you have trouble with the API calls, 9 times
> out of 10 the problem is mismatched variable types. Refer to the Palm
> OS SDK and TechNotes often.

Shared Libraries

Even with the addition of SysTrapSub and SysTrapFunc, there are a large number of API calls that can't be accessed by NS Basic. Many of the API traps require the use of pointers or structures that just aren't within the capabilities of NS Basic. Even those functions that *are* accessible through the API calls are somewhat cryptic. How in the world are you ever supposed to remember that the API trap numbers for cut, copy, and paste are 308, 307, and 316? Which one is which? And what about obtaining the active form and object pointers first? Am I making you dizzy?

Shared libraries to the rescue! OK, maybe I'm getting a little dramatic. Although I've already referred to them throughout this book, let me describe the shared libraries, and what they have to offer, and you can make up your own mind.

Have you ever used a shared library before? You say you don't know? You probably have one on your Palm device, and don't even know it. One of the most popular shared libraries, MathLib, is so widespread that most users don't know they have it, don't know what it's for, and never give it a thought. Unless they delete it, that is (actually, MathLib is usually difficult to delete, and it's even in the Handspring Visor ROM!). MathLib is a shared library that adds a large number of mathematic functions that would otherwise be difficult or time-consuming to create in C or NS Basic.

Similarly, there are a number of new shared libraries available for NS Basic that add functionality and ease of use that only a month or two ago would have been impossible without using C. The secret behind this is that the shared libraries are written in C, but encapsulate the API calls and C code in a way that makes them compatible with NS Basic. The power of C with the ease of use of NS Basic – what a combination!

> **Note** just a reminder – you must have the registered, full version of
> NS Basic in order to include any of NS Basic's shared libraries (other
> than MathLib) in your applications. You won't be able to compile the
> projects otherwise. However, feel free to read this chapter anyway, and
> see what shared libraries can offer you. You may never need to use
> them, but it's nice to know that they're there, and some of the functions
> that they can supply.

Why not just have NS Basic add these functions to the runtime, and avoid shared libraries? Well, many of these functions will only be useful to a subset of NS Basic programmers, and adding them to the runtime would increase its size for everyone. Since the Palm memory space is so limited (especially compared to most desktop, laptop, and notebook computers!), conserving memory is a necessity, so programmers can include only those additional functions that they need, without unnecessary "code bloat".

Like MathLib, any shared library that you decide to use must be installed on your user's Palm device, but you'll see that these individual libraries don't consume a great deal of memory by themselves. Just don't forget to include them!

So, what are these shared libraries, and what do they have to offer the NS Basic programmer (and user)? The table below lists the available shared libraries and their descriptions.

Shared libraries available for NS Basic (more may have been added by the time you read this).

Library Name	Description
BitsNBytes	Adds support for logical (bit level) and related functions
NSBHandera	Adds functions to control HandEra devices
NSBKyocera	Adds support for Kyocera SmartPhone
NSBScreenLib	Adds support for controlling display features
NSBStringLib	Adds additional string functions
NSBSymbolLib	Adds support for Symbol barcode scanner
NSBSystemLib	Adds support for many system functions

Although some of these libraries are designed to work with specific devices, the NSBSystemLib is a good example of how shared libraries can make your life easier, and can provide functions previously unavailable.

For this example, we'll create an app that lists all the applications installed on a Palm device with their respective Creator ID's. There aren't any "native" NS Basic functions that provide this level of support, but the NSBSystemLib allows us to list databases, libraries, and apps according to their type, and can return information specific to each item, including Creator ID, memory card number, size, etc. For our purposes we'll create an app (Creator ID List) to allow our user to list all apps with their Creator ID's.

LoadLibrary

Syntax:

LoadLibrary libraryname, abbreviation

Description:

Instructs the compiler to load an existing shared library

In order to use shared libraries, we need to tell NS Basic to load them, and for that we'll use the LoadLibrary in the StartUp code for our app to load the NSBSystemLib shared library (you *did* start the IDE, didn't you?):

```
LoadLibrary "NSBSystemLib", "NSL"
```

> **Note** I told you that I'd give you a way to determine which applications used shared libraries, and this is the most sure-fire method: look in a project's Startup code in the IDE. If you see the LoadLibrary

statement, you can be certain that the project uses shared libraries. If you don't see the statement, then the only shared library supported is MathLib, which NS Basic supports by default.

The LoadLibrary statement identifies the library that we'll be loading (NSBSystemLib), and a "shortcut" (NSL) that we can use when calling the library. This way we can refer to a library function like DatabaseCardNo like:

```
CreatorIDFound=NSL.DatabaseCreatorID()
```

rather than having to use:

```
CreatorIDFound=NSBSystemLib.DatabaseCreatorID()
```

Although this is a minor point, using the shorter library name improves the readability of the code, cuts development time, and reduces the risk of typographical errors.

Note Talk about making the programmer's life easier! NS Basic didn't need to use these shortcuts – they could have forced you to type the entire library name each time. It's attention to this kind of detail that builds user loyalty!

Since our app will only perform a single function (and will only have a single code section outside of the StartUp code), there's no need for Global variables, so we can leave the StartUp code and concentrate on the program code.

As I've mentioned several times, it's best to flowchart or pseudo-code our app before writing any actual code. Here's how I picture the app:

- Initialize (we did that in the StartUp code)

- Perform the reading of apps and their Creator ID's

- Finalize

Well, that's about as simple as it gets! Hopefully, our code will be as simple. I already hinted that we could use the NSBSystemLib to perform this task, so we'll see if there's some way to get a list of applications.

It turns out that the NSBSystemLib has a very useful function "GetNextDatabaseByTypeCreator" that has the following syntax:

```
dbID = GetNextDatabaseByTypeCreator(newSearch, dbType,_
dbCreatorID, onlyLatestVersion)
```

Each of the parameters has multiple values, but for our purposes we'll set newSearch as 0 (to search for all apps), dbType to the integer for "appl" (the database type for applications), dbCreatorID to 0 (to match all apps), and onlyLatestVersion as 0 (for all versions).

The function returns a dbID value, which is an integer that identifies the LocalID, a non-zero Palm OS internal identifier for the database. If there is no database found, dbID will be zero. If a database is found that matches the given parameters, we can then use two other NSBSystemLib functions - DatabaseInfo and DatabaseCreatorID – to give us the name and Creator ID to display for our user.

Since we're going to be creating a list of apps and their Creator ID's, it makes sense to use a List object, so place one on our app's form, make it as large as you can (why waste space?), and give it a useful name, such as lstDirectoryList (we *are* creating a mini-directory). While you've got the form displayed, give it a useful title as well, like "Creator ID List".

Looking at the GetNextDatabaseByTypeCreator function, it's clear that the function doesn't return a list of items, but we can easily create a loop that calls the function until it returns a zero (remember, the dbID returned is a non-zero value, so the function is designed to return zero when there is no match). We'll put the code to perform this search in our main (and only) form's After code, starting with a declaration of the variables needed:

```
Dim dbID as Integer
Dim newSearch as Integer
Dim dbCreatorID as Integer
Dim CreatorIDFound as Integer
Dim onlyLatestVersion as Integer
Dim dbType as Integer
' isn't the type a 4 char string? We'll discuss that later...
Dim dbName as String
Dim dbListItem as String ' to use with the .Add list method
```

Before we use our List to display the information returned in our loop, we need to clear it (you'll forget to do this from time to time, but not while I'm teaching you!):

```
lstDatabaseList.Clear
```

Now, let's set up our parameters with their default values:

```
onlyLatestVersion = 0
dbCreatorID = 0
newSearch = 1
dbType = NSL.String4ToInt("appl")
```

I had to sneak in another NSBSystemLib function here, since the Palm OS internally uses an integer for this call, not our four-character string. The String4ToInt function takes the database type and returns an integer value. It's easy to see how we can expand this application by providing other four-character database types, such as "data" and "libr" to search for data and library databases (the Directory project on the CD uses these additional database types).

Now we're ready to read our "appl" databases. Since we will be checking in our loop for a non-zero return value, we don't want the loop to fail before we actually run it, so we'll assign a non-zero value to dbID (which we'll use for our return value), then run through the loop:

```
dbID=1
```

```
Do While dbID <> 0
    dbID = NSL.GetNextDatabaseByTypeCreator(newSearch, dbType,_
    dbCreatorID, onlyLatestVersion)
    If dbID <> 0 Then ' we have a database, so get its info
        dbName = NSL.DatabaseInfo(0, dbID)
        CreatorIDFound=NSL.DatabaseCreatorID()
        dbListItem=dbName+" - ID: "_
        +NSL.IntToString4(CreatorIDFound)
        ' format the list item
        lstDatabaseList.Add dbListItem ' and add it
    End If
    newSearch = 0
Loop
```

If you have a large number of applications, loading the list can take a long time, and it may appear to your user that the app is "frozen". So, add a field "fldStatus" to the right of the form title, and use it to let your user know that list items are being added. You could use a counter, and give a "Reading app: " message with the counter, but it's just as easy to display the dbName in the field, and this will give your user good feedback. Our loop will add this updating code:

```
dbID=1
Do While dbID <> 0
    dbID = NSL.GetNextDatabaseByTypeCreator(newSearch, dbType,_
    dbCreatorID, onlyLatestVersion)
    If dbID <> 0 Then ' we have a database, so get its info
        dbName = NSL.DatabaseInfo(0, dbID)
        CreatorIDFound=NSL.DatabaseCreatorID()
        fldStatus.text="Reading:" + dbName
        dbListItem=dbName+" - ID: "_
        +NSL.IntToString4(CreatorIDFound)
        ' format the list item
        lstDatabaseList.Add dbListItem ' and add it
    End If
    newSearch = 0
Loop
fldStatus.text="" ' clear status field
```

Compile the project (don't forget to give it a unique Creator ID!), HotSync it to your Palm device (or load it in POSE), and run it. Voila!

> **Note** Louis Pasteur is credited with saying, "Serendipity favors the prepared mind" (but in French). While writing this chapter and creating the Creator ID List app, I resized the List object to occupy the entire form (except for the form title). In doing so, I discovered how to do something I had often thought about – creating a List without a border. It turns out that if you make the List large enough to cover the form, you lose the border edges! Tuck that away in the back of your mind. You never know when you'll need it again!

Each shared library in NS Basic has a TechNote that explains the functions, their parameters, and return codes. If you wish to experiment with creating your own shared libraries, there are even TechNotes and sample code to get you started. For the

NSBSystemLib, the SysLibTest project provides examples of the incredible capabilities available with this small library. Take a look in the TechNotes directory on the CD for more information.

Chapter XVIII - Special Topics

You've done it! From the history of Basic through the nuances of NS Basic syntax, you've explored virtually everything that NS Basic has to offer. In this chapter we'll cover some special techniques and concepts that will help you integrate general programming algorithms with Palm OS-specific ideology, and I'll give you some techniques for optimizing the speed of your applications (including knowing when to break the rules of structured programming).

Printing in NS Basic

Storing information in your Palm device is great, and HotSync allows you to transfer this data to your desktop computer, where you're likely to do most of your printing. However, you may need to print directly from your Palm device, either through the serial port or to an IR-enabled printer. NS Basic doesn't have any "Print" keyword, or any built-in print routines, so currently the only way to print from NS Basic is to do so using the serial I/O functions (which we've already discussed), or through the use of third-party applications such as SCSPrint or PalmPrint (a shareware version of each is included on the enclosed CD, in case you don't already have either one). Printing through PalmPrint in NS Basic is somewhat different from how you may be used to printing in other dialects of Basic (printing using SCSPrint is handled using the same code, so I'll just refer to PalmPrint for either PalmPrint or SCSPrint).

The easiest way to print to PalmPrint in NS Basic is through the use of the AppLaunch statement. Since it's not always easy to remember the syntax of this statement or the launch code used, there's a code module PalmPrint.COD included with the projects and modules on the CD. Here are the contents of that module as seen when you load it into NS Basic's IDE:

```
Sub PalmPrint(PrintString as String)
Dim CardNo as Integer
Dim LaunchCode as Integer
Dim result as Integer
CardNo=0
LaunchCode=32768
result=AppLaunch(CardNo,"PalmPrint",LaunchCode,PrintString)
If result<>0 Then
    result=alert("PalmPrint", "Error printing to_
    PalmPrint",1,"OK")
End If
End Sub
```

If you load this code module into your application, when you need to print to PalmPrint from any of your forms or objects, all you need to provide is the name of the subroutine and the string to be printed:

```
PalmPrint "This is the print string"
```

   or

```
Call PalmPrint("This is the print string")
```

I prefer the first version, as it involves less typing, and is less prone to typographical errors. Plus, it acts like a built-in statement, which improves the readability of the code.

This is fine if all you want to do is print a single line of text. Most of the time, however, you'll need to print multiple lines (or pages) of information. Using the PalmPrint statement with each individual line will work, but with an undesirable side effect – each line will be printed on a separate page! The AppLaunch statement (and the PalmPrint subroutine that uses it) runs PalmPrint as a separate "print job" each time it's called, so PalmPrint faithfully ejects the page after each job.

To print multiple lines on the same page, you'll need to modify your string so that it contains all of the lines to be printed PLUS codes to tell the printer to move to the next line as needed. Luckily for us, the code for moving to the next line when printing is the same as the code for moving to a new line in a field – the Chr(10), or "line feed" character:

```
Dim PrintString as string
PrintString="This is the first line."
PrintString=PrintString+chr(10)+"This is the next line."
PrintString=PrintString+chr(10)+"and so on…"
PalmPrint PrintString
```

PalmPrint allows you to determine whether you want a line feed, a "carriage return" (the ASCII code Chr(13)), or both at the end of a line (even if your lines end with the line feed alone, as above). Most printers will print properly if the line feed and carriage return pair is used (but you may have to experiment with your printer). PalmPrint also allows you to select from a wide variety of printers, and knows which codes to send to tell the printer to print using different fonts, point sizes, and other settings.

Printing with PalmPrint is easy with supported IR-enabled printers, and printing through the serial port is only slightly more complicated. Your application won't need to handle printing any differently, but you'll need to make sure that PalmPrint and your printer are set to use the same baud rate and other serial parameters. You may also need to use a "null modem" cable or adapter, depending on your printer, if you are printing through the Palm serial port connected directly to a printer.

Note that if you are using a serial printer, you may not need PalmPrint at all. Just as we sent text to HyperTerminal in the chapter on Serial I/O, we can print directly to a serial printer instead. The same caveats apply regarding the serial settings and the use of a null modem. You may even be able to redirect serial output through the IR port if your printer can handle "raw" data (most use an IrDA protocol, which isn't currently directly supported by NS Basic, although a few users have been able to get acceptable results in special circumstances).

Directly printing using serial I/O give you the most flexibility, but also requires that you maintain complete control over the flow of data, including handling errors in transmission. It's not a job for the faint of heart, and you may find PalmPrint much more stable. It's also likely that most of your users already have PalmPrint installed, and even if they don't, the low registration price for PalmPrint (or its "stripped-down" sibling SCSPrint) is reasonable enough for most users. Luckily, whether you use PalmPrint or SCSPrint, the AppLaunch statement and PalmPrint cod module can be used "as-is" for either application.

Advanced Printing – Formatting with Control Codes

For most purposes, PalmPrint works well "out of the box", since it knows internally how to print to many different printers. In fact, PalmPrint was written to be "printer independent", so that if you have something that you print on one type of printer, then switch to another type of printer, you'll still get the same (or very similar) output. However, there may be times that you'll want to "spice up" your output with bold, double-wide, condensed, or other print formatting. PalmPrint makes this easy by allowing you to embed special "escape" codes to tell your printer what formatting you'd like to use. Not all of the special formatting codes work the same with all printers, however, so you end up trading printer independence for this added formatting power.

Formatting codes are inserted in strings sent to PalmPrint as one to three digit numeric values surrounded by the "double-less-than" and "double-greater-than" ("<<" and ">>") characters. Note that these refer to ASCII 171 and 187, NOT merely two less-than or two greater-than signs together, but the characters found in the lower right corner of the "Int'l" portion of the popup keyboard on the Palm (normal and shifted).

Many of the formatting codes use the "ESC" (ASCII 27) character to tell the printer that formatting commands follow, so only the value 27 needs to be in the "<<>>" string. For example, "ESC"W1 turns on a special "double-wide" mode on a Canon printer, and "ESC"W0 turns it off. So the following string would print with a special "double wide" string at the top (27 is the numeric value of the ESC character), followed by normal text:

```
Dim EscStart as byte
Dim EscEnd as byte
EscStart=chr(171)
EscEnd=chr(187)
Msg=EscStart+"27"+EscEnd+"W1This is double-wide"
Msg=msg+chr(10)+ EscStart+"27"+EscEnd+_
"W0And this is back to normal"
PalmPrint Msg
```

As an added "bonus", PalmPrint expects only numeric values between the "<<>>" characters, so non-numeric strings are ignored, and can be used to embed comments in the string:

```
Msg="<<This text is double-wide>>"+ EscStart+"27"+EscEnd+_
"W1 Profits 2nd Quarter"
Msg=msg+chr(10)+"<<Back to normal>>"+_
+EscStart+"27"+EscEnd+"W0Region: Northwest"
PalmPrint Msg
```

For some printers, you may need to enter the ESC character without the "<<>>" delimiters:

```
Dim EscChar as string
EscChar=chr(27)
Msg=EscChar +"W1 Profits 2nd Quarter"
Msg=msg+chr(10)+EscChar +"W0Region: Northwest"
PalmPrint Msg
```

Remember that these "escape sequences" are printer-dependent, although many printers have "Epson-compatible" or "HP-compatible" modes, allowing you to use standard Epson or Hewlett-Packard codes. Consult your printer manual for the specific codes to use. The following table gives common escape sequences and their functions for Epson and compatible printers:

Epson Printer Control Codes (Esc=chr(27)).

Code String	Effect
Esc @	Reset Printer
Esc -1	Turns underlining on
Esc -0	Turns underlining off
Esc E	Turns emphasized (bold) on
Esc F	Cancels emphasized mode
Esc G	Starts double-strike mode
Esc H	Cancels double-strike mode
Esc P	10 character per inch (CPI) mode (pica)
Esc M	12 CPI mode (elite)
chr(15)	Condensed print
Esc S0	Starts superscript mode (S0)
Esc S1	Starts subscript mode (S1)
Esc T	Cancels subscript/superscript modes
Esc W1	Starts double-wide mode
Esc W0	Cancels double-wide mode

Starting with version 2.0, PalmPrint provides yet another way to control print formatting, and this method maintains printer-independence. It's a little more involved, and sacrifices a little printer control (e.g., you don't have the ability to select printer-specific fonts), but it may work better for routine formatting when you don't have control over which printer will be used.

The secret to this method of formatting is the fact that PalmPrint can accept launch codes in the AppLaunch statement (like the 32768 used to tell PalmPrint to print the string passed to it):

```
result=AppLaunch(CardNo,"PalmPrint",32768,PrintString)
```

The following table gives the Launch codes that are available from within NS Basic (there are other codes available, but require pointers not available using the AppLaunch statement):

PalmPrint Launch Codes available using NS Basic

Launch Code	Description
32768	Print string, then eject page when finished
32770	Marks the start of a series of print commands ("print job")
32774	Marks the end of a series of print commands
32771	Marks the start of a series of transmit commands
32775	Marks the end of a series of transmit commands
32772	Sends a string of characters to the printer, without ending the "print job" like 32768
32773	Transmits a string of characters
32800	Sends a form feed to the printer (ejects the page)
32802	Sets plain printing
32804	Sets bold printing
32828	Sets printer into portrait mode (PCL and Postscript only)
32830	Sets printer into landscape mode (PCL and Postscript only)

As seen in the above table, you can tell PalmPrint to start a "print job" (series of print commands), send the necessary formatting commands, use 32772 instead of 32768 to print your text, then tell PalmPrint to end the print job. Here's an example of printing the same report as in the previous example, but using the different launch codes rather than escape sequences:

```
result=AppLaunch(CardNo,"PalmPrint",32770,"") ' start print job
result=AppLaunch(CardNo,"PalmPrint",32804,"") ' set bold
result=AppLaunch(CardNo,"PalmPrint",32772,"Profits 2nd Quarter")
result=AppLaunch(CardNo,"PalmPrint",32802,"") ' set default print
result=AppLaunch(CardNo,"PalmPrint",32772," Region: Northwest")
result=AppLaunch(CardNo,"PalmPrint",32774,"") ' end print job
```

You'll also notice in the table above that there are launch codes for controlling character transmission. PalmPrint allows you to send output to terminal programs like HyperTerm, as well as to printers. By using codes 32771 (start transmission), 32773 (transmit line), and 32775 (end transmission) you can send your output to a serial program for capture, rather than a printer. You will most likely need a null-modem adapter, and will also need to make sure that PalmPrint and your receiving application are set to the same baud rate (PalmPrint's other serial parameters: 8 data bits, 1 stop bit, no parity, hardware flow control). If you are using PalmPrint for this feature, consult its documentation for more specifics.

One last point about printing using PalmPrint. You may have certain applications that require you to send a null (chr(0)) as a character embedded in the print string. However, the Palm OS uses the null character to mark the end of a string, so using the actual null character will cause the output to be cut off past the null. If you need to use the null character, use chr(255) instead – PalmPrint will translate it into the null character for output (however, this means that you won't be able to send a chr(255) to your printer).

PalmPrint is a very flexible application, so study its documentation thoroughly, and check at www.stevenscreek.com to see if your specific printer is supported. PalmPrint may work with printers not specifically mentioned, but you risk causing compatibility problems that might be difficult to debug.

If you don't want to use either PalmPrint or SCSPrint, another method for printing may be available for NSBasic programmers by the time this book hits the shelves. Be sure to check the book's support site, www.nsbasicprogrammingforpalmos.com, as well as the NSBasic message board (currently at groups.yahoo.com/group/nsbasic-palm/) for a shared library being produced by Douglas Handy, one of the more active and helpful members in the group. This shared library is being created to allow you to print signatures and have finer control over print layout including font changes, precise alignment of text (including columns with proportional spaced text), and other features.

String parsing

From time to time you may need to take a string of characters, and break it down into substrings. For instance, you may have a database that's tab-delimited (data separated by tab characters), and you have to break each record into its individual data elements. Comma-separated values (CSV) files are commonly used in many applications (Excel, HanDBase, and others) to allow data to be passed in a common format between applications. In CSV files, data elements are separated by commas (and may be surrounded by quotations marks as well).

Parsing refers to taking a string and breaking it down into individual substrings, and the easiest way to accomplish this is through the use of InStr to determine the first incidence of the delimiter, extracting the first portion of the string up to the delimiter, then proceeding through the rest of the string in the same manner. For example, let's parse the following string into separate strings, placing each substring into a string array, using the "space" character as a delimiter:

"NS Basic programming can be extremely rewarding"

The process will be to initialize the array pointer, and loop through the string, with each array item consisting of characters up to the space. Using InStr, we'll find the position of each space until InStr gives us a result of 0 (string not found), and chop the string down as we remove each element. We don't really have to chop the string, but if we don't, we have to keep track of the starting and ending points of each substring – and I don't want to work that hard!

Let's initialize our variables and array:

```
Dim ParseArray(100) as string
Dim ArrayPointer as integer
Dim StartString as string
Dim ChoppedString as string
Dim SpacePosition as integer
```

Now that we have the variables, let's set up our loop to parse through the string:

```
ArrayPointer=1
StartString="NS Basic programming can be extremely rewarding"
ChoppedString=StartString
SpacePosition=Instr(1,ChoppedString," ",1)
Do While SpacePosition <>0
   ParseArray(ArrayPointer)=left(ChoppedString,SpacePosition-1)
   ChoppedString=mid(ChoppedString,SpacePosition+1,_
   len(ChoppedString)-SpacePosition)
   SpacePosition=Instr(1,ChoppedString," ",1)
```

```
    ArrayPointer=ArrayPointer+1
Loop
```

The first pass through the string will return "NS Basic" as the first array item, "programming can be extremely rewarding" as the new ChoppedString, SpacePosition as the position of the next space, and ArrayPointer increments to point to the next array item. As long as there is a space in the remaining string, SpacePosition will be non-zero, and the loop will repeat. However, when we get to the last word "rewarding", there won't be any space at the end. Since this must then be the last item in the string, we can save this substring in the array, then end:

```
ParseArray(ArrayPointer)=ChoppedString
```

We can encapsulate this routine in a subroutine, and reuse it as needed. However, since we'd like to make this routine as "portable" and reusable as possible, we'll change the delimiter from a space to a variable that can be any character – even a string of characters. The final subroutine will look like this:

```
Sub ParseString(StartString as string, Delimiter as string)
Dim ArrayPointer as integer
Dim StartString as string
Dim ChoppedString as string
Dim DelimPosition as integer
ArrayPointer=1
ChoppedString=StartString
DelimPosition =Instr(1,ChoppedString,delimiter,1)
Do While DelimPosition <>0
    ParseArray(ArrayPointer)=left(ChoppedString, DelimPosition -1)
    ChoppedString=mid(ChoppedString, DelimPosition +_
    len(delimiter),len(ChoppedString))
    DelimPosition =Instr(1,ChoppedString,delimiter,1)
    ArrayPointer=ArrayPointer+1
Loop
ParseArray(ArrayPointer)=ChoppedString
end sub
```

You'll notice that the line:

```
Dim ParseArray(100) as string
```

is missing – but only because it will need to be declared outside of the subroutine as a global array. Otherwise, the routine is a good, general purpose parsing routine that you'll probably find a good use for. You'll find an example of this method of string parsing in the Parse Test project.

Data Encryption

You've worked hard on your applications, and when you decide to distribute them, you have a very difficult decision to make: what is the best way to keep your data safe from prying eyes (or worse, from unscrupulous persons who wouldn't think twice about stealing your data and calling it their own)? The easiest answer is to encrypt your data, and perform decryption in your program's code.

Before you actually decide to encrypt your data, however, you need to decide how difficult you want the encryption to be to break. No form of encryption is completely unbreakable, and someone determined to break your encryption scheme can find a way. If you're distributing nuclear arms secrets, you'll need stronger encryption than if you're writing a cookbook app, but that shouldn't stop you from using some form of simple encryption. You may not be able to stop every hacker, but you can make it difficult for the casual snooper to get at your data, and that might be enough for your needs.

I won't talk about some of the more sophisticated encryption methods, because, quite frankly, I don't know them. I don't need to use them, and haven't studied them. I'm not a professional programmer, and I don't claim to be one. I will give you something useful, however, and you can decide if it will suit your purposes. If so, great! If not, don't let me stop you from pursuing better methods.

One of the simplest encryption methods is the substitution cipher, where each character is substituted with a different, unique character. There are even several methods of substitution ciphers available, from simply using the next letter of the alphabet:

"NS Basic can handle encryption."

becomes

"OTCbtjd!dbo!iboemf!fodszqujpo/"

This encryption isn't hard to code (in the Encryption Demo project):

```
Sub Encrypt(InputText as String, outputtext as String)
Dim CharPointer as Integer
Dim TempString as String
Dim TestChar as String
TempString=""
For CharPointer=1 to len(InputText)
    TestChar=mid(InputText,CharPointer,1)
    If asc(TestChar)=255 Then
        TempString=TempString+chr(1)
    Else
        TempString=TempString+chr(asc(TestChar)+1)
    End If
Next
OutputText=TempString
End Sub
```

Note that this encryption uses a couple characteristics of strings to its advantage. First, strings in NS Basic are null (chr(0)) terminated, so we'll never run into a character with ASCII code 0 – this means that when we get to the routine to decrypt this string, we shouldn't run into a character with code (1). However, the highest ASCII code is 255, so if we get a character with code 255, we can't save one with a code of 256. Since a code of 1 in the output string wouldn't normally exist, we'll use a code of 1 instead of 256.

Decrypting this string is the reverse:

```
Sub Decrypt(InputText as String, outputtext as String)
Dim CharPointer as Integer
```

```
Dim TempString as String
Dim TestChar as String
TempString=""
For CharPointer=1 to len(InputText)
   TestChar=mid(InputText,CharPointer,1)
   If asc(TestChar)=1 Then
      TempString=TempString+chr(255)
   Else
      TempString=TempString+chr(asc(TestChar)-1)
   End If
Next
OutputText=TempString
End Sub
```

A more secure form of the substitution cipher uses 2 cipher strings, where each character in the input string is used as an index to the first cipher string, and the output character written from the second string. This is actually pretty easy to code as well, but suffers from a potential security "hole" (I'll let you think about what that might be, and tell you later):

```
Sub Encrypt2(InputString as String, OutputString as String)
Dim CharPointer as Integer
Dim TempString as String
Dim TestChar as String
Dim cypherstring1 as String
Dim cypherstring2 as String
cypherstring1="abcdefghijklmnopqrstuvwxyzABCDEFGHIJKLMNOPQR_
STUVWXYZ"
cypherstring2="ZYXWVUTSRQPONMLKJIHGFEDCBAzyxwvutsrqponmlkji_
hgfedcba"
TempString=""
For CharPointer=1 to len(InputString)
testchar=mid(inputstring,charpointer,1)
If instr(1,cypherstring1,testchar,0)=0 Then
   TempString=TempString+testchar
Else
   TempString=TempString+mid(cypherstring2,
instr(1,cypherstring1,testchar,0),1)
End If
Next
OutputString=TempString
End Sub
```

Decryption is the reverse:

```
Sub Decrypt2(InputString as String, OutputString as String)
Dim CharPointer as Integer
Dim TempString as String
Dim TestChar as String
Dim cypherstring1 as String
Dim cypherstring2 as String
cypherstring2="abcdefghijklmnopqrstuvwxyzABCDEFGHIJKLMNOPQR_
STUVWXYZ"
cypherstring1="ZYXWVUTSRQPONMLKJIHGFEDCBAzyxwvutsrqponmlkji_
hgfedcba"
```

```
TempString=""
For CharPointer=1 to len(InputString)
   testchar=mid(inputstring,charpointer,1)
   If instr(1,cypherstring1,testchar,0)=0 Then
      TempString=TempString+testchar
   Else
      TempString=TempString+mid(cypherstring2,_
       instr(1,cypherstring1,testchar,0),1)
   End If
Next
OutputString=TempString
End Sub
```

Can you tell where the security problem lies? The main problem with this form of encryption is that the encryption and decryption strings are embedded in your application, which means that a hacker could get at them. Of course, if you make them as obvious as I have they're extremely easy to recognize. However, you can see how this decryption could defeat the casual snooper.

As I mentioned before, there are many more secure methods of encryption than these, including methods in the BitsNBytes shared library (see the Tech Notes), but if you just want to keep casual snoopers away, these should be useful.

Sorting Data

When your applications revolve around data, at some point you'll need to arrange that data in sorted order. We've seen that by using keyed database access you can usually avoid having to worry about the sorting algorithms – NS Basic did a wonderful job of isolating you from this necessary, but tedious job. I even introduced you to the Bubble sort when we looked at Lists and PopUps, with the disclaimer that the Bubble sort may be easy to understand, but it's horribly inefficient. And as slow as molasses. Luckily, there are more efficient sorting algorithms available. Unfortunately, most of these algorithms exist in dialects of Basic that aren't easily converted to NS Basic. And one of the best sorts – the Quick Sort – is usually written with a technique know as recursion (where a routine calls itself) that isn't applicable to NS Basic at all.

One of the faster sorting routines, the Shell-Metzner sort, is easily adapted to NS Basic. In contrast with the Bubble sort, which sorts data by comparing each item against all other items, the Shell-Metzner sort begins comparisons between items a fixed distance apart, then closes this distance with each pass, arranging data as it goes. For a ten item list, the first pass compares items 5 apart: 1 and 6, then 2:7, then 3:8, 4:9, then 5:10. The next pass decreases the distance to 4, with each successive pass smaller until a 1:1 comparison is made through the list. By first starting far apart, the ends of the list are found early, reducing unnecessary comparisons, and decreasing the number of swaps needed.

You can attempt to write this routine yourself, but I've included the Sorting Comparison project that contains code for both the Bubble and Shell-Metzner sorts, documented to help you understand how each sort works (thanks to Nick Morton for making a small modification to the Shell-Metzner sort that I missed when translating the sort from a previous dialect of Basic.

For those of you who need faster sorting than the Shell-Metzner routine can provide, here's a version of the QuickSort that doesn't use recursion. The routine was created to sort a 256 element string array, but you can modify it for other data types (or even databases) as needed. I'll warn you right now – it isn't pretty:

```
'non-recursive QuickSort variation

Dim StringArray(256) as String ' use whatever size you need here
Dim SortStackLow(128) as Integer ' half of the string array size
Dim SortStackHigh(128) as Integer ' ditto
Dim stackpointer as Integer
Dim LowPointer as Integer
Dim HighPointer as Integer
Dim low as Integer
Dim high as Integer
Dim middle as Integer
Dim LowBoundary as Integer
Dim HighBoundary as Integer
Dim compare as String
Dim tempstring as String

LowPointer=1
HighPointer=128 'use half of array size
StackPointer = 1
SortStackLow(StackPointer) = LowPointer
SortStackHigh(StackPointer) = HighPointer
StackPointer = StackPointer + 1

Do WHILE StackPointer <> 1
   StackPointer = StackPointer - 1
   Low = SortStackLow(StackPointer)
   High = SortStackHigh(StackPointer)
   Do WHILE Low < High
       LowBoundary = Low
       HighBoundary = High
       Middle = (Low + High) / 2
       Compare = StringArray(Middle)

       Do WHILE LowBoundary <= HighBoundary
          Do WHILE StringArray(LowBoundary) < Compare
             LowBoundary = LowBoundary + 1
          Loop
          Do WHILE StringArray(HighBoundary) > Compare
             HighBoundary = HighBoundary - 1
          Loop
          If LowBoundary <= HighBoundary Then
             TempString=StringArray(LowBoundary)
             StringArray(LowBoundary)=StringArray(HighBoundary)
             StringArray(HighBoundary)=TempString
             LowBoundary = LowBoundary + 1
             HighBoundary = HighBoundary - 1
          End If
       Loop
       If (HighBoundary - Low) < (High - LowBoundary) Then
          If LowBoundary < High Then
             SortStackLow(StackPointer) = LowBoundary
             SortStackHigh(StackPointer) = High
             StackPointer = StackPointer + 1
          End If
          High = HighBoundary
```

```
        Else
            If Low < HighBoundary Then
                SortStackLow(StackPointer) = Low
                SortStackHigh(StackPointer) = HighBoundary
                StackPointer = StackPointer + 1
            End If
            Low = LowBoundary
        End If
    Loop
Loop
'end of non-recursive QuickSort
```

(I warned you it wasn't pretty!)

When you sort data on your Palm device, you'll eventually come upon sorts that don't seem to work, and you'll be dumfounded to explain why. I've scoured the documentation, and have never seen any mention of the Palm sort order. Of course, I took that as a personal challenge, and wrote an app to sort the various characters, including non-printable characters. What I discovered shocked me – the Palm OS doesn't sort string data according to ASCII order. The sort order is loosely based on the order of characters as they appear in the standard fonts, but there are so many exceptions that attempting to generate a sorting algorithm on non-Palm systems is an extremely complicated matter.

> **Note** Why does this even matter? As long as the data gets sorted, what's the problem? Well, the problem is that the Palm data is often transferred to non-Palm systems (such as Windows or Mac OS applications) that are more likely than not to use a different sorting order. This isn't a problem if numeric values are being sorted, or if strings to be sorted consist of all upper or lower case characters, but strings with non-alphanumeric data (like punctuation, for instance) will not necessarily sort the same in different systems. Making matters worse is that most Windows applications ignore the apostrophe and hyphen when sorting or comparing strings! Take-home message: if you'll be working with data on different systems, make sure all functions work as expected, or write your own.

A table with the Palm OS string sort order is included in the appendices.

Running HotSync from NS Basic

You may wish to perform a HotSync immediately after users manipulate databases, in order to keep the data synchronized between your applications and the desktop. One method, devised by both Ron Glowka and Douglas Handy uses SysTrapSub, and is listed below (and in the ChainToHotsync.cod code module):

```
Dim KeyChar as Short
Dim KeyCode as Short
Dim KeyModifiers as Short
KeyChar=521
KeyCode=521
KeyModifiers=8
SysTrapSub 301,3,KeyChar,KeyCode,KeyModifiers
```

This routine calls HotSync, and immediately starts the HotSync process (so be sure your user knows to place his Palm device in its cradle prior to running this code). Control doesn't get passed back to your application after HotSync, so this acts like the Chain statement.

Soundex

You may have no idea what Soundex is, and may never need to use it. However, it's a great routine, and you probably don't realize that you might be using it every day.

Put simply, Soundex is a way of representing words in a simplified manner based on how they sound. Actually, it's even simpler than that. Soundex creates an alphanumeric code based on letters of a word, and how the first part of the word would sound in an extremely simplified format, where individual letters and groups of letters are treated as being equal.

In Soundex, certain letters are treated as being the same, and given a numeric code. If the Soundex routine finds a B, F, P, or V, the numeric code is 1. C, G, J, K, Q, S, X, and Z are given a code of 2, D and T are given a code of 3, L gets a 4, M and N get a 5, and R gets a 6. All other characters are ignored, as are duplicates of any character. Once the Soundex routine creates a code with 4 characters, or it hits the end of the word, it ends.

Sounds like a lot of work to generate a simple code, so what good is it? Well, it's amazing what you can learn when you're writing a book. When I decided to write a Soundex routine for this book, I though it would be useful to search for the origin of the routine. It turns out that the Soundex routine was created for use by the United States Census, to make it easier to represent different names. Since there are many different ways to spell names, and so many names sound alike, the routine has found a great deal of utility for census taking. Soundex is also great when you're looking for information but don't know exactly how to spell it; sometimes just being close is good enough. Many computerized dictionaries also use Soundex to provide a list of possible matches for a word that doesn't exist in their word lists.

If you think you might find a use for Soundex, you'll find the code in the Soundex Generator project.

Staying alive

The Palm devices are battery powered. You already knew that, but I thought I'd remind you. Why is this so important to remember? Battery life is a premium, so the Palm OS has to have a way to automatically turn off the device when it's not in use.

You're probably used to this by now, but I lied again! The device never *really* gets turned off, but instead is put into low power mode if the buttons aren't pressed - or the screen isn't tapped – for a period of time that you have some control over in the Prefs application.

But what if you need to keep the Palm active, for a continuous display or to receive data over the serial port, for example? Well, by calling the Palm OS EvtResetAutoOffTimer routine we can reset the AutoOff Timer:

```
SysTrapSub 304,0 ' reset auto off timer
```

There's a slightly less elegant way to do this; the Delay statement resets this AutoOff timer, so by using Delay with a tiny value we can achieve a similar result:

```
Delay 0.01
```

This adds a tiny delay to the application, and should be avoided if possible. However, what this means is that if you are already using a Delay statement, the SysTrapSub call to keep the app "alive" isn't necessary.

Saving State

Use most Palm applications, and you'll notice that you can usually exit the app, run some other application, then return to your initial app, in the same spot where you left off. Now that you've become an NS Basic expert, you can apply these same techniques to your own apps.

All that's needed is a way to determine what your app is doing when it exits, code to save any temporary or "session-specific" data, and some way to restore the data and status when you return. The obvious (and correct) place to put the "save what I'm doing" code is the Termination Code section of your application. Any data on the current form, along with the name of the current form, can be saved to a database. When the app is run, it checks to see if this database has data from a previous session, and restores the previous state from this data. Check out the "Save State" project for my solution to this programming task in a multiple-form app.

MegaMemo also uses this technique to allow my users to go to a different app, save data to the clipboard, then return to MegaMemo to insert the data in the previously opened memo.

System Info

Since NSBasic can function on a wide variety of devices, each having different hardware capabilities and various versions of the Palm OS, you may need to use different routines based on device-specific information. Through the use of SysInfo, you can determine a number of different characteristics of the device running your application.

SysInfo

Syntax:
    SysInfo(arg)

Description:
    Returns various types of system information based on the value of arg

SysInfo arguments and return information

Argument	Return information
0	Runtime version (as xxx, e.g. 201 = version 2.01)
1	Number of clock ticks since device was last reset
2	Ticks per second for current device
3	PortID used by Palm OS to refer to an open serial port
4	Current Form ID (used with SysTrapSub, SysTrapFunc, shared libraries)
5	Number of bytes waiting on serial port

Real Estate - location, location, location!

I've mentioned this before, but it bears repeating. Your Palm forms are tiny, so consider your object placement carefully. Rather than using Lists, consider PopUps to reduce the amount of screen space that is occupied by Lists that don't require constant display. The same goes for menus and status lines. If they don't need to be constantly displayed, don't waste valuable screen real estate with them. Even the title itself can occupy nearly 10% of the screen space. If the title isn't needed, consider removing it.

Graphics should be used to increase the usability and appeal of your apps. Use them wisely, keep them as small as practical, and consider removing unnecessary, "cute" graphics.

Optimizing applications for speed

NS Basic has made considerable improvements in features and speed since its original release, but no matter fast you make your applications, at times you'll want to eke out the best performance possible. Some of the techniques presented below fit nicely within the paradigm of structured programming, while others break the rules a bit for the sake of performance. Whenever practical, opt for the best performance you can get while maintaining good structure. Only break the rules when absolutely necessary!

Plan *before* coding

The best way to create efficient programs is to plan them that way from the beginning. Flowchart or pseudo-code your applications before you start to write a single line of code, and you'll have a much better chance of creating compact, smooth-running programs. Believe me when I tell you that it's easier to structure a program *before* you write it than it is to try to restructure it later!

Avoid string concatenation whenever possible

When it comes to performance, string concatenation is one of the most "expensive" operations in NS Basic (and in most versions of Basic). Because of this, string concatenation should be avoided when possible. Unfortunately, as we've already discussed, string literals can only contain up to 255 characters. If you have a large amount of text to place in a field, such as help text or other instructional messages, it's tempting to create long strings by adding literals together:

```
HelpText="To put this toy together, place tab A into slot B,"
HelpText=HelpText+chr(10)+"then place box C next to circle D,"
HelpText=HelpText+chr(10)+"being careful not to disturb the"
HelpText=HelpText+chr(10)+"alignment of triangle E and_
trapezoid F. "
fldHelp.text=HelpText
```

A faster way to perform this would be to maintain this help text in a database as a single field, then read it and place it in the appropriate field. Placing help text in a database, rather than hard-coding in into your program, also allows you to distribute new help text to existing users without having to recompile the application. Additionally, you can provide multilingual support by having databases of help text in various languages.

Reduce time spent initializing variables

When your application starts, NS Basic creates a database to contain the variables used in your application. Creating this database takes time, so the fewer variables that you declare in your startup and first form's "before" code, the faster your application will display its first form. Eventually, all of the variables still need to be declared, but if you spread the variable declaration out among the various forms and subroutines, the initial loading of your application will be faster, which to your user translates into a snappier appearing application.

Avoid performing unnecessary operations in loops

Looping can take a great deal of time, so any instructions you can remove from within loops will improve their speed. Take the following code that loops through 20 bitmap ID's for display:

```
For BitmapNumber=1 to 20
   BitmapID=1000+BitmapNumber*2
   DrawBitmap BitmapID, x, y
Next
```

A more efficient method is to code the bitmap ID into the For…Next loop counter:

```
For BitmapID=1002 to 1040 step 2
   DrawBitmap BitmapID, x, y
Next
```

Initializing/Clearing Arrays

If you have a large array that you need to initialize or clear, you might be tempted to perform code like this:

```
'clear a 100x100 string array for a table
For CurrentRow=1 to 100
For CurrentCol=1 to 100
     TableArray(CurrentRow,CurrentCol)=""
Next
Next
```

Even on a fast device, this code takes a long time. Once again, a database gives you a faster alternative. Write a small application that performs the code above, then save the entire array to a database as an array. Then, when you need to clear the same size array in your main app, read the cleared array instead of running through the loop.

Initializing User-Defined Type Variables

The UDT is one of NS Basic's most powerful structures. From a programming standpoint, UDT's make it easy to write code that functions and reads well. Modifying and debugging code using UDT's is greatly simplified, compared to code that uses individual variables. If you use UDT's with a large number of elements, you probably initialize them like this:

```
Type PersonnelDescriptor
LastName as string
FirstName as string
SSN as string
Address1 as string
Address2 as string
CityState as string
ZIP as string
PhoneNum as string
FaxNum as string
PagerNum as string
End type

Global Employee as PersonnelDescriptor

'...code to manipulate employee record...
'now, clear record for next employee
Employee.FirstName=""
Employee.LastName=""
Employee.FirstName=""
Employee.SSN=""
Employee.Address1=""
Employee.Address2=""
Employee.CityState=""
Employee.ZIP=""
Employee.PhoneNum=""
Employee.FaxNum=""
Employee.PagerNum=""
```

If you have to clear the employee record more than once, each time you do so requires that each element get cleared separately, which adds up to a lot of time. A faster method is to have a second variable declared as a Global of type "PersonnelDescriptor", clear it once, then set the Employee variable to the cleared variable:

```
Global Employee as PersonnelDescriptor
Global BlankEmployee as PersonnelDescriptor
 'clear BlankEmployee record
BlankEmployee.FirstName=""
BlankEmployee.LastName=""
BlankEmployee.FirstName=""
BlankEmployee.SSN=""
BlankEmployee.Address1=""
BlankEmployee.Address2=""
BlankEmployee.CityState=""
BlankEmployee.ZIP=""
BlankEmployee.PhoneNum=""
BlankEmployee.FaxNum=""
BlankEmployee.PagerNum=""

'...code to manipulate employee record...
'now, clear record for next employee
Employee=BlankEmployee
```

Although this seems like a lot of work to accomplish the same task, the savings pay off if you need to clear the Employee variable multiple times. You can also use the database approach as we did with arrays and long strings, although this method is slightly faster (and easier to debug).

Load lists and popups at design time

Do you have lists and popups that always get loaded with the same information when your application is run? You can make a HUGE difference in the speed of your applications by removing the list and popup loading routines altogether, and creating the list/popup data at design time.

Load lists with only a subset of data

If you don't want to load large lists ahead of time (the data changes, you don't want to make the compile application too big, the database already exists anyway, etc.), you can use a list as a virtual "window" into a database by reading a small subset of records – enough to fill the visible area of the list without causing the list's scroll arrows to appear – and "scrolling" the list by changing which range of records to read and display. Using this method you can scroll a 50,000 item database as quickly as one containing 50 items, one chunk at a time. See the LargeListScroll project for an example.

Modify database data in place

Palm, Inc. recommends that database editing be performed with the data still in the database, rather than copying the data to a variable (or field or other object), editing it there, then writing it back to the database. Although for a single record this may not seem like it would make such a difference, if you have a database of hundreds or thousands of records, and read the entire database into an array (or list or popup), perform editing, then rewrite the entire database back, you'll be in for serious delays – and unhappy users. Besides, copying an entire database (or even sections of it) into memory wastes memory, since the databases exist in memory anyway.

If disk systems ever become available for the Palm devices this situation might change, but the Palm OS will have to maintain backwards-compatibility to avoid having existing software crash, so you'll still be safe following Palm's advice. Besides, even if you have to rewrite sections of your code for new devices, you will have already taken my advice and documented your code thoroughly, right?

Evaluate common values in expressions first

Compare the two routines below, and at first glance, you'd think they would be equivalent:

```
If Salary > 50000 then
   Bonus=Salary*0.1
Else
   Bonus=Salary*0.075
End if

If Salary <= 50000 then
   Bonus=Salary*0.075
Else
   Bonus=Salary*0.1
End if
```

However, if the variable Salary is usually > 50000, the first expression will run slightly faster. A similar situation occurs using Case statements:

```
Select Case FirstName
Case "Mike"
'code here
Case "John"
'code here
Case "Eggbert"
'code here
Case Else
'code here
End Select
```

Since "Mike" and "John" are more common than "Eggbert", this set of Case statements will run more quickly than if "Eggbert" was the first name in the list. Arrange the different possibilities in your If and Case statements so that the most common conditions are evaluated first.

Keep databases open if possible

I usually open databases as I need to use them, carry out my database manipulation, then close the databases when I'm through. In general, I try to avoid keeping databases open while waiting for user input. Although this helps avoid losing data in the event that the user causes the Palm device to crash, each database open and close statement takes additional processing time. You need to weigh the risks of data loss with potential performance gains.

Avoid the use of subroutines or functions

What's going on here? I've worked hard to promote the use of subroutines and functions to help you "streamline" your code, and here I go, telling you to avoid them! From a code reusability and maintainability standpoint, subroutines and functions are great. However, each subroutine or function call adds additional processing over the same code placed "in line", and exacts a small price in performance.

I'm not advocating eliminating subroutines and functions altogether. However, once you have your application working properly, you can often gain a modest performance advantage by converting subroutines and functions into straight, in line code. Make sure that you save the original version of your code, though, in case you want to go back to the more structured version.

Chapter XIX – Appendices

Appendix A. Palm OS sort (string comparison) order.

When NS Basic keyed databases are written, the Palm OS determines the record position by key order. Unfortunately, the Palm OS doesn't sort string keys according to ASCII codes, but uses a somewhat arbitrary order. The table below lists the characters and ASCII codes in the order the Palm OS uses for sorting and comparing strings. Note that many of the ASCII values don't have characters displayable using Palm Font 0 (the default font for most Palm apps). This sort order is absolutely non-intuitive, and my search of the Palm OS documentation didn't explain just how this sort order came about.

The most important take-home message is that if you are preparing non-Palm software to sort data prior to syncing with the Palm for use in NS Basic keyed databases, use the ASCII number order as shown, or NS Basic applications may not find all records using keyed access methods.

The thought of implementing this sort order in code gives me a headache (it's best to use some form of lookup table).

Palm OS sort order

Char*	ASCII	Char	ASCII	Char	ASCII	Char	ASCII	Char	ASCII
(nd)	0	%	37	¥	165	C	67	ò	242
(nd)	1	&	38	(nd)	128	ç	231	Ò	210
(nd)	2	(	40	§	167	Ç	199	ô	244
(nd)	3	)	41	©	169	d	100	Ô	212
(nd)	4	*	42	¬	172	D	68	ö	246
(nd)	5	,	44	®	174	_	240	Ö	214
(nd)	6	.	46	˘	176	_	208	õ	245
(nd)	7	/	47	µ	181	e	101	Õ	213
(nd)	8	:	58	¶	182	E	69	ø	248
(nd)	14	;	59	·	183	é	233	Ø	216
(nd)	15	?	63	†	134	É	201	œ	156
(nd)	16	@	64	‡	135	è	232	Œ	140
(nd)	17	[	91	•	149	È	200	p	112
(nd)	18	\	92	…	133	ê	234	P	80
(nd)	19	]	93	‰	137	Ê	202	q	113
(nd)	20	^	94	0	48	ë	235	Q	81
(nd)	21	ˆ	136	_	188	Ë	203	r	114
(nd)	22	_	95	_	189	f	102	R	82
(nd)	23	˜	96	_	190	F	70	s	115
(nd)	24	{	123	1	49	f	131	S	83
(nd)	25			124	_	185	g	103	_	154

(nd)	26	}	125	2	50	G	71	_	138
(nd)	27	~	126	‾	178	h	104	ß	223
(nd)	28	¡	161	3	51	H	72	t	116
(nd)	29	‾	166	‾	179	i	105	T	84
(nd)	30	··	168	4	52	I	73	˜	254
(nd)	31	¯	175	5	53	í	237	_	222
(nd)	127	´	180	6	54	Í	205	™	153
(nd)	129	,	184	7	55	ì	236	u	117
(nd)	141	¿	191	8	56	Ì	204	U	85
(nd)	142	˜	152	9	57	î	238	ú	250
(nd)	143	'	145	a	97	Î	206	Ú	218
(nd)	144	'	146	A	65	ï	239	ù	249
(nd)	157	,	130	ª	170	Ï	207	Ù	217
(nd)	158	"	147	á	225	j	106	û	251
'	39	"	148	Á	193	J	74	Û	219
-	45	„	132	à	224	k	107	ü	252
(nd)	173	‹	139	À	192	K	75	Ü	220
(nd)	150	›	155	â	226	l	108	v	118
(nd)	151	+	43	Â	194	L	76	V	86
space	32	<	60	ä	228	m	109	w	119
(nd)	160	=	61	Ä	196	M	77	W	87
(nd)	9	>	62	ã	227	n	110	x	120
(nd)	10	±	177	Ã	195	N	78	X	88
(nd)	11	«	171	å	229	ñ	241	y	121
(nd)	12	»	187	Å	197	Ñ	209	Y	89
(nd)	13	_	215	æ	230	o	111	_	253
!	33	÷	247	Æ	198	O	79	_	221
"	34	¢	162	b	98	(nd)	186	ÿ	255
#	35	£	163	B	66	ó	243	Ÿ	159
$	36	€	164	c	99	Ó	211	z	122

*nd = nondisplayable

Appendix B. Palm OS Fonts

Font 0 – Standard

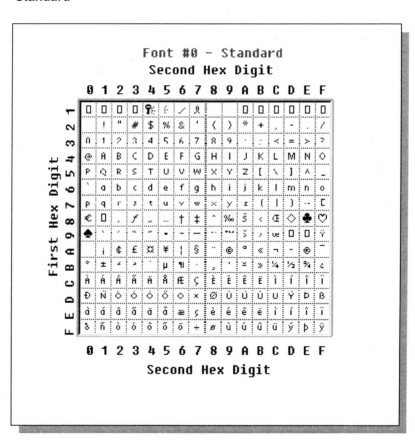

Font 1 – Standard Bold

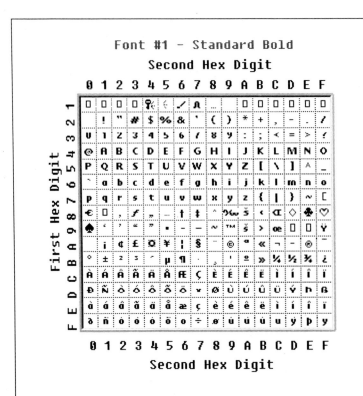

Font 2 – Large

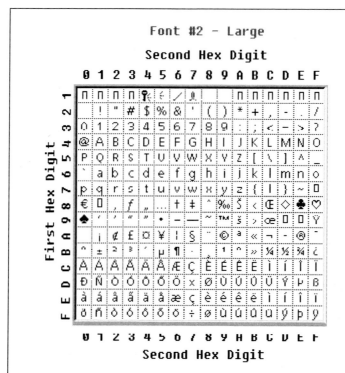

Font 3 – Symbol

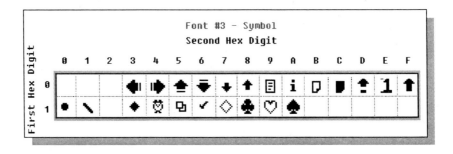

Font 4 – Symbol 11

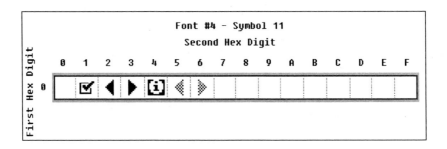

Font 5 – Symbol 7

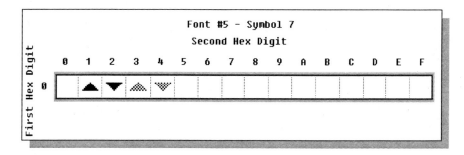

Font 6 – LED

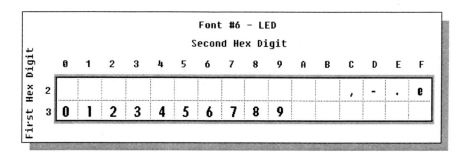

Font 7 – Large Bold

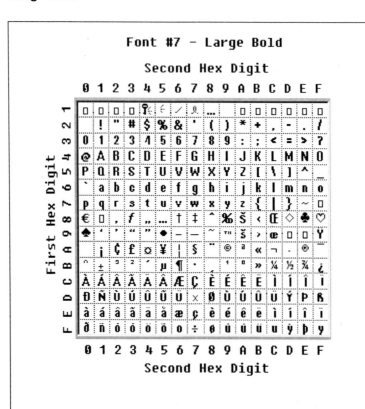

Appendix C. Accessory Programs

The CD included with this book includes several programs designed to assist in programming with NS Basic, perform database conversions, provide printing support, and manipulate Palm programs and databases outside of your NS Basic applications, to name a few. Although you may not find all of these programs useful, you're not likely to see this amount of support and extensibility anywhere else. There's a current surge of interest in NS Basic programming and the creation of helpful tools. Many of these were developed by NS Basic programmers (including me) for our own personal use; we then realized that others could benefit from them as well. If the authors of these utilities happen to make a few bucks from the registration, that's not bad either (although not all of these programs are shareware or require registration).

Each program resides in its own subdirectory on the CD, and each has a brief file describing the program and its installation. If all goes well, these files will have obvious names like README.TXT, INSTRUCT.DOC, or the equivalent. If not, the program will include an installation file named SETUP.EXE, SETUPEX.EXE, INSTALL.EXE, or something similar, with easy to follow instructions for installation.

Please note that most of these programs will probably have updated versions available by the time this book is published. Check the documentation for each application for upgrade information. You'll also find some hidden goodies on the CD, including many Palm apps I created while writing this book to explore the various NS Basic and Palm objects and their functions. Many of the apps are standalone products that I've released as shareware or freeware, and they've been tested, updated, and modified according to my users' needs. I've included the source code to these apps, as well as dozens of other projects, to help you learn everything that I can teach you.

Code Tools

I wish I had created this program. But I didn't, so I can't take the credit for it. Christien Lee started creating this great programming utility back when NS Basic had a simpler, less "Visual" IDE. Code Tools combines several tools into one, including a bitmap and icon converter, form and object previewer, message and alert box generator, Font/character map/picker, shape drawing tool, API viewer, and text width calculator. In addition, Code Tools can automatically launch the NS Basic IDE and POSE, tying everything together nicely.

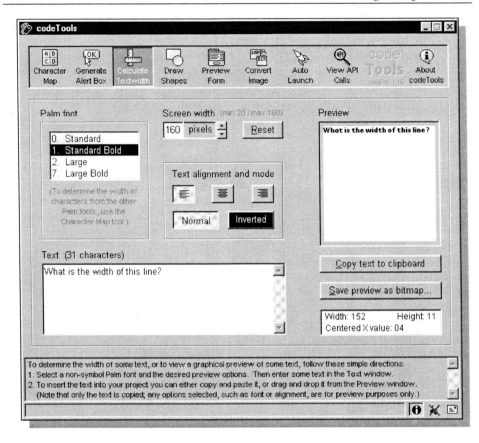

PDB Converter

In the chapter on database access we saw how to create databases using NS Basic, which is fine if you or your user are going to be producing the data entirely from within you application running on a Palm device. But, what if you already have data that you wish to use – a LOT of data? You could write a separate app to write the data, but wouldn't it be easier to convert your data from its existing format to a format readable by NS Basic – preferably a Palm PDB database? What if you've created a large database, and want to edit it outside of the Palm environment?

I initially wrote PDB Converter as a simple way to experiment with NS Basic database access, and the program blossomed into a full-fledged database converter/creator/editor capable of converting Microsoft Excel worksheets, comma-separated values (CSV) files, text files, and even HanDBase (TM) databases into NS Basic-compatible PDB databases. Although PDB Converter currently only handles string data, it can accommodate databases with up to 16384 records, 255 fields per record, and 255 characters per field. Even if you never use it to convert databases between PDB and other formats, you'll find PDB Converter a powerful way to create and edit string-based databases that are easily readable by NS Basic.

PDB Converter can run in its normal, interactive mode, giving you a familiar spreadsheet interface to work with. PDB Converter can also accept command line arguments, allowing it to read, convert, and write databases from batch files, and even install PDB's for any HotSync user – automatically.

PDB Converter writes records one row at a time, with columns representing separate fields within a record. A PDB Converter worksheet containing 100 rows and 25 columns would be written as a PDB database of 100 records, each containing 25 fields. PDB databases can be written with variable length fields (minimizing the size of the database by eliminating excess spaces at the beginning or end of fields), or with fixed length fields, padded with spaces to equal the length of the longest string in each field. Fixed length fields make access to each individual field using non-keyed access very rapid, since the dbPosition function can be used to allow access of any record at any field offset. In other words, if your records contain 200 fields, you can access the data in field 186 without having to read the first 185 fields, as long as you know the offset of field 186 in the record – which will remain constant in each record when fixed length fields are written.

PDB databases written using PDB Converter can be read from, and written to, using non-keyed methods. Additionally, as long as the databases are in sorted order by the first (key) field, and there are no records with duplicate keys, the databases can be accessed using keyed methods as well. See www.mverive.com/pdbconverter.htm for the most up-to-date information.

PDB Converter - C:\WINDOWS\DESKTOP\ZIPCODES.PDB						
File Edit Format Recalc Sort Options Transaction						
Creator ID ZIPx ? PDB Type DATA ?						
PDB Name zipcodes ?			Save Creator ID, PDB Type, and PDB Name as defaults			
	A	B	C	D	E	F	G
1	22026	VA	Dumfries				
2	53020	WI	Elkhart Lake				
3	53132	WI	Franklin				
4	55110	MN	Saint Paul				
5	60007	IL	Elk Grove Village				
6	60101	IL	Addison				
7	60102	IL	Lake in the Hills				
8	60103	IL	Bartlett				
9	60106	IL	Bensenville				
10	60108	IL	Bloomingdale				
11	60153	IL	Maywood				
12	60160	IL	Melrose Park				
13	60177	IL	South Elgin				

Sheet1

Status: Ready

PDB Info

I'm almost ashamed to include this tiny app. PDB Info doesn't do much, but what it *does* do it does well, and may save you a lot of time and frustration. Remember that part about needing to have unique Creator ID's? What about the fact that databases need to be accessed by their case-sensitive internal name, not the Windows' filename? And how many records are *really* in that zip code database you've been using, but has started to get sluggish? PDB Info can reveal the Creator ID, data type, internal Palm name, database size, and number of records for PDB and PRC files (number of records for PDB's only). Not exactly rocket science, but if knowing the Creator ID of an app BEFORE creating one that conflicts with an existing app can keep you from pulling your hair out, my endless hours were spent wisely (actually, it only took about 2 hours to put PDB Info together, but that doesn't sound as dramatic...).

Also, if by chance you already created a database or application with a name, Creator ID, or data type that you wish to change, you can do this with PDB Info without having to recompile your app or rewrite your database. Careful, though – if you change the data type of a PRC from "appl" to "libr" or something else, you won't be able to see the application on the Palm screen. You can use this to your benefit, however. If you have an application that is getting too big and cumbersome, and want to break it down into multiple, smaller apps, you can change the data type from "appl" to "libr" for each of the smaller apps, and use a main app (with its default type of "appl") as a main app, using Chain to call the smaller apps.

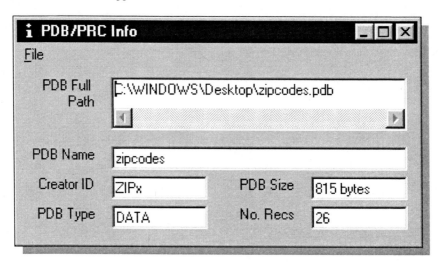

OnBoard RsrcEdit

C programmers seem to have all the fun, at least when it comes to creating really neat apps that allow you to "tweak" and modify another applications bits and pieces. OnBoard RsrcEdit, available from Quartus (www.quartus.net), is a Palm resource editor that you use on the Palm device itself. Palm programs are built from many components, or resources. These resources have characteristics that you can modify with OnBoard

RsrcEdit to allow you to do some cool stuff that you just can't do easily with NS Basic or other Palm programming tools. You can directly edit an application's icons, bitmaps, manipulate properties of objects (change the usual oblong buttons to rectangles, for example), and so much more that you'll have to see it to believe it. Be careful, though, since this power comes with a price. Save your work often, and be prepared to perform many hard resets (not due to program bugs, but you can easily make changes that will render your applications useless, and freeze your Palm).

PalmPrint

From StevensCreek Software (www.stevenscreek.com), PalmPrint was the first Palm application to provide printing capability for the majority of Palm users, and it remains one of the most powerful and flexible. NS Basic provides a simple interface to PalmPrint (or SCSPrint, previous mentioned in "Printing in NS Basic") through the AppLaunch function, and should serve most of your printing needs. A large number of different printers are supported, including most IrDA and serial printers, as well as Monarch and SiPix printers created for the Palm devices. IrDA adapters are available that allow the use of virtually any standard parallel or serial printer, in case your printer isn't IrDA compatible.

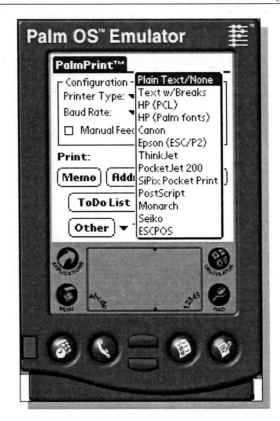

PilotInstall

HotSync'ing isn't the only way to install applications to your Palm device. PilotInstall (from envicon.com) allows you to install individual applications to your Palm, without having to go through the HotSync process.

PilotInstall features:

- Installs Palm OS software directly from the web
- converts plain text files to the DOC format (on the fly)
- installs MIDI sounds to your system MIDI database
- installs Bitmaps
- desktop install replacement
- you can select the speed up to 256000 baud
- multiupload
- can be executed from command-line
- time measure (and current transfer display)
- no dll needed (you can use it in your installer...)
- drag and drop capability

I think you'll find PilotInstall a great addition to your Windows system.

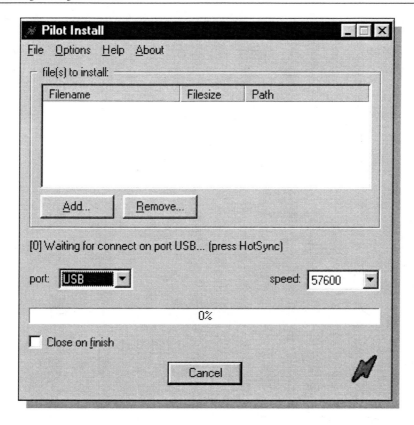

NS Basic PalmAPI Viewer

The Palm OS SDK is indispensable for writing Palm apps in any language, including NS Basic. Unfortunately, it's not easy to navigate, and any help in this regard is more than welcome. The NS Basic PalmAPI Viewer presents the API calls available from NS Basic in an easy to read format, indexed by API trap number. I keep it running when I'm using SysTrapSub or SysTrapFunc, and I suggest that you do the same.

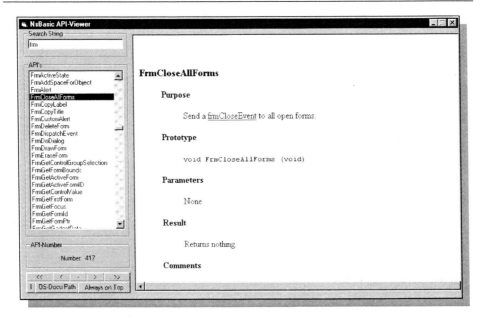

Sig2Bmp

This command-line utility allows you to convert captured signature strings saved in databases into standard Windows bitmaps. These bitmaps can then be read, edited, and printed using any standard Windows graphics application (including Windows Paint, and the Windows graphics applications on the CD). Refer to the readme.txt file that accompanies Sig2Bmp in the "Accessory Programs" directory.

CrannSoft's TUIG for NS Basic

If you have a lot of data in Access databases, you'll find this tool the easiest way to convert the individual tables into NS Basic-compatible PDB's, including conversion of date and time fields into NS Basic format. TUIG also supports conversions between CSV and PDB, and supports up to 250 fields per table, 32000 characters per field, and can handle tables of up to 32100 records.

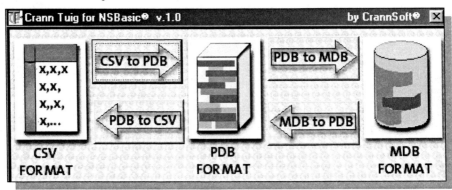

Miscellaneous Fun Stuff

I couldn't resist! After playing with my Palm devices, I've had the opportunity to experiment with various tools and utilities. Look in the Fun Stuff directory of the CD for various font, speed, graphics, and other utilities – including the popular HackMaster. These aren't really programming utilities *per se*, but can help optimize your use and enjoyment of your Palm device. Enjoy!

Appendix D. Running POSE

NS Basic doesn't contain its own embedded Palm emulator or debugger, but instead uses the Palm OS Emulator, commonly known as POSE. By using POSE, NS Basic allows you to test your applications using a wide variety of OS versions.

NS Basic will install a version of POSE ("bound" with a built-in ROM) in its working directory. Other bound emulators are found in the "Bound Emulators" directory (in "Accessory Programs") on the CD.

If you want to work with the full Palm OS Emulator, the CD contains version 3.4 of POSE, and also the necessary "skin" files to allow POSE to look like the actual devices. The skins aren't necessary for POSE to function properly, however - they're just for looks. We'll discuss them in the next section.

If you want to experiment with different device ROM's, you will need to either download your own device's ROM (using a serial cable and the "ROM Transfer" app that comes with POSE) or get ROM's from Palm, Inc. (or your device's manufacturer). From Palm, Inc.'s web site at www.palmos.com/dev/tools/emulator/:

> "For legal reasons, you must sign an agreement with Palm Inc. to download ROM images. To obtain the agreement, you must be a member of the Palm OS Developer Program. After joining that program, we recommend that you also join the Developer Seeding Program, which requires that you return a signed agreement to us. This allows you to access pre-release ROM images and other valuable tools. If you are based in the USA, you may also obtain images using a "clickwrap" agreement that does not require a signed agreement."

I couldn't have said it any better.

Installing POSE

To install POSE, extract the emulator files into a new directory (I'd call it "POSE", but you can use whatever name you'd like). Create a subdirectory named "Skins" within this directory, and extract the skin files here. This directory MUST be named "Skins", and the skin files MUST be in this directory, in order for POSE to find them. Note that when you attempt to extract them, they will go to their previously stored directory names unless you tell your uninstaller (I use WinZip – you can get the latest version at www.winzip.com) to ignore the directory names. If you forget this step, and POSE always starts with the default "generic" skin, look at the "Skins" directory, and you'll probably see another directory within it that contains the skins. Move the skins to the "Skins" directory, and everything should work appropriately.

These skins aren't merely close approximations – they have the exact look *and feel* of the real Palm devices, like this PalmIIIc:

Note OK – I lied again – the skins don't *really* make POSE *feel* like the actual device. But they do look impressive!

NS Basic will default to using its own bound emulator for testing unless you tell it otherwise. In the Tools section of the IDE, select Options, then while in the General section, click the Browse button next to "Path to POSE" and locate the unbound emulator.

Using POSE with your device's ROM

Unlike the bound emulator, POSE doesn't ship with any ROMs. However, it does come with a ROM Transfer app that you can load to your Palm device, and use it to transfer a copy of your ROM to your hard drive (currently this only works with devices with a serial cradle, but as more and more devices use USB, this may change by the time you read this).

To transfer the ROM, start POSE (the full version, not the bound emulator) on your desktop computer, then with POSE running, right-click on POSE, and select "Transfer ROM". Follow the directions step by step, and within a few minutes you should have your ROM downloaded and ready to use.

Using POSE with NS Basic

Included in the POSE directory are the SDK's for Palm OS 3.5 and 4.0. You may wish to go to www.palm.com and search for newer versions of these files, as well as updates to POSE and the skins. While you're there, you should consider joining the developed program. It's free, and it's the only way to get access to all of the Palm ROMs, including special debug versions (not yet supported by NS Basic, however).

Although you can run POSE from within NS Basic, and have NS Basic automatically load and run your applications after they are compiled, I personally prefer to have POSE running in one window, the NS Basic IDE in a second window, and a third window open to the NS Basic download directory. I set the compile options to neither download to POSE nor install to device – I prefer to install the applications into POSE myself. Navigating among the windows is only a few key strokes or mouse clicks away, and loading an app into POSE is easily accomplished by dragging its PRC into POSE (as long as POSE isn't currently running the app).

That's enough talking about POSE – let's walk through the steps and get POSE running. If you haven't installed POSE yet, now would be a good time to do so.

Running POSE for the first time

To make running POSE as simple as possible, I prefer to have a shortcut to POSE on my desktop. You can do this easily by locating the Emulator.exe file that you installed from the emulator-win.zip archive, right-click on the file, and drag it to the desktop. Windows will ask you if you want to copy, move, or create a shortcut – choose the shortcut. Then, when you want to run POSE, just double-click on the shortcut, and you're in business.

Before POSE will actually run, you'll need to give it a ROM. The first time you attempt to run POSE, you will be asked to select a few different options, including starting a new session.

Click "New", and select a Palm ROM (the ROM from your device, if you used the ROM Transfer application, or a ROM from Palm, Handspring, or other manufacturer) for your POSE session. You should see POSE display the Palm startup screen, then the Prefs screen. Click on the application launcher "silk screen" button, and you should see the familiar Palm screen with application icons. You're in business!

Tip You don't *really* want to go through all these steps each time, do you? Before going any further, right click on POSE, select "Save", and save your POSE session (as an Emulator Session File, with a .psf extension). You can then directly run POSE with this ROM by selecting this session file. Later, when you have applications installed into POSE, you can save additional session files, effectively saving different Palm "devices", each with different applications installed. Note that you don't have to these steps with the NS Basic emulator (actually, you couldn't even if you *wanted* to, since there's no "save" option with the bound emulator).

Installing applications and databases into POSE

As I briefly mentioned earlier, you can install applications and databases into POSE by dragging them into POSE while it's running, or by right-clicking on POSE, and selecting the "Install Application/Database" option (remember, these PRC and PDB files must be in Palm format – don't just drag an Access database or Word document into POSE and expect them to load).

Automatically loading applications and databases into POSE

If there are PDB's or PRC's that you always want to load each time you run POSE or the NS Basic emulator, create a subdirectory named AutoLoad in the directory that contains POSE or the NS Basic emulator (this will usually be c:\NS Basic\tools). Any PDB or PRC file in this AutoLoad directory will be loaded automatically.

Caution This can be a blessing or a curse, since you can easily forget to include these files with your applications for distribution!

Exporting applications and databases from POSE

Exporting databases and applications from POSE is a different story, however - you can't simply drag databases and applications from POSE to your Windows desktop. Instead, to export from POSE, right click on POSE while it's running, and select the "Export database" option. You can export any of the existing Palm applications or databases. This makes it easy for you to use your NS Basic applications to create databases within POSE, then you can export the databases to share with other users. Also, if you experiment with the Onboard Resource Editor (RsrcEdit, one of the accessory applications on the CD), you can even make changes to your NS Basic applications that you can't do with the NS Basic IDE, then transfer the modified application to the desktop for redistribution.

> **Note** With some versions of the bound emulator you won't be able to export databases this way. However, you can use the POSE dbexport application (load the posedbexport.prc file into the emulator) to export any of the databases on the emulator.

POSE Error messages and debugging options

POSE is a great tool, and you'll be tempted to assume that an application that runs on POSE will run on the actual Palm device. While I haven't found an exception to this, it's always possible that the actual device will behave differently than POSE. Actually, POSE is much more strict and unforgiving that the actual Palm devices, and will surprise you from time to time with very strange error messages. While many of these messages can be ignored, it's essential to test your applications on real devices before distributing them.

With POSE 3.4, you have considerable control over just how strict POSE is with how applications behave, and can tailor the error reporting to your needs. Right click on POSE, select "Settings", "Debugging...", and you'll see numerous Debug Options:

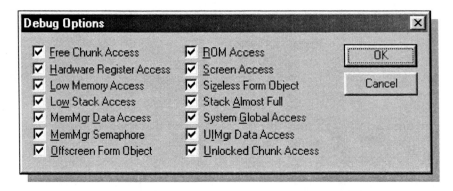

> **Tip** For most NS Basic applications, you can safely avoid common, "ignorable" errors by unchecking the "MemMgr Data Access", "Offscreen Form Object", and "UIMgr Data Access" options. These errors don't occur on the actual Palm OS devices, so having POSE ignore these errors can speed up your debugging process considerably, allowing you to focus on "real" errors.

Letting POSE be your first beta tester

When you get around to experimenting with POSE, you'll come upon gremlins. I swear to you that I didn't make this up! Right click on POSE, and you'll see "Gremlins". Basically, Gremlins are best thought of as tireless users who try to enter any kind of information in any field, tap and scroll anywhere – in short, *really nasty beta testers*. If you select "Gremlins", "New" you'll be given the chance to create a New Gremlin Horde (POSE's nomenclature, not mine!) that will run any application or group of applications. You can also determine how many times to run each app, and how to log the different events, errors, and activities that might occur.

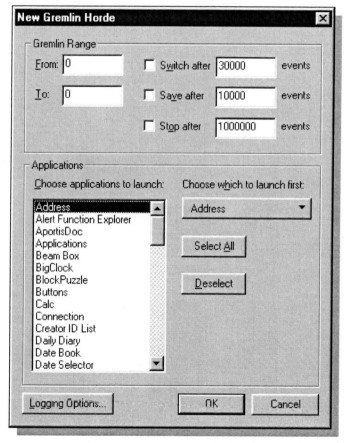

I strongly suggest that you use Gremlins to test your software – not in place of beta testers, but to complement them. POSE has many, many options – so many that you can easily get overwhelmed. Relax, only try one new technique at a time, and you'll do just fine.

HotSyncing POSE

You can even HotSync your POSE session as though it were a really device, although it's a little tricky (and slow!). You'll need two serial ports on your Windows machine that's running POSE. One should be already set up to run HotSync. In order to allow POSE to HotSync on this machine, right click on POSE, select "Settings", "Properties", and under "Serial Port", select the other serial port for POSE to use. Connect the two ports through the use of a null modem, and with HotSync and POSE both running, select "HotSync" from the "System" group on POSE. You should see the familiar HotSync dialog, and will be prompted for the user name if you haven't already wet it up through the same "Settings", "Properties" option in POSE. HotSync will be much slower when running on the same machine as POSE, but you can speed it up by making sure that POSE is the "foreground" application, with HotSync running in the background.

Quitting your POSE session

Before I go, I should probably tell you how to exit POSE, since it doesn't have the same Windows interface that you're accustomed to. To exit your POSE session, right click on POSE, and select "Exit".

Experiment with POSE, and learn to use it well. However, I must stress this again: don't rely on POSE for the final testing of your applications. There's no substitute for the real thing!

Index

RTSauto, 247
Running external programs, 62
Running POSE, 304

S

Saving State, 280
Scanner, 262
Scientific Notation, 152
SciNot, 152
Screen Graphics, 77
Scroll arrows, 122
ScrollBar, 129
    code, 129
    methods, 129
    properties, 129
Searching Strings, 168
Second, 183
Select, 51
Select Case, 51
Selected, 99, 115, 123, 126
Selector, 132
    code, 133
    methods, 133
    properties, 133
Serial, 243
Serial I/O, 243
    POSE, 255
    return codes, 249
SerialClose, 244, 245
SerialDial, 244, 252
SerialHangup, 244, 253
SerialOpen, 244
SerialReceive, 244, 250
SerialReceiveWithEvent, 254
SerialSend, 244, 249
SerialSet, 244, 246
SerialSet parameters, 247
SetCurrentWindow, 77
SetEventHandled, 73, 237
SetFocus, 104
Shared libraries, 20, 262
Shared Libraries, 261
Shell-Metzner Sort, 116, 124, 276
Shift Indicator, 105, 135
Short, 260
Show, 94, 97, 101, 105, 106, 111, 127, 129, 131, 134
Show Titlebar, 70
ShowAlphaKeyboard, 259
ShowDefaultKeyboard, 259
ShowInternationalKeyboard, 259
ShowNumericKeyboard, 259
Sidebars, 15
Sig2Bmp, 302

Sign, 140, 144, 149
Signature Capture, 105
Sin, 141
Single Line, 102
Sinh, 141
Soft-key, 30
Sony, 238
Sort order, 287
Sorting, 276
Sound, 30, 235
Soundex, 279
Space, 166
Special Topics, 267
Sqrt, 140
StartSignatureCapture, 107
Startup code, 68
Statements, 40
Status, 98, 125, 127
Staying alive, 279
Step, 53
StevensCreek, 299
Stop, 65
Stopbits, 247
Str, 156
String, 167, 260
String conversions, 155
String Handling, 155
String literals, 155
String Parsing, 169, 272
String variables, 155
Structured programming, 21
Sub, 42
Subroutines, 42
    arguments, 43
    variables, 42
Subscript, 35
Substring, 164, 168
SubtractDays, 178
SubtractHours, 184
Subtraction, 139
SubtractMinutes, 184
SubtractMonths, 178
SubtractSeconds, 184
SubtractYears, 178
Support web site, 10
Symbol, 262
SysInfo, 253, 280
System Information, 280
SysTrapFunc, 31, 259
SysTrapSub, 31, 258

T

Table, 136
Tan, 141

Tanh, 141
Termination code, 65
TestNum, 103
Text, 96, 99, 102, 110, 115, 120, 123, 133
Then, 47
Time, 173, 181
Timeout, 247
TimeVal, 183
Tips, 14
ToDate, 176
TODAY, 174
Top, 96, 101, 110, 128, 131, 133, 135
Top-down programming, 20
ToTime, 182
Trapping user actions, 237
Trigonometry, 153
Trim, 157, 163
True, 30, 99
Trunc, 140, 144
Truncation, 160
Type, 33

byte, 31
database, 31
date, 31
declaring, 32
double, 31
float, 31
global, 30
integer, 31
long, 31
NS Basic, 31
short, 31
single, 31
string, 31
subroutines, 42
time, 31
variant, 31
Visual Basic, 31
Vertical, 130
Visible, 128
Visible Items, 122
Volume, 247

U

Ucase, 159
UDT, 33
UInt, 260
Underline, 101
User-Defined Type, 33

V

Val, 156
Value, 131
Variable names, 33
    case sensitivity, 33
Variables, 29, 30

W

Width, 96, 101, 128, 131, 133
Word, 13

X

XonXoff, 247

Y

Y2K, 173
Year, 175
YearMonth, 175